ARE WE THERE YET?

Are We There Yet?

VIRTUAL TRAVEL AND VICTORIAN REALISM

Alison Byerly

The University of Michigan Press
Ann Arbor

Published in the United States of America by
The University of Michigan Press
Manufactured in the United States of America
⊗ Printed on acid-free paper

2016   2015   2014   2013   4   3   2   1

A CIP catalog record for this book is available from the British Library.

Library of Congress Cataloging-in-Publication Data

Byerly, Alison.
    Are we there yet? : virtual travel and Victorian realism / Alison Byerly.
        p.   cm.
    Includes bibliographical references and index.
    ISBN 978-0-472-07186-9 (cloth : acid-free paper)—ISBN 978-0-472-05186-1 (pbk. : acid-free paper)—ISBN 978-0-472-02876-4 (e-book)
        1. English fiction—19th century—History and criticism. 2. Realism in literature. 3. Travel in literature. I. Title.
    PR878.R4B94   2012
    823'.80912—dc23   2012033642

For Steve, Laramie, and Ryan

ACKNOWLEDGMENTS

I am very grateful to Middlebury College, and to President Ron Liebowitz, for the generous leave support that made it possible for me to complete this book even in the midst of an appointment as provost.

Research for this project began in the John Johnson Collection of Printed Ephemera at the Bodleian Library, Oxford, and ended in a virtual reality lab at Stanford. I benefited greatly from the opportunity to participate in the vibrant intellectual communities of these two universities. An appointment as Visiting Fellow at Harris Manchester College, Oxford, in 2001–2, allowed me to spend a year doing research in England, and I thank Harris Manchester College, and Principal Ralph Waller, as well as Ann-Marie Drummond, Claire Harman, and many other Oxford colleagues for their warm hospitality during that time.

In 2008–9, I was fortunate in having the opportunity to be a visiting scholar in English at Stanford University. I am grateful to Bryan Jay Wolf, Ramon Saldivar, Jennifer Summit, Andrea Lunsford, and John Bender for helping me to feel welcome at Stanford, and to Dagmar Logie for helping me to figure out how everything worked. I owe special thanks to Jeremy Bailenson, founder of Stanford's Virtual Human Interaction Lab, for allowing me to visit the lab, and to Nicole Fernandez for her tour and demo.

For assistance in making research materials available, I am grateful to Mrs. Julie Lambert at the John Johnson Collection of Printed Ephemera, Bodleian Library; the Museum of London, and former assistant curator Gail Cameron; the Museum of London–Docklands; the National Railway Museum, York; the British Library; and Henry Lowood, Curator for the History of Science and Technology Collections and Film and Media Collections at the Stanford University Libraries. At Middlebury, I have benefited from the assistance of our own excellent staff in Library and Information Services, as well from substantial legwork at the book's inception by research assistant Sarah de Guzman.

For permission to reprint material that appeared originally in *Nineteenth-Century Contexts*, "'A Prodigious Map Beneath His Feet': Virtual Travel and the Panoramic Perspective," vol. 29, nos. 2–3 (June–September 2007): 151–69, I thank the editors of that journal, as well as Taylor and Francis/Routledge, and Keith Hanley and John Kucich, coeditors of *Nineteenth-Century Worlds: Global Formations, Past and Present* (2008), where the same essay was reprinted. An early version of some material in Part Two appeared as "Rivers, Journeys, and the Construction of Place in Nineteenth-Century English Literature," in Steven Rosendale, ed., *The Greening of Literary Scholarship: Literature, Theory, and the Environment* (Iowa University Press, 2002), 77–94. My thanks to Iowa University Press for permission to use it here.

I greatly appreciated the advice of colleagues who were kind enough to discuss this project with me at various points, or to read portions of the manuscript. These include David Bain, Jim Buzard, Jennifer Green-Lewis, Jonathan Grossman, David Herman, Antonia Losano, Jason Mittell, Paul Monod, Sujata Moorti, Jay Parini, Ted Perry, John Plotz, Lisa Rodensky, Marie-Laure Ryan, Margery Sabin, Elaine Scarry, and Susan Zlotnick. I am also grateful for the comments of the anonymous University of Michigan Press readers, and for the expert guidance of my editor at UMP, Tom Dwyer.

This book would not have been possible without wide-ranging conversations in its earliest stages, and detailed editorial advice in its final stages, offered by my husband, Steve Jensen. Nor would it have been possible without the willingness of Laramie and Ryan Jensen to follow the project from our home in Middlebury, Vermont, to Oxford and California. They often wondered, but seldom asked, when this book's journey would be over. I am glad to be able to tell them that we are finally there.

A.B.

CONTENTS

INTRODUCTION

Travel and the Art of the Real

If it had not been a wet morning, Mr. Irwine would not have been in the dining-room playing chess with his mother, and he loves his mother and chess quite well enough to pass some cloudy hours very easily by their help. Let me take you into that dining-room, and show you the Rev. Adolphus Irwine. . . . We will enter very softly, and stand in the open doorway, without awaking the glossy-brown setter who is stretched across the hearth, with her two puppies beside her. . . .

—George Eliot, *Adam Bede*, chap. V, 1859

Jump in.

—Xbox 360 ad campaign, 2006–9

Looking at an *Illustrated London News* picture of viewers "visiting Paris" by way of a room-sized panorama, reading newspaper accounts of women swooning at an elaborately staged train wreck at Drury Lane, or opening a novel in which the narrator faithfully promises to take you to a nonexistent place called Wessex, the twenty-first-century media user may marvel at the simplicity of a culture that found such representations "realistic." With a wide range of complex technologies constantly competing to provide us with intensely vivid aesthetic experiences, we can scarcely imagine being fooled by such naive stratagems.

Victorian realism can be seen as a distant phenomenon that encapsulates a specific age, a period now more than a century removed from our own. Professors have to explain to students that this was a culture in which people voluntarily read 900-page, triple-decker novels simply because they enjoyed being immersed in a narrative for as long as possible. This cultural predilection seems less remote, however, when we recognize the continuities between the realistic worlds that the Victorians sought in their literature and visual culture, and the "virtual" worlds we create today through a variety of digital media. These representations aim not just to create alternative worlds but to give us the illusion of entering them, a journey that is itself part of the process of creation. In the Victorian period or in the present, art that aspires to realism must do more than just depict a real-seeming world. It must take you there.

This book is about the persistence of a powerful construction of the act of imagining, one that is exemplified in the sentence I have just written: the idea of travel as a metaphor for the imaginative displacement of the self.

The study is rooted in an apparent paradox. The nineteenth century saw an explosion of new transportation technologies that, as critics have shown, made travel accessible to a broader public than ever before.[1] Yet even as actual travel became easier, staying at home and fantasizing about travel became a favorite pastime. A booming market developed for realistic representations of popular locations, and new ways of representing place—360-degree panoramas, foldout river maps, exhaustive railway guides—seemed to offer themselves as substitutes for actual travel. While many of the best-known travel accounts of this period recount epic journeys of exploration across the globe, an enormous number of self-styled "travel" narratives describe experiences that do not involve physical movement at all. Satiric accounts of the countries visited through the "panoramic-dioramic mode of conveyance"; verbal and visual balloon's-eye views of a city already quite familiar to both balloonist and reader; humorous stories about aimless trips up and down the Thames; descriptions of the confusion felt by the railway traveller who enters a station in London and emerges six hours later in Liverpool: these accounts share a sense of pleasurable disorientation that is unrelated to the specific place being visited but is connected instead to the activity of travel itself. Their object is not to describe someplace new but to replicate the experience of going somewhere through a rhetoric I describe as "virtual travel."

This study strives to expand our understanding of the genealogy of realist fiction by identifying key narrative strategies that, I will argue, evolved directly out of the virtual travel narratives created through a wide range of nonfiction prose forms and visual media. Through close examination of such disparate texts as panorama advertisements, maps of the Thames, pocket railway guides, and little-known periodical accounts of various forms of travel, I will chart the evolution of a discourse of virtual travel that cut across a range of genres and media. I will then suggest that Victorian novelists borrowed from these popular cultural forms many descriptive techniques and rhetorical gestures that position the reader or viewer as a kind of traveller, a conception of the reader's role that was fundamental to the operations of literary realism. I use the idea of virtuality to describe what is, in essence, a fictive component to nonfiction narratives, a pretense that they are something they are not. When elements of virtual travel are transposed into a novel, however, this sense of fictiveness is flattened into the already-fictional context. Within this framework, the virtual becomes the (fictional) real. Thus, I will argue, the cultivation of virtuality in nonfictional genres was a crucial step toward the Victorian construction of narrative realism.

Travel, as a temporary relocation, seems to encapsulate the sense of hypothetical belonging that characterizes our interaction with compelling fictional worlds. In depicting the activity of imagining as an experience so strenuous it is almost physical, Victorian novelists enhanced the tangibility of their worlds. But what is perhaps more important, in depicting this displacement as contingent—as temporary, hypothetical, experimental—they introduced a crucial element of self-reflexivity into their narrative structures. Tom Boellstorf offers the following definition of the virtual: it "connotes approaching the actual *without arriving there*" (19; original emphasis). I will argue that the strategies of virtual travel allowed novelists to chart a pathway to immersion in their fictional worlds, while at the same time acknowledging that the reader would be on a perpetual, inconclusive journey.

Virtual travel as it will be defined in this analysis is inherently reflexive, a continuous feedback loop. Travel itself is a form of repetition; defining the body's movement as a journey implies that the ground covered conforms to some sort of itinerary, even if the itinerary is to take a spontaneous, unplanned trip. As James Buzard (*Beaten Track*, 4) has shown, many forms of nineteenth-century travel had a self-consciously programmed quality to them, hence the recurrent image of "the beaten track, which succinctly designates the space of the 'touristic' as a region in which all experience is predictable and repetitive."[2] The replication of such journeys through panoramas, guidebooks, or nonfiction travelogues introduced another layer of mediation. By imitating those imitations, I will argue, Victorian novelists incorporated a layer of self-reflexivity into their narratives that seemed to substantiate the underlying reality.

This study relies on a disparate, perhaps idiosyncratic, range of materials. It began with an examination of panorama advertisements in the John Johnson Collection of Printed Ephemera at the Bodleian Library and railway guidebooks from the National Railway Museum in York. It ended with a visit to a virtual reality laboratory at Stanford. In between, I have sought commonalities among a variety of nineteenth-century texts that do not simply describe, but attempt to reproduce, an experience of travel. Although the goal of this book is to illuminate a certain dimension of Victorian realist fiction, a central role is also played by advertisements, travel guides, and periodical literature. I have applied the term *media* to these texts advisedly, for I hope to demonstrate how such forms mediated between the physical or perceptual experience of travel, and its fictional representation. In making this argument, I work out of the field of Victorian studies as a primary context but make some use of current media theory that I believe is helpful in engaging questions about narrative immersion.

Although I do not attempt to chart a continuous historical progression between the Victorian forms that are at the center of this study and the contemporary media that will occasionally surface around the edges, I do suggest that there is a strong relationship between these mid- to late nineteenth-century forms and their twenty-first-century counterparts. Jay David Bolter and Richard Grusin have popularized the term *remediation* to describe the way in which new media are seen as "reforming or improving upon" earlier media in a continual drive toward greater "immediacy and transparency" (59–60). As influential as this concept has been, more has been done to map the route whereby new visual media—photography, film, television, digital graphics—overlap with and challenge each other than to understand how *textual* representation fits into this framework. If a "medium" is, in Bolter and Grusin's words, "that which appropriates the techniques, forms, and social significance of other media and attempts to rival or refashion them in the service of the real" (65), then I would argue that nineteenth-century literature can take its place among other literary and visual forms as part of the Victorian media landscape. Understanding the evolving interrelationship among these forms, and their shared role in constituting some influential dimensions of Victorian culture, calls for an approach that can perhaps be described as Victorian media studies.

By looking at a Victorian phenomenon in part through the lens of contemporary conceptualizations of media and its effects, this study inserts itself into a gap between cultural studies and literary or aesthetic theory. Other critics who have applied current theories about media to nineteenth-century cultural forms have focused productively on the social or economic dimensions of these forms in order to examine topics like representations of empire, ideas about gender, or commodity culture.[3] But the excellent work that has been done in Victorian cultural studies in general over the last two decades has tended to overshadow interest in aesthetics and narrative. In the meantime, some of the most interesting work in narratology has moved to the fresher fields of film and media studies.[4] Thus, there are few studies of Victorian narrative form that take advantage of new insights offered by contemporary theorists working in other media.

Interest in the relationship between Victorian literature and visual media has been strong for many years, starting with Martin Meisel's *Realizations: Narrative, Pictorial, and Theatrical Arts in Nineteenth-Century England*. This interest is reflected not only in many works devoted specifically to that relationship but in the de rigueur use of Pre-Raphaelite paintings and Victorian advertisements to illustrate works in literary and cultural studies. This is not surprising, given the astonishing array of realistic representational forms that emerged over the course of the nineteenth century. As Martin Hewitt writes in his cogent summary of Victorian "visual regimes," "A new graphic engagement with the contemporary world; an unprecedented investment in 'illustration'; and—at least in part—the predominance of realist strategies, narrative modes, and 'genre' subjects, were encouraged by the visual mechanisms for the collection and dissemination of social and economic knowledge that were established in the 1830s and 1840s" (413). The rise of realism in these earlier visual forms was ultimately amplified through technology into the new medium of photography, and a number of critics have traced the relationship between fictional realism and photographic attention to physical and material reality.[5] The continuous evolution of more and more advanced optical apparatuses has made it possible for historians to trace the roots of film and other contemporary visual media in such nineteenth-century devices as the stereoscope and the kinescope.[6] I see this study as continuous with many earlier works of "interart" comparison, including my own. There is still room, however, to connect this varied visual landscape more specifically to the literary landscape of the period. Whereas other critics have looked at broad thematic or ideological parallels between works of visual art and literature, this study seeks to identify some of the formal or aesthetic similarities between them.

I believe that a defining feature of the nineteenth-century realist novel is its effort to generate an almost physical sense of presence within the fictional world—a sense of locatedness and embodiment—that depends on a strategic positioning of the reader. This assertion brings together two important strands of commentary about realism, one emphasizing place, and the other materiality and embodiment. Nineteenth-century realism has always been recognized as a genre anchored in a firm sense of physical location. J. Hillis Miller's *Topographies* and Franco Moretti's *Atlas of the European Novel, 1800–1900*, among others, explored the role of place in the nineteenth-century novel in general, and many analyses of Dickens's London or Hardy's Wessex reflect the centrality of those specific locations in those authors' works.[7] More recently, Victorian criticism has become preoccupied with the role of nineteenth-century novels in creating a sense of Britain as an imperial space extending over many continents.[8] But at the same time that the field of Victorian studies has worked to expand its mapping of British nationalism, it has also focused inward, on the Victorian body itself, as a gendered, racialized, sexualized, even traumatized subject.[9] These outward and inward trajectories converge here in an examination of the Victorian obsession with representations and evocations of the body's movement from place to place through the act of travel.

This obsession with travel, and the dual perspective it provides, reflects a tension between the competing claims of subjectivity and objectivity that is in many ways the fundamental subject of Victorian realist fiction. James Buzard has already connected travel to a process of engaging alternative perspectives that he sees as having an important impact on the Victorian novel: that of the emerging science of ethnography. Buzard (*Disorienting Fiction*, 2005) describes an "ethnographic impulse" that allowed Victorians to distance themselves from their own culture by making it an object of study. He sees Victorian novels as "anticipating modern field-working ethnography *in reverse*, by construing its narrator's (and many character's) desired position vis-à-vis the fictional world it depicts as that of an *insider's outsidedness*—'outside enough' to apprehend the shape of the culture . . . yet insistently positioned as the outsidedness of a *particular* inside" (19). Buzard's analysis of various fictional "narratives of displacement" as constituting a genre of "English autoethnographic fiction" (17) rests on a nuanced reading of the way in which specific characters or narrators alternate between these insider and outsider perspectives.

There has been strong interest in epistemological questions in Victorian fiction over the last two decades, with several critics noting, like Buzard, an alternation between the competing claims of immersion in subjective experience, and efforts toward detachment or objectivity. Amanda Anderson has made a compelling case for the importance of detachment as a cultivated virtue in a range of Victorian texts. She sees literary forms like "omniscient realism and dramatic monologue" as representing the "aspiration to a distanced view" (4, 6). Victorian novels in particular, she suggests, demonstrate a "dialectic between detachment and engagement" (6). George Levine also argues that objectivity is a central goal in many realist novels. He claims that in Victorian fiction, "one can only achieve truth through objectivity," and that the struggle for objectivity lies behind the self-conscious narrative interventions that are so characteristic of Eliot, Charlotte Brontë, and Thackeray (149). Levine suggests that in spite of these narrators' best efforts, perfect objectivity is an unattainable goal. It is, however, something to which the novel aspires. While these novels acknowledge how important it is to "affirm the value of personal desire" and recognize the pull of subjectivity, "it feels as though the culture's imagination of what is possible simply requires *something like* objectivity" (12; original emphasis).

Levine's phrase "*something like* objectivity" seems to align his statement with my claim that Victorian novelists understood realistic representation to be, like virtuality, an effort at similitude that is ultimately unrealizable. The word *vir-*

tual evokes an imaginative experience that is not fully realized, but aspirational. It is a state of *almost* being, of tending toward realization. The truly objective perspective, too, can never be fully attained. But virtual travel offered the opportunity to experiment with a range of perspectives along a continuum between complete detachment and complete immersion.

It is not irrelevant to note that the tropes of virtual travel that the Victorians developed as they grappled with the new art forms of their day continue to resonate in our descriptions of the new media of the twenty-first century. When we use a web browser called Internet Explorer to "navigate" our way to a new "site," take a "virtual tour," and then return "home," we are using geographic metaphors that have their origin in the Victorian panorama advertisement that promises a "visit to Niagara Falls" and the Thames guidebook that invites the reader to accompany the author on a leisurely journey. Examining the formation of this descriptive framework allows us to trace relationships among a range of textual and visual media that form a trajectory of aesthetic development over three centuries. Collectively, these media demonstrate the importance of self-positioning to creating a sense of realism.

Travel in the Nineteenth Century

Although this study is in its conception more aesthetic and cultural than historical, my examination of different modes of virtual travel will include detailed discussion of the material aspects of travel, in particular the challenges and possibilities posed by the development of new modes of transport in the period. Understanding Victorian travel as an experience is a necessary precondition to understanding its attraction as an imaginative medium. I will outline here some general contours of travel in the period, discuss the ways in which its cultural impacts have been assessed by critics and historians, and use some contemporary theories of travel to unpack the meaning of travel for the Victorians and in the present. I will then turn to the emerging genre of travel literature in the period, a subject that has generated a great deal of critical commentary, before moving into a discussion of virtual travel and virtuality to conclude this introduction. In the analysis of specific forms of travel that will follow in each of the book's three major parts, I will highlight some recurring social and cultural issues, such as the class distinctions associated with different modes of transport, and the gradual blurring of those distinctions over time; the tension between the public space of travel and the interior focus cultivated by guidebooks and travel reading; and the connection between travel and other emerging modes of communication.

Any discussion of travel in the Victorian period must begin with the observation that the building of the railway, the development of the steamboat, and the proliferation of tour operators and transport companies over the course of the nineteenth century enabled an increasingly broad range of people from all social classes to experience the pleasures of travel.[10] Leisure travel was no longer limited to scions of wealthy families taking the Grand Tour but might include workingmen from a provincial Mechanics' Institute taking an excursion train to London, London workers' families enjoying a Sunday steamer to Margate, and people of all classes using the railway for weekend holidays at the seaside. This widening of access turned an existing class dichotomy, between those who could afford leisure travel and those who could not, into a realm of opportunity that extended through the middle class and even into the working classes. A growing appetite for the travel experience was fed by an explosion of representations of travel: pictures, narratives, lectures, and photographs depicting journeys to popular tourist destinations at home and abroad. These media forms helped foster the expectation that some experience of travel should be possible at any income—or, to put it another way, that knowledge of other places was no longer limited to direct personal experience: one could know a place without having seen it.[11]

Even the familiar British landscape, the Victorians found, could provide a stimulating sense of otherness when viewed through the lens of the traveller, and a new domestic literature of travel helped to train the eye. Though much critical commentary on travel in the Victorian period focuses on increased opportunities for foreign travel, the Victorians also developed an unprecedented appreciation for the touristic possibilities of their own country. The dramatic expansion of domestic travel in nineteenth-century Britain can be seen as an inverted manifestation of the imperialist agenda that had made foreign travel and exploration so popular in the early decades of the nineteenth century. Now, travellers sought to replicate within England's borders the same kinds of experiences their predecessors had enjoyed in foreign lands.

Patrick Brantlinger (*Rule of Darkness*, 38) has described a "waning of adventure" in late nineteenth-century imperialism in terms that acknowledge the paradox: "Despite or perhaps because of the greatness of the major Victorian explorers, exploration after the 1870's rapidly declined into mere travel, Cook's Tours came into vogue, and the 'penetration' of Africa and Asia turned into a sordid spectacle of tourism and commercial exploitation" (37–38). This study seeks to interrogate the relationship between "despite" and "because," locating the impulse toward the replication of travel in its paradoxical relationship to travel itself. As we will see, the exploration of exotic lands was mimicked by writers and artists who recreated such journeys in a variety of attenuated forms. The use of travel as a metaphor for aesthetic engagement represents, among other things, a growing interest in understanding aesthetic response as an *experience*, as a sensory and time-bound activity.

Ian Baucom (4, 37) has noted that British nationalism is deeply rooted in specific sites of cultural memory, and sees England struggling to "define the relationship between the national 'here' and the imperial 'there.'" Baucom's emphasis on the space *between* here and there suggests that transit is an important part of the project of defining the self, whether of a nation or an individual. Historians have shown, of course, that British travellers typically imported much of their "home" culture to the places they visited, as well as attempting to assimilate certain elements of foreign cultures by bringing them home and incorporating them into familiar surroundings.[12] Many domestic travel accounts show a desire for a taste of the exotic, as authors attempt to look at the familiar British landscape with the sense of distance previously applied to foreign parts. Even as they appreciate its thorough Englishness, they attempt to experience that "here" as if it were elsewhere, in a sense of "organized dislocation" that can be intensely pleasurable (Rojek and Urry, 6). Travel is always a "vehicle for estrangement and reassessment" (Huggan, 39), a way of taking a fresh look at oneself by visiting someplace new.

Travel was the ideal medium for achieving this dual perspective. In the texts explored here, we see the Victorians experiment with the sense of "elsewhereness" that was initially associated with exotic, foreign travel, applying it first to local landscape, and finally creating it through a variety of media that construct a simulated sense of place. Domestic travel by boat or train becomes, as we will see, a miniaturized version of foreign travel, replicating many of its tropes and structures. The experience is attenuated further through virtual travel that recreates the experience of a journey through the power of verbal or visual representations. As an activity that allows the participant to engage imaginatively with two places at once, travel functioned as a kind of paradigm for aesthetic absorption. The traveller's sense of being both an outsider and an insider to the world surveyed would prove a powerful metaphor for the realist novel's alternation between empathy and critical distance.

Like art, travel implicitly calls for some kind of judgment. The potential for transformation often associated with travel derives in part from the shape of the travel experience, which offers a series of contrasts over time. "Travel"—as distinct from commuting, migration, displacement, or exile—generally refers to a voluntary journey from which the traveller returns. Most travel narratives are structured around the idea of a voyage out and a return, with the end implicit in the beginning, a teleology that has important consequences for the traveller's experience of the trip. The conventional trip is defined by the contrast among these various points along the way: the point of origin; the places encountered throughout the journey; the destination or destinations; the home to which one returns, which may look a bit different when seen in contrast to the places just visited. Virtual travel, as we will see, compresses this teleology into a structured aesthetic experience that provides many of the same contrasts, offering the reader or viewer the opportunity to experience the same redefinition of self that defines actual travel. If a traveller is, in Richard Kerridge's words, always a "proxy, venturing into foreign space on behalf of the reader at home" (167), then it is easy for that traveller to become an avatar, substituting for the reader within a virtual landscape.

By combining discussion of some characteristically Victorian forms of travel with analysis of literary and artistic forms of "virtual travel," I will show that the literal and the metaphoric journeys of this period share a kind of perceptual discontinuity that challenges the linearity generally associated with narrative. Modes of travel differ, as we will see, in their emphasis on the travel *process*, on what happens between point A and point B on the map. In what I call "panoramic travel," the sensation of being elsewhere first associated with panorama exhibitions, the space of transit disappears entirely. One walks into the room and is presented with the illusion of being somewhere else, without any sensation of having gotten there (fig. 1). River travel, by contrast, was a form of transportation that involved savoring the journey, with the actual destination often a matter of complete indifference. There, what drops out of the equation is the purposiveness associated with going somewhere in particular. Instead, the physical dimension of travel is the focus of the experience. Eventually, the impression of being magically transported to another place created by panorama exhibitions would be physically realized in the experience of train travel, which created a similar disjunction between one's perceived space and one's actual geographic location. The Victorians felt, and cultivated, a fascination with the phenomenon of imaginative dislocation that is still with us today.

Travel is of course different from mere transportation in its most mechanical definition: the movement of people from one place to another for utilitarian purposes. But it is important to recall how recent a concept "transportation" is. The evolution of the mass transit industry in the nineteenth century is marked by a blurring of boundaries between the categories of travel, tourism, and transportation. The development of the railway as an efficient means of moving goods and people was based on the assumption that for most people, the object of travel was getting to the specific place they wanted to go as quickly as possible. This

Fig. 1. C. V. Nielson, "Viewing platform with spectators and detail of a panoramic view of Constantinople by Jules-Arsène Garnier." Wood engraving, ca. 1882.

assumption proved by and large to be correct, yet Victorians immediately felt the difference between rumbling along by carriage at seven to ten miles per hour and being, in John Ruskin's famous words, "sent like a parcel" on the train.

The railway passenger's disorienting yet exhilarating sense of imaginative detachment from his own physical experience resembles the "fracturing of presence," in Edward Castronova's (2007) words, that takes place in virtual worlds, where "we have people moving their attention, not their bodies" (*Exodus to the Virtual World*, 70). Collectively, these new forms of travel made the Victorians familiar with a kind of freedom and mobility that they would ultimately seek to replicate in many aspects of their literature and art.

Travel Literature

During this great age of exploration, the Victorians enjoyed reading about exotic locations that were beyond the reach of the average reader. They devoured Sir Richard F. Burton's *Pilgrimage to Al-Madinah and Meccah* and numerous accounts of his African explorations; followed Isabella Bird Bishop's travels over many years in the American Rocky Mountains, Japan, Tibet, China, Korea, and

Morocco; and made a best seller of David Livingstone's *Missionary Travels and Researches in South Africa*.

Many critical analyses of travel literature present travel as a kind of imaginative appropriation that reflects or nostalgically recreates the acts of political appropriation that defined the nineteenth century, and travel writing as a celebration of this gesture.[13] Within the field of Victorian studies, Mary Louise Pratt's *Imperial Eyes: Travel Writing and Transculturation* established an understanding of the way in which the signifying practices of travel writing both "encode and legitimate the aspirations of economic expansion and empire" and, at times, "betray them" (5). Other critics have focused so forcefully on the legitimating role of travel writing within an imperialist agenda that they may seem to "render the whole genre intrinsically invidious" (Clark, 3).[14] Even postcolonialist writers who are exempt from complicity with an imperialist agenda must still contend with what Graham Huggan calls "the perceptual legacy of *exoticism*: a mode of vision in which travel writing, fuelling European fantasy, has acted as a primary vehicle for the production and consumption of cultural 'otherness'" (56).[15]

The pseudo-travel writing I will discuss here, however, does not focus on the exotic "other." It uses the distancing effect of the traveller's perspective to reorient the reader to a place that is already familiar. The Victorians were increasingly drawn to travel accounts and guidebooks describing familiar places. While earlier accounts of travel around England generally reflect an assumption that most readers would not have the opportunity to see the distant cities and remote hamlets to which the narrator is able to travel, nineteenth-century narratives and guidebooks increasingly position themselves in relation to an audience that has wider opportunities and is presumed to share many of the experiences described.

As we will see, the rhetoric of accounts and guidebooks describing popular boating routes on the Thames, or standard trips along the major railway lines, is designed to evoke the sense of a fictive journey that is shared by author and reader. Appeals to the reader's own experience, present-tense descriptions that suggest a scene is being viewed simultaneously by both reader and writer, and detailed instructions directing the reader's gaze to specific sights as they pass, all combine to create an engaging representation that treats the narrative itself as a journey that is either physically enacted by the reader or imaginatively performed through the act of reading. The value of this reading experience clearly lies not simply in the acquisition of new information but more crucially in the sensation of being imaginatively transported from place to place. Even the most factual guidebooks took on an aura of fiction in their capacity to immerse the reader in an imaginary space.

The rhetoric of invitation employed by these travel guides, I will suggest, influenced many of the narrative devices that characterize realist fiction, as novelists sought to create a sense of movement that would reinforce the solidity of their own fictional worlds. From Fielding onward, direct addresses to the reader form an important part of the novel's development, and the Victorian reader is often invited to accompany the narrator as he or she moves through the various physical settings described. Dickens invites us to "pass from one scene to the other, as the crow flies" (*Bleak House*, chap. 2), while Thackeray begins the "Vauxhall" chapter of *Vanity Fair* by suggesting, "Let us step into the coach with the Russell Square party, and be off to the gardens. There is barely room between Jos and Miss Sharp" (chap. 6). The obtrusive, sometimes awkward insistence of the narrator of George Eliot's *Scenes of Clerical Life* that we must "look at [Amos Barton] as he winds through the churchyard," or "go there, and hear whether Mr. Pilgrim has reported their opinions correctly" (2), makes more sense if we recognize that these devices strive to create not just a sense of vividness, but of *movement*. We are not merely standing and watching with the narrator, we are following him, and that sense of a shared journey is an essential part of our immersion in the story. The idea of a narrative as a kind of journey is as old as literature, of course, and inherent in the form. As Garrett Stewart notes, "fictional reading is inductive. In every sense, it leads you on" (7). But allegorical journeys like those depicted by Spenser and Bunyan, or picaresque novels like *Tom Jones* focus on the various challenges encountered by the hero as he travels through the world. The journey is both a plot device that allows things to happen, and an allegory of the hero's life as a whole. The realist novels of the Victorian period, on the other hand, are not specifically about a hero's epic journey, yet they require us to keep up with their characters as they make the rounds of their ordinary lives. The techniques these novels employ to create a sense of shared movement echo the conspiratorial rhetoric of travel narratives and guidebooks.

Moreover, we will find that a classic descriptive mode of Victorian fiction, the sweeping, panoramic survey of a scene that appears so often in Hardy, Dickens, and Eliot, is in fact derived from a mode of landscape description that developed in connection with two forms of Victorian travel: the virtual travel embodied in the experience of viewing the massive panoramic displays that were so popular in the middle of the century, and the physical experience of balloon travel, whose similarly disorienting, bird's-eye perspective felt almost fictive. These tropes helped Victorian novelists to give a sense of realism to their descriptions by reminding the reader of highly mediated forms of visual experience that were themselves successful in imaginatively transporting the viewer.

It is not by representing real travel, but by representing *virtual* travel, that the novelist mobilizes the reader within his or her own work.

Self-referentiality has long been seen as a defining feature of realism, and one of its strongest defenses against charges of oversimplification and naïveté. The Victorian novelist's penchant for reminding the reader that he or she is narrating a novel, and that its characters are merely characters, is recognized as a disarming admission of the work's artifice that ultimately strengthens its credibility. Thus, the novel is "realistic" in presenting itself not as "the real world," but as "a realistic representation of the real world." I have argued elsewhere for the central role that representations of art play in this kind of self-reflexivity. The Victorian novel often incorporates references to painting, music, theater, or other arts as a way of affirming the reality that underlies the representations scattered across its surface.[16] Here too we will see that, paradoxically, realism is reinforced by the representation of a mode of experience that is already mediated, and an acknowledgment that "realistic" is not the same as "real." Even the most vivid manifestations of virtual reality, as we will see, do not function as substitutes for reality. They are merely vacations from it.

A Detour through the Virtual

Using contemporary ideas of the virtual as a starting point for this examination helps bring into focus the specific characteristics that make any kind of simulation or fiction feel "real." The brief overview that follows highlights the importance of movement to creating the sense of immersion that is fundamental to the perceived realism of a fictive environment. Travel, as an activity that allows the participant to engage imaginatively with two places at once, functioned as a kind of paradigm for aesthetic absorption. In the nineteenth century, the traveller's sense of being both an outsider and an insider to the world surveyed would prove a powerful metaphor for the realist novel's alternation between empathy and critical distance. Contemporary media seem to engender a similar oscillation between competing states of consciousness.

I use the term *virtual travel* here in recognition of the distinction between the nineteenth-century phenomenon under discussion and the contemporary technology known as "virtual reality." My discussion of Victorian texts will occasionally be punctuated by allusions to a variety of new media that attempt to evoke a realistic sense of place: virtual reality environments, tourist websites, travel blogs, game worlds. These texts and media take very different material forms, but they share an awareness of the way in which an illusion of physical movement can help the reader or viewer to feel fully engaged in the fictive environment. In looking ahead to future developments rather than backward to historical antecedents, I may seem to gesture in the direction of what Richard Grusin *Premediation* (2004, 19) has described as "premediation": an assumption that "the future itself is also already mediated, and that with the right technologies . . . the future can be remediated before it happens."[17] My goal here, however, is not to suggest that the Victorians envisioned, anticipated, or consciously worked toward the creation of the new media of today. Rather, it is to consider some contemporary theories of virtuality as a context for understanding the nineteenth-century forms to be discussed in the following parts. Over the course of the study, I will use contemporary developments as occasional touchstones for comparison that allow us to trace a genealogy that includes some Victorian forms seldom thought of as "media."

Although the word *virtual* is often loosely used to describe any artificial situation that even gestures toward real experience, at its core it refers to an imitation that is not simply viewed, but experienced "as if" it were real. In this sense, the term *virtual reality* is not so much an oxymoron, as some commentators have suggested, as a kind of organic metaphor in which the virtual is the vehicle and reality the tenor. Pierre Lévy (*Becoming Virtual*, 24) notes that "the virtual should, properly speaking, be compared not to the real, but to the actual." The virtual is that which "*tends* toward actualization" (original emphasis) or "concretization." The virtual is trying to get somewhere.

The term *virtual reality* was coined by Jaron Lanier, founder of VPL Research, in 1989 as a broad rubric under which to consider a variety of technologically based experiences and simulations. As Howard Rheingold points out in his account of the birth of virtual reality, Lanier and others had been working on simulations of various kinds for years before anybody "uttered the word 'virtual' to describe anything a computer was likely to do" (159). In its most specific sense, *virtual reality* refers to a digitally simulated environment, an "immersive, interactive system based on computable information" (Heim, 6). Pierre Lévy (*Cyberculture*, 52) describes it as a form of "interactive simulation in which the explorer has the physical sensation of being immersed in a situation defined by a database." Lévy's use of the term *explorer*, and his reference to physical sensation, emphasize the degree to which virtual reality involves a transference of imaginative experience into a perception of physical experience.

At its most basic level, virtual reality involves a projection of the self into a fictive environment. It creates what is known as *telepresence*: perceived or simulated presence, a sensation of not just looking at something but *being* somewhere else. Although *telepresence* is now often shortened to simply *presence*, the term with its original prefix describes a paradox: being present at a distance, being both here and there. Samuel Weber (116) has noted that the word *tele-vision* reflects the way in which the medium "transports vision as such." Television "overcomes distance and separation; but it can do so only because it also *becomes* separation" (original emphasis). It is a method of transmission, and "transmission, which is movement, involves separation." *Telepresence*, which refers to two separate points and the jump that occurs between them, encapsulates a similar feeling of suspension.

The primary component of virtual reality and the standard against which it is judged is the level of "presence" it generates, and there is a growing body of literature on the technical, aesthetic, and, to a lesser degree, philosophical components of mediated presence.[18] Presence defines a mode of perception that feels embodied, that creates a sensation of physical location in an alternative space. The illusion of movement is essential to creating that sense of locatedness. As Mark B. N. Hansen (5) puts it, "The body forms an ultimate background, an absolute here, in relation to which all perceptual experience must be oriented." Hansen notes the role of "self-movement" as the "tactile . . . face of perception." Movement enhances the tactile dimension, which in turn "serves to confer a bodily—that is, sensory—reality on external perceptual experience."

As I will argue in relation to Victorian novels, a sense of locatedness provides a crucial connection between the physical self and the imaginative environment. The recent explosion of technologies designed to help us, literally, find ourselves is a testament to the high value we place on navigation and orientation in the real world. When we use Google Earth to zoom in on specific addresses all over the world, or when we use a GPS system to track our car's movement from one street to the next, we feel reassured by the fact that as large and complex as the world is, we can locate our own place within it. In addition to the convenience or efficiency increased mobility offers, it is also clear that we simply enjoy its ongoing affirmation of our sheer physical presence. The archetypal cell phone conversation that consists primarily of a caller reporting his or her minute-by-minute location to the person on the other end is another reflection of our childlike pleasure in the magical sense of "being" two places at once.[19]

This sense of dual citizenship, of belonging to two worlds, is similar to the pleasure we derive from a fully engaged reading of fiction. Over the centuries we have struggled to find language to express our ability to occupy a new imaginative or intellectual space in a way that conveys a sense of aesthetic response as an experience. While using the language of travel might seem a logical consequence of the need to describe getting to an imagined space, I suggest that the reverse is true: our sense of there being a "place" there at all results from our sense of having *gone* there. Representing a leap of consciousness as if it were a physical action implies that the place one has landed is equally solid. Thus, the metaphor of travel does not simply reflect, it helps constitute an imagined world.

In connecting the idea of virtual travel in the nineteenth century to developments in contemporary media, I am suggesting that virtual travel has both a historical-cultural dimension and a universal aesthetic dimension. As we will see in Part Three, virtual travel played an important role in the specific nineteenth-century British project of entering the age of modernity. We may understand that project better when we recognize that it continues to perform similar cultural work today. The evolution of a standard vocabulary for describing imaginative experience has facilitated our assimilation of new technologies that are rendered more comprehensible through their absorption into a familiar descriptive framework. By conceiving of the huge body of information available on the World Wide Web as a series of spaces that can be visited, for example, we establish a structure for our interaction with that information. We speak of navigating pathways and travelling through cyberspace as if following a series of computer links involved physical movement from place to place. This language may feel natural and intuitive, but one could imagine relying on an alternative vocabulary of "opening boxes" or "turning pages" or "accessing folders" to describe the process of looking at electronic packages of information, rather than "visiting sites." The effect of creating a topography out of our mental processes, of "mapping . . . real places onto virtual places," one geographer notes, is to suggest that the relationship between a communicator and a communication system is analogous to the relationship between an inhabitant and the place he or she occupies (Adams, 89).

Two different spatial metaphors are generally used to define the "virtual topography" of cyberspace, as Mark Nunes has noted: the idea of the Internet as an "information superhighway" and the idea of the Internet as a smoother, more fluid space that can be "surfed." Nunes suggests that these two figurations correspond to Deleuze and Guattari's description of striated and smooth space: "The highway metaphor calls to mind a system that facilitates and regulates the flow of traffic from destination to destination. . . . In 'surfing' smooth space, however, 'the points are subordinated to the trajectory'" (62). We will return to this distinction in Part Three, where the role of connectivity among specific points in a network is considered in relation to Victorian depictions of railway junctions. But Nunes's analysis underlines the general point that descriptions of using the Internet rely almost exclusively on metaphors of travel, and that these metaphors serve to characterize our relationship to the content that we find there.

As we have seen, the idea of travel as it evolved during the Victorian period challenged a number of boundaries: between home and abroad, domestic and foreign, or simply here and there—a dichotomy that is really a dichotomy between self and other. Virtual reality, by its very nature, embodies that same kind of permeability. "Immersiveness," a sense of confusion about whether one is outside or inside an artwork, is a primary goal of all virtual environments. As Janet Murray has pointed out, all media, including literature, find "exploration of the border between the representational world and the actual world" to be an important part of their self-definition and evolution (103). Immersion involves participation, an "active creation of belief" (110), a willingness to insert oneself in the fictional space. Murray notes, "Immersion can involve a mere flooding of the mind with sensation . . . but in a participatory medium, immersion implies learning to swim" (99). Virtual environments attempt to surround and envelop the viewer, rather than providing a flat interface. They seek where possible to create a multisensory environment, or a visual environment so rich it over-whelms the other senses, extending the participant's own sensory perception so as to minimize the sense of boundary between self and environment.

Other new media rely on the visual environment to engage the viewer's attention in a way that seems very familiar to students of Victorian spectacle. The massive screens of IMAX theaters, like the painted panoramas we will ex-amine in Part One, attempt to capture a large enough percentage of the viewer's field of vision to create a sense of immersion in the scenes displayed. Three-dimensional displays are used in many computer and video games to create a sense of depth that allows the viewer to feel that he or she has entered the scene.[20] Following that sense of initial immersion, a continuing sense of move-ment and engagement is needed to maintain the illusion.[21] A sense of move-ment is integral to the unique "feel" of the game, "the way that the game's me-chanics are orchestrated to create both a compelling experience for the player and the illusion of an internally consistent world" (Bissell, 81). The physical experience or "feel" that a game offers affects our perception of it as a world that has the coherence of reality.

William Gibson, the novelist who coined the term *cyberspace*, has acknowl-edged that the concept was inspired by early arcade games, but said that it was less the games themselves than the players' experience of them that led him to imagine the creation of an alternative reality. "'I wasn't as taken by the graphic content of the early arcade games as I was by the posture of the kids playing the games. . . . It was so evident that they wanted to get *through* the screen: you could see them yearning for some kind of surround, and doing everything they could to just be there'" (quoted in Poole, 22; original emphasis). The boundary between game space and real space is temptingly permeable, and effective games make the players want to "jump in."[22] Our ability to cross between these spaces, to move fluidly from here to there, feels like a physical rather than purely imaginative journey.

Immersion in virtual environments has been described as a psychological state in which one feels that one is "enveloped by, included in, and interacting with an environment that provides a continuous stream of stimuli and experiences" (Sallnas, 175). Game theorists often cite psychologist Mihaly Csikszentmihalyi's work on the sense of "flow" generated by "optimal experience," a form of complete involvement in the task at hand that leads to a pleasurable "loss of self-consciousness" (King and Krzywinska, 33). The continuous flow of the experience, the sense of it unfolding over time, can be enhanced either through a sense of movement on the part of the user or through continuity in the representation itself.

As we will see, similar qualities that one might call "seamlessness" and "continuousness" were central to the Victorian experience of virtual travel. The elaborate staging of panoramas, with foreground scenery and even actors to bolster the illusion; the endless "pageant" of images presented to the view during a leisurely trip up the Thames; the rapid blur of scenery through the window of a railway car, which confuses the traveller into feeling he has never really left his point of departure: all of these forms of continuous stimuli create an essential indeterminacy about the physical location of the body within a dynamic environment. This propriocentric indeterminacy fascinated Victorians in much the same way that virtual reality fascinates us today: it creates access to an imaginative perspective that feels grounded in physical experience.

The immersiveness of a virtual environment is enhanced by some degree of interactivity. The user's capacity to take an active role of some kind, whether through "navigation, manipulation of objects, or interaction with other agents" (Regenbrecht and Schubert, 426), augments his or her perception of the reality of the environment.[23] These interactions can be just as important as accuracy of visual representation in creating a sense of realism. The perceived quality of a virtual environment, Blascovich et al. (112) write, is not simply a matter of its "photographic realism" but also reflects the "behavioral realism" of the social interactions that take place within it.[24]

The Victorians understood the value of interactivity in persuading audiences to suspend their disbelief. Many of the enormous panorama displays of the period were supplemented by costumed actors, narrators, or souvenir sellers who provided opportunities for dialogue, suggesting that participants desired active engagement with the setting. As we will see, the river and railway guidebooks that were so popular during this time relied heavily on a participatory rhetoric that implies that the viewer is accompanying the author on a journey.

This development contributed to an increased degree of what might be called *interactivity* in Victorian fiction, a term that encompasses direct addresses to the reader and other strategies that shape what Garrett Stewart has described as "the conscripted audience" of nineteenth-century fiction.

Clearly, this level of engagement with a text is not the same as complete interactivity, and some would argue that in fact such interactivity is inimical to the processes of fiction. Michael Chaouli, for example, has recently suggested that real interactivity, of the kind found in hypertext fiction, "interferes with the unfolding of literature, particularly with writing that means to lead us into fictional worlds" (607). To be what Chaouli calls an "active reader" (610), you must be receptive to the one-way communication of the text. The full interactivity of hypertext, which turns readers into authorial collaborators, does not seem thus far to generate fictional worlds as compelling as those created by traditional narratives.[25] Nonetheless, we can describe some traditional literary texts as more interactive than others in the degree to which they encourage the reader to think self-consciously, throughout the text, about his or her relationship to the narrative.

Interactivity has the effect, Pierre Lévy suggests, of authenticating the virtual environment. Operating within it "as if" it were real helps make it so; by interacting with the virtual world, "users explore and actualize it at the same time" (*Cyberculture*, 57). Such users are like the Victorian reader who is both addressed and created by Charlotte Brontë with the words, "Reader, I married him." The reader, who is not simply the person holding the book but the ideal reader conjured by Brontë's narrative, cannot refuse this gesture of recognition, and thus is born a relationship that makes the reader a participant in the storytelling activity and a visitor to the world it describes.

Given the power of virtual reality technology to "realize" a place and give it a sense of presence, it seems surprising that the vast majority of virtual environments do not create exciting new worlds, but reproduce places that already exist. Although virtual reality is often associated with fantasy in the popular imagination, it was initially developed for functional, real-world purposes. Virtual environments were first created for military training, for purposes ranging from flight simulations to the staging of complex battle scenarios, and that use continues. More recently, psychologists and therapists have explored the use of virtual reality scenarios that allow patients with severe phobias to accustom themselves to situations they find frightening.[26] Social science researchers have recognized the potential usefulness of distributed research environments where human behavior can be imitated and analyzed. Recent virtual reality research that demonstrates consistency between online and real-world behavior has raised the possibility of conducting research that substitutes virtual environments for real ones.[27]

One might expect that by now the Internet would be fully populated with holodeck-style fantasy sites, but in fact "virtual tours" of real places are among the most popular experiences available on the Internet. Many tourist sites now have electronic equivalents that combine textual description with plentiful, high-quality images or streaming video that convey a sense of the visual landscape. Some offer 360-degree panoramic views that allow the user to navigate an independent pathway. Many sites are designed to entice visitors, of course, by whetting their appetite for the real thing. Others present themselves, either implicitly or explicitly, as a substitute for an actual visit.[28]

The success of these electronic tours, I would argue, is due in part to their capacity to build on a long-standing tradition of virtual tourism as developed in the nineteenth century. The famously inaccessible Caves of Lascaux, in France, are now most easily reached by way of the web. Damage to the real caves had already led to the creation of a full-scale facsimile on the website, while the real caves remain closed to most visitors. Now, the French government has created a virtual tour that leads you through the various rooms of the caves and allows you to stop and examine any of the wall art close up. Jonathan Taylor (185) describes such sites as "museums of the real," a way of preserving endangered sites by allowing people to experience them without actually being there. Many museums now offer virtual "tours" for school groups that require computers rather than buses.

As this brief overview suggests, the capacity of a virtual environment to create a sense of immersion in the viewer depends on a variety of features that reinforce its own internal coherence. In this sense, virtual reality technology operates much like fiction. The fact that the virtual environments of multiplayer games are generally referred to as *game worlds* suggests that, like the fictional world one finds in a novel, the environment of a game can have an internal coherence and logic that make it feel comprehensive.[29] This does not make a game identical to a fictional narrative, of course. An ongoing debate exists in the discipline of video-game criticism about whether narrative expectations can and should be applied to video games. Ludologists, those who study games, generally feel that narratologists who examine games for their similarity to cinema or literature are simply colonizing a new medium without recognizing the fundamental differences between games and narrative-based media.[30]

The idea that immersiveness involves a sense of what was earlier called *continuousness*, of occurring over time, is reinforced by Marie-Laure Ryan's description of virtual reality as a "process," one that unfolds according to rules that often resemble those of narrative. Virtual reality resembles fiction in that both forms offer the opportunity to "test a model of the world", (*Narrative*, 63). In a sense, Ryan is arguing not that virtual reality resembles fiction, but that fiction resembles virtual reality in its depiction of possible worlds. Nevertheless, when the makers of *World of Warcraft* assert in their advertisements, "It's not a game. It's a world," they are underlining the degree to which successful immersion requires that the medium itself become invisible. I will suggest here that the preoccupation with virtual travel we find in Victorian fiction demonstrates that the reader's feeling of transportation is not a by-product of narrative world-making, but a fundamental step in the process.

The Victorians were interested primarily in exploring aspects of their own world, rather than inventing new ones. Some of their virtual travel destinations are foreign, many are familiar to the point of irrelevance, but none of them are entirely imaginary. Their passion for creating representations of things that were already available to them in reality suggests that they valued these virtual travel experiences *as representations*. The repetition involved was an important element of the experience. Travel itself, as a form of repetition, provided the model for a continuing loop of replication. The attraction of the virtual travel experience was the opportunity it provided for disorientation and self-reflection. The places visited seem largely incidental.

It may be useful here to consider Foucault's distinction between resemblance and similitude. Resemblance "predicates itself upon a model it must return to and reveal; similitude circulates the simulacrum as an indefinite and reversible relation of the similar to the similar" (44). Mark Taylor describes the self-reflexivity referred to by Foucault as a play of signs that is akin to the "strange loops" of feedback described by Douglas Hofstadter in *Gödel, Escher, Bach* (75). This circularity describes the Victorian affinity for reading imaginary guidebooks describing panoramas that in turn represent real places they may have already been. The effect is one not of resemblance but of similitude; the guidebooks do not refer back to real locations but reinforce the realism of the panorama that is caught between reality and its re-representation.

Marc Augé has described "the traveller's space" as "the archetype of *non-place*" (70; original emphasis), a space that forms a gap that the traveller seeks to fill with guidebooks or narratives (68). In many of the examples we will explore, the space that is carefully evoked does turn out to be a kind of nowhere, a nonspace that exists only as an arbitrary end point to a journey that is the real locus of interest. In this sense, the traveller's space is always virtual.

The virtual, Marcus Doel and David Clarke note, "like all images, concepts, and ideas," is assumed to be "subservient to that which it re-presents and/or displaces." Of course, the critiques leveled at virtual reality echo critiques leveled at art since Plato.[31] As Janet Murray (97) points out, Cervantes's *Don Quixote* offers the same critique of literature that modern critics level at virtual reality: it can be mistaken for the real. That displacement or confusion is in fact the source of the attraction of the virtual. Its combination of likeness to, and difference from, reality ensures that the reader is always in transit.

Are We There Yet? focuses on three forms of travel that the Victorians used to map the imaginative journey between representation and reality. The book's three parts unfold along similar trajectories. Each begins with the material, bodily experience of travel; analyzes its nonfictional representation in advertisements, guidebooks, and memoirs; and describes the transmutation of that experience into fiction. The brief novel readings that conclude each part emphasize their status and operation as realist fiction, but they do so by uncovering traces of rhetoric borrowed from nonfiction prose accounts of travel. These virtual travel narratives serve to mediate between the actual experience of travel and fictional efforts to construct the reader as a kind of traveller.

Part One, "Going Nowhere: Panoramic Travel," analyzes the "panoramania" of the nineteenth century as an early manifestation of our attraction to visiting "non-places." Enormous, realistic, 360-degree paintings of actual places, as well as moving panoramas that unfolded continuous tableaux of scenery, were a staple of Victorian entertainment culture for decades. Through close examination of reviews and descriptions of panoramas; surviving preparatory sketches for panoramas; advertisements, handbills, and other ephemera generated by panorama exhibitors; and literary or satiric accounts of the panorama experience, I argue that these displays were prized less for their aesthetic or theatrical value than for their supposed capacity to transport the viewer to another place.

Looking at this specific dimension of Victorian visual culture allows us to see the ways in which the rural and urban landscape descriptions of Hardy, George Eliot, and Dickens, in such novels as *Jude the Obscure, Tess of the D'Urbervilles, Adam Bede, The Mill on the Floss,* and *Bleak House,* were influenced by journalistic evocations of panoramic travel. These novelists, I will suggest, capitalized on the popular associations generated by panoramic views of landscape in order to give their readers a sense of immersion in the fictional scene that was analogous to the kind of virtual reality attributed to the panorama experience.

Part Two, "Total Immersion: Navigating the Thames," explores the way in which Thames travel narratives constructed a sense of immersion and continuity that gave the feel of virtual reality to depictions of the Thames travel experience. The navigation of the river, like the navigation of branching pathways through a computer-generated game scenario, becomes an exercise in illusory agency that directs the participant toward a series of predetermined destinations. Geographers distinguish between spatial representations that are topological, like maps, and those that are "projective," giving a sense of the route one would follow in travelling a space. Both the verbal and the visual representations discussed in Part Two unfold, over time, in a linear dimension that attempts to recreate the experience of travelling the river.

The late nineteenth-century craze for journeys along the Thames spawned an entire subgenre of guidebooks, topographical poems, and personal accounts devoted to description of the river. In many of these accounts, the Thames journey is presented as a form of exploration, described in language that consciously evokes journeys taken by explorers of the Nile and other travellers to exotic locations. In addition, a journey up the Thames provides the central organizing principle for two novel-length prose works, Jerome K. Jerome's massively popular *Three Men in a Boat* (1889) and William Morris's utopian fantasy *News from Nowhere* (1890). Both books use a journey on the Thames to create a timeless space that is, paradoxically, an ideal setting for exploration of the most current social issues. The unique characteristics of river travel, as described in these narratives, render it remarkably similar to the kind of virtual travel provided by the panoramic perspective. The impression of a moving landscape passing before one's eyes encourages the viewer to see the riverbanks as, in the words of one writer on the Thames, a "pageant" that displays characteristic scenes in a manner that immerses the viewer in a seamless visual environment. But the traveller is able to alternate a more distant, aesthetic perspective with frequent stops that involve direct engagement with the environment.

These river narratives provided an important model for novelists who use the image of the Thames as a darker reflection of life in industrial London. Where the pastoral Thames journey was a replication of more exotic river travels, the urban Thames journey, as seen in Dickens's *Our Mutual Friend* and *Great Expectations* and in George Eliot's *Daniel Deronda*, presents a concentrated vision of the anxieties of nineteenth-century culture.

Part Three, "High-Speed Connection: The Railway Network," shows how the leisurely linear narratives of panoramas and river journeys were compressed into rapid transit along railway networks, a development that drastically reconfigured the Victorian understanding of the traveller's relationship to the space he or she traverses. Beginning with the groundbreaking work of Wolfgang Schivelbusch, critics have long recognized that the development of the railway was a crucial cultural event that transformed popular understandings of space and time in the second half of the nineteenth century. By the end of the century,

I will suggest, travel no longer meant taking a journey of significant length with the expectation of seeing things along the way. Instead, we will see that the idea of travel was gradually sifted into two distinct and opposing categories: first, the kind of individualized leisure travel that was valorized in Thames river narratives; and second, the mass transportation epitomized by rail travel. The nostalgic displacement of the more leisured sense of travel onto specific forms like river journeys or walking tours made it possible for the Victorians to revel in the brute efficiency of the railway journey.

My discussion of the railway makes extensive use of some little-known non-fiction representations of rail journeys, including personal accounts and short stories, from periodicals such as *Blackwood's, Bentley's Miscellany,* and *The Cornhill,* as well as some railway guidebooks and travelogues. These accounts show the Victorians' pleasure at being able to travel more quickly to a wider range of places, while also revealing a nostalgia for a fully embodied travel experience in which the traveller occupies the space of the journey itself. They differ radically from earlier travel narratives in saying very little about the actual landscape being traversed, focusing instead on the mechanisms of travel—processes and procedures, arrival and departure. Railways redefined the spatial context of travel, focusing the attention of the traveller inward, either on the new social world created by the diverse mix of passengers in a carriage or on the interiorized space of a newspaper or novel to be read.

Part Three highlights the connection between the expansion of railway networks and the evolution of information networks, such as the telegraph and telephone, that prefigure the Internet in their capacity to provide virtual agency, or "telepresence," to those who travelled these early information superhighways. These networks play a critical role in the information systems known as novels. In the Sherlock Holmes stories of Arthur Conan Doyle and in Bram Stoker's fin de siècle novel *Dracula,* railway networks form the nexus of multiple avenues of communication, and rail lines provide an extension of personal power and agency to those who master them. A brief exploration of the connection between railways and the development of early cinema demonstrates the crucial role played by technologies of travel in stimulating the development of new forms of art and media. The book concludes by examining the implications of my argument for current debates about the relationship between the Victorian period and modern and postmodern culture.

Armchair Travel / Virtual Travel

Although this study involves a variety of forms of representation, it is fundamentally a book about texts and their capacity to mobilize the imagination. The kind of virtual reality that can be experienced today by sitting in a chair with controls, datagloves, and visors hearkens back to the idea of "armchair travel" first popularized in the nineteenth century. In 1854, the term was common enough to provide the structure for a travel book entitled *The Old Arm-Chair*, in which the author's comfortable chair allows him to travel "more rapidly than the lightning-speed of the telegraph" (15); and "armchair travel" is still a commonly used phrase today, though it carries more overtones of irony than it did in the Victorian period. The image perfectly encapsulates the contradiction inherent in the idea of virtual travel: the contrast between the cozy, stable, domestic space of the reading experience, and the movement across vast spaces it inspires in the imagination.

Of course, the sense of being completely immersed in a fictional work is often described in spatial terms, as in the phrase "lost in a book." Neuropsychologist Victor Nell uses the phrase as the starting point for outlining a model of readerly absorption that links fully absorbed reading to a state of hypnosis (213). Nell cites Hilgard in noting the imaginative "disjunction" that allows a reader to be "involved and to maintain a safe distance" from the world of the book.[32] Sven Birkerts describes the "state of being elsewhere while reading" (84) in *The Gutenberg Elegies* and admits, "Book to real world, real world to book—I am in perpetual transit" (102). Nineteenth-century writers adopted this common trope and turned it into a metaphor that extended across a range of cultural forms.

Birkerts's quotation emphasizes a central aspect of fictive travel that we will return to throughout this study: it is an activity that focuses attention less on the places being visited than on the self. The self is defined in response to an experience of place. As we will see, this can be a disorienting experience. Georges Poulet, in his analysis of the phenomenology of reading, describes what he calls a "strange displacement of myself by the work" (59). This process of alienation turns him, temporarily, into a different person, "a self who is granted the experience of thinking thoughts foreign to him" (56). He himself becomes a foreigner. Poulet sees two possible reactions to this sense of "invasion": "in the first case I lose myself in that alien world, and in the other we keep our distance and refuse to identify." The oscillation between these two poles of "extreme closeness and extreme detachment" (63), as described by Poulet, resembles the transition from subjectivity to objectivity that, as we saw, is integral to the travel experience.

The idea of fiction as armchair travel is elegantly articulated in the opening pages of George Eliot's *Mill on the Floss*, where a vivid and lyrical description of the scene outside Dorlcote Mill prefigures many of the descriptive elements that will define "virtual travel" throughout this study. The book opens with a sweeping vista that evokes the panoramic paintings we will examine in Part One. The distant perspective encompasses the "wide plain, where the broadening Floss hurries on between its green banks to the sea," the black ships visible in the distance, and the pictorial contrasts created by the red rooftops of St. Ogg's and the "rich pastures and patches of dark earth." The narrator is able to survey the overall topography of the scene while pausing to admire the prospect: "And this is Dorlcote Mill. I must stand a minute or two here on the bridge and look at it" (53). The visual expanse before her emphasizes her own position in relation to the scene, allowing her to engage it imaginatively and emotionally.

Rivers were a common subject for panoramas, and descriptions of river trips were a particularly popular form of travel narrative, as we will see in Part Two. River travel often evokes the idea of a journey through time, or across a different and larger space, and here too, the river seems to transport the narrator back to the past. The narrator's movement through the scene enhances her sense of physical presence: the flowing river is "like a living companion while I wander along the bank and listen to its low placid voice." She returns to the scene through memory, writing, "I remember those large dipping willows . . . I remember the stone bridge . . ." (53). The narrator stresses her specific location and sensory experience, describing what she sees, hears, and feels as the late-afternoon scene becomes cooler and darker.

The sensory isolation that is essential to creating a feeling of immersiveness is here created through an auditory filter: "The rush of the water and the booming of the mill bring a dreamy deafness which seems to heighten the peacefulness of the scene. They are like a great curtain of sound, shutting one out from the world beyond" (54). The narrator brings the reader along with her as she points out specific details—"See how [the horses] stretch their shoulders. . . . Look at their grand shaggy feet that seem to grasp the firm earth" (54). Like visitors to a holodeck, the narrator and reader are in their own world, cut off from external reality, ready to experience whatever this world has to offer.

Eliot uses yet another method to place us directly in the scene: she creates an avatar, a figure in the landscape with whom we can identify. The figure of the "halted traveler" was common trope in Romantic poetry, and is a prominent feature of the landscape paintings of Caspar David Friedrich, where such foreground figures serve as "a surrogate for the artist and the audience" (Koerner 182). Eliot's figure acts on our behalf in much the same way an avatar represents the player of a computer game. Looking at the mill, the narrator sees a mirror image of herself: "That little girl is watching it too: she has been standing on just the same spot at the edge of the water ever since I paused on the bridge." After lingering a few more moments, she writes, "It is time the little playfellow went in, I think. . . . It is time too for me to leave off resting my arms on the cold stone of this bridge" (55). The narrator's identification with the girl, and our identification with the narrator, creates a regression that pulls us into the scene.

The intensity of this imaginative transportation is represented as an almost physical action. The narrator actually feels that she is leaning on the cold railing of the bridge and only gradually realizes that this is part of the illusion. "Ah, my arms are really benumbed. I have been pressing my elbows on the arms of my chair and dreaming that I was standing on the bridge in front of Dorlcote Mill as it looked one February afternoon many years ago" (55). Eliot literalizes the idea of the "armchair traveller" in her step-by-step description of the virtual journey taken by the narrator while she is sitting at home in her chair. The physical link she establishes between the real world and the imaginative one makes her seem equally present in both, and allows her to invite the reader to make the same trip. "Before I dozed off, I was going to tell you what Mr. and Mrs. Tulliver were talking about," she tells us, and with a turn of the page, we have entered their left-hand parlor.

By framing her novel in this way, Eliot invites us into an imaginative space that is characterized not as a state of mind but as a location. This gesture, I will argue, is typical of the way in which the Victorians conceptualized aesthetic engagement. As we will see, many nineteenth-century commentaries on travel are less about places visited than about the journey there. Through their detailed exploration of the activity of travel, the Victorians created a powerful paradigm for the way in which the mind of a reader, viewer, or audience member can be moved to a place beyond his or her own subjective experience. This movement, the Victorians suggested, is an end in itself.

The phenomena examined here establish a trajectory toward an increasingly sophisticated use of narrative techniques that attempt to immerse the reader in a coherent and convincing illusion. The blending of aesthetics and technology embodied in the Victorian vogue for virtual travel is an important precursor to the twentieth-century transformation of art into "media." When compared to 3-D game environments, 360-degree panoramas may seem crude, and *Adam Bede* may seem a long way from hypertext, but this book suggests that the "willing suspension of belief" demanded by literature eventually points us toward what William Gibson famously described as the "consensual hallucination" of cyberspace. We still struggle to find a way to express the ontological status of a place we experience "as if" it were reality. Travel, as a way of belonging to two places at once, became in the nineteenth century the perfect metaphor for the virtuality of realism.

Part One

GOING NOWHERE
Panoramic Travel

> So wonderful is the effect produced by this enchanting scene on the spectator,
> that they cannot help fancying themselves imperceptibly transported into
> the very interior of the province of Switzerland . . . viewing in reality, the very
> identical spot, on which their admiration is so intensely fixed.
>
> —Advertising handbill, "Grand View of a Lake and Waterfall in
> Switzerland," Leicester Square, 1831

> Digital living will include less and less dependence on being in a specific place
> at a specific time, and the transmission of place itself will start to become
> possible. If I really could look out the electronic window of my living room in
> Boston and see the Alps . . . in a way I am very much in Switzerland.
>
> —Nicholas Negroponte, *Being Digital*, 1995, 165

The panorama is a unique space where the nineteenth century meets the present. Contemporary developments in panoramic videography have repopularized the word and helped to restore its specific visual meaning after a century in which it had come to signify any form of broad overview. Panoramic photographs can now be easily assembled by stitching overlapping digital images together, video "virtual tours" can be created with rotating line cameras such as Panoscan, and panoramic digital mapping using Shuttle Radar Topography Mission (SRTM) data allows computers to generate swooping panoramic images for GIS applications like Google Earth. And yet the panorama somehow retains the aura of the nineteenth century. In Katsuhiro Otamo's 2005 anime film *Steamboy*, the Victorian world that provides the setting for its steampunk science fiction plot is evoked in wide-angle shots of Manchester and London. The hero's flights aboard a steam-powered zeppelin initiate panoramic, wide-angle views of London that begin at the top of St. Paul's and zoom down into "a virtual tour of the twisting, intertwining streets of 19th-century London," a visual tour de force that is often cited as an example of the film's widely admired "detail and realism" (Audrey Doyle). As many Hollywood films from *Mary Poppins* onward reflect, panoramic views over rooftops make us think, in an almost subconscious way, of Victorian London.

The noted video-game designer Cliff Breszinski may not be aware that one of the most famous panoramas of the Victorian period was a view of London taken from St. Paul's Cathedral. Yet in his account of the evolution of his best-known game, *Gears of War,* Breszinski identifies the panoramic vista seen from St. Paul's as the inspiration for his game's uniquely timeless atmosphere.

> I'll never forget the first time I went to London and experienced, firsthand, the beauty of Hampton Court Palace, Westminster Abby, and Saint Paul's Cathedral. The afternoon was bright as the sun set on the last tours of the day. I had just climbed all 532 of the damp cathedral steps to the very top. As I emerged into the open air, the clouds parted to reveal a beautiful sunset, and I had an epiphany. Seeing all of London sprawled out beneath me was humbling and inspiring. Right then I knew that the next universe I would help craft wouldn't be about aliens or tournaments; it would be character-driven, centered on themes of loyalty, redemption, paranoia, and "destroyed beauty."[1]

Breszinski has said that one of his goals in *Gears of War* was to create a setting that seemed like an unexpected blend of the old and the new, and the sweeping city views seen in the game seem to evoke both the nineteenth century and the present. A screenshot from *Gears of War* (fig. 2) shows a panoramic vista that includes St. Paul's on the right, and the avatar in the foreground closely resembles the spectator figures that were common in nineteenth-century landscape paintings like Caspar David Friedrich's *Traveler Looking Over a Sea of Fog* (1818).

Breszinski's comment also demonstrates that the view itself seemed to evoke an imaginative world, a "universe" he sought to recreate in a game that has been praised as having "an experiential depth rare in the genre" (Bissell, 4). This world, though fictional, would not be fantasy. Breszinski's response, as we will see, mirrors the experience of Victorians who viewed the panorama of London that Thomas Horner painted from the very same spot. The sense of transportation or immersion that Breszinski creates in his game was anticipated by this quintessentially Victorian art form.

In this part, I will explore the nature of the panoramic perspective and the specific methods by which it cultivates a sense of virtual travel. Beginning with

Fig. 2. Gears of War. Copyright 2006 Epic Games, Inc. All rights reserved. Image used with permission.

an overview of the development of painted panoramas as a visual medium and the cultural significance they accrued in the nineteenth century, I will turn to a detailed examination of textual representations of these visual representations. By applying some theories of travel writing to these pseudo-travel narratives, I show how handbills, advertisements, panorama guides, and reviews of panorama exhibits adopted the tropes of "real" travel writing to powerful effect. Using concepts elaborated by narrative theorists such as Gérard Genette and David Herman, I then suggest that Victorian realist novels continue this self-reflexive gesture, using the panoramic perspective to create a realistic sense of immersion in their narratives. A close examination of descriptive passages from Dickens, Eliot, Thackeray, and Hardy shows that they borrowed the descriptive rhetoric of the panoramic view, and in particular the way in which it positions the spectator as a traveller to another place, as a way of reinforcing the realism of their own fictional worlds.

Cultural theorists have long recognized the panorama as emblematic of the nineteenth century. The collection of materials assembled in volume 5 of the complete works of Walter Benjamin under the title *Das Passagen-Werk*, first published in 1982 and translated in 1999 as *The Arcades Project*, explores, through a montage of quotations interspersed with brief commentaries by

Benjamin, the shopping arcades (*passages*) of Paris as archetypes of the "primal history" (*Urgeschichte*) of the nineteenth century. Among the related cultural phenomena that Benjamin returns to again and again in these sketches, drafts, and "exposés" is the panorama or diorama.[2] Just as the Parisian *passage* organizes the flow of commerce into "'miniature worlds'" ("Exposé of 1935," *Arcades*, 3) that compel and direct the attention of consumers, so the panorama presents a synthesis and condensation of an entire landscape that allows the viewer to comprehend and consume it. Benjamin notes the "tireless" effort of artists "to make panoramas the scenes of a perfect imitation of nature" (5) and connects this to the general "phantasmagoria of capitalist culture" that he sees unfolding in the urban landscape (8).

Benjamin's fragmentary account leads to a conception of the panorama as itself a kind of *passage*, a liminal space that both reflects and sustains the illusions of capitalist culture. The "connecting or mediating function" of arcades ("Hauss-mannization, Barricade Fighting," *Arcades*, 125) renders them emblematic of the way in which all the phenomena Benjamin describes create a transitional space between past and present, distance and interior, nature and art. The "interest of the panorama is in seeing the true city—the city indoors" ("Panorama," *Arcades*, 532), and its capacity to bring the complex outside world into a controlled interior space was clearly an important aspect of its appeal to Victorian audiences. As we will see, contemporary accounts of the experience of viewing panoramas emphasize the perceptual shifts involved in viewing something that one knows is an illusion, yet feels like reality. These accounts display an oscillation between resistance and surrender to the illusion of the panorama that evokes the dialectical movement Benjamin sees as characteristic of the nineteenth century.

> The development of the forces of production shattered the wish symbols of the previous century, even before the monuments representing them had collapsed. . . . these products [of literature and art] are on the point of entering the market as commodities. But they linger on the threshold. From this epoch derive the arcades and *intérieurs*, the exhibition halls and panoramas. They are residues of a dream world. The realization of dream elements, in the course of waking up, is the paradigm of dialectical thinking. ("Exposé of 1935," *Arcades*, 13)

Though Benjamin refers here to the late nineteenth century in particular, the Victorian obsession with panoramas clearly reflects the beginnings of the transitional cultural moment he identifies. The popularity of the panorama, as we will see, derived from its ability to mediate between different levels of the increasingly complex geography of the Victorian world. The panorama created a transitional, hypothetical, "virtual" space that offered an opportunity to "try out" a certain kind of experience or worldview.

The panorama seemed so emblematic of the nineteenth-century zeitgeist that Dolf Sternberger, who was acquainted with Benjamin, used it as the central leitmotif for an overview of the century in his 1938 work *Panorama oder Ansichten vom 19. Jahrhundert* (translated in 1977 as *Panorama of the Nineteenth Century*)—a work that Benjamin bitterly described in a letter to Adorno as plagiarized from his own arcades project (Buck-Morss, 59 note 2). Sternberger suggests, for example, that the development of the railway "elaborated the new world of experience, the countries and the oceans, into a panorama. . . . since travelling became so comfortable and universal, it turned the eyes of travellers outward, offering them a rich diet of changing tableaux, the only possible experience during a trip" (39). As we will see when we explore the relationship between train travel and the panoramic perspective in Part Three, the panorama phenomenon was deeply implicated in the changing perceptions of time and space that, as many commentators have noted, marked the passage of the Victorian age into the modern age.[3]

Panoramas, and textual evocations of what I will call the "panoramic perspective," provided a form of "virtual travel" that seemed to expand the horizons of the Victorian gaze. By condensing, packaging, and commodifying the travel experience, panoramas exploited the Victorian fascination with travel while providing a safe alternative to it. Panoramas were not evaluated as works of art, or even as visual exhibitions: they were evaluated according to their capacity to recreate the experience of a real place. As we will see, the panoramic perspective created the sensation of being in two places at once, of being both a viewer/reader and an actual traveller. This bifurcation of the viewer's subjectivity created a unique space for perception, a Benjaminian *passage*, in which the viewer could "try on" the experience of travelling elsewhere without having to invest time and energy in the real thing. The appeal of the panorama derived in large part, I will argue, from the provisional or hypothetical nature of the experience. The panoramic perspective encouraged viewers to position themselves neither as full participants in, nor as detached spectators of, the scene displayed. Instead, they were situated in a liminal space between these two experiential poles—among other things, as consumers, who could sample the product before deciding to buy. The provisional or contingent quality of the panoramic perspective makes it the earliest example of what would later be called "virtuality."

The panorama has generally been considered in relation to other forms of visual culture, other precinematic modes of exhibition and display, rather than in relation to literary texts. Here I will focus primarily on verbal panoramism,

looking at the ways in which the panoramic perspective influenced the construction of landscape, both rural and urban, in a variety of literary and nonliterary
texts from the 1830s through the 1880s. In promotional and journalistic descriptions of the panoramas themselves we see the specific qualities that made them
so vividly appealing to viewers. The 360-degree panoramas displayed in venues
like the Colosseum and Leicester Square promised a comprehensive and synop-
tic view of scenes, like the burgeoning London metropolis, that seemed to have
grown too large to grasp. Moving panoramas, long canvases that were unrolled
before the spectator in imitation of a journey, added a dynamic and temporal
dimension to this perspective, inviting the viewer to undertake a complete journey in the company of an expert guide. When the *Illustrated London News*, in its
mission statement (May 1842, 1), promised "to keep before the eye of the world
a living and moving panorama of all its activities and instances," it was invoking
a power to synthesize, reflect, and channel the disparate forms and events of
modern life into a unified representational stream that would carry the reader/
viewer along with it. This synthesis of word and image would allow the public
to have "under their glance, and within their grasp, the very form and presence
of events as they transpire, in all their substantial reality."

Unlike the static, fragmentary, and ahistorical framing of landscape embodied in the "picturesque" perspective that dominated scenic description earlier
in the century,[4] the panoramic perspective reflected an urge toward comprehensiveness, continuity, and dynamism. Moving panoramas invited viewers to
contemplate a landscape over time, in a sequence of different places. Circular
panoramas required the viewer to turn, walk, and consider them from a variety
of angles. This mode of contemplation was far more active than the kind of
reaction called forth by picturesque landscape paintings. Yet it was more passive
than engagement with a real landscape would be. It was a form of virtual travel,
an experience partaking of both movement and vision, without fully embracing
either. The panoramic perspective enforced a destabilization of one's own point
of view, offering a model for aesthetic experience that would lay the groundwork
for the development of new media that would focus even more intensively on
evoking these same effects.

The relationship created between the panoramic scene and the stationary
spectator, who felt that he or she was actually floating down a river or across
a landscape, is closely related to that created in a similarly destabilizing scenic
experience popular at this time: hot-air balloon travel. Brief examination of several popular accounts of balloon journeys will show that air travel created an
inverted panoramic effect: a sense that the viewer was standing still while the

landscape below was "unrolled," like "a grand natural panorama" (Glaisher, 20). The freedom and detachment felt by balloon travellers is linked, I will suggest, to the kind of mediated perspective we see in panorama descriptions. In both cases, the traveller revels in his unique perspective on the landscape he surveys. His or her access to a scene that was previously invisible provides a unique vision of its structure and constituent parts. At the same time, this perspective occludes other, nonvisual aspects of the scene, allowing the viewer to avoid confronting the street-level reality of the cities and landscapes he enjoys.

This mode of vision is somewhat different from the all-encompassing "imperial gaze" often associated with conventional forms of Victorian travel. As Mary Louise Pratt and others have shown, efforts to map the empire, both literally and conceptually, rely on the adoption of a stable vantage point from which to define the "other." The conceptual space created by the panoramic perspective, however, is delimited by moving coordinates. The viewer is forced to define his or her own point of view in the constantly shifting space between himself or herself and the scene below. In their attempts to describe the world they see stretched out before them, nineteenth-century panoramic travellers are constructing a world that has never before been seen. At the same time, they are constructing an identity for themselves, a place from which to grasp that newly expanded world. Floating above the boundaries between city and suburb, metropole and colony, core and periphery that would define their own places *within* the scenes they survey, the panoramic traveller is able to reduce his increasingly complex world into what balloonist James Glaisher would call a "map . . . beneath his feet" (5).

I. A ROOM WITH A VIEW:
THE VICTORIAN PANORAMA

It is difficult to overstate the popularity of scenic panoramas in mid-nineteenth-century London. Interest in panoramas among people of all classes surged in the years 1845 to 1850, but they were a staple of the London entertainment scene from the 1830s through the 1870s, with numerous competing panoramas running concurrently during most of that time. Richard Altick, in his indispensable book *The Shows of London*, describes the panorama craze as one example among many of the Victorian fascination with "mimetic effects." Dioramas, moving clockwork figures, tableaux, waxworks, and other simulations of reality were immensely appealing to a culture that loved exhibitions of all kinds, some of which provided "tangible evidence of nature's variety and man's ingenuity," others of which "depicted an illusory reality" (51). As we will see, panoramas often bridged these two categories, presenting scenes that conveyed real information about natural landscapes and man-made structures, but that also pleased viewers with their illusionistic virtuosity.[5]

In the period between 1820 and 1860 there were often dozens of panoramas or panorama-type scenic exhibitions in London at any one time. There were several exhibition spaces devoted exclusively to panoramas, most notably the Panorama in the Strand, which opened in 1802 and lasted until 1831, and the Panorama in Leicester Square, operated by John and Robert Burford from 1823 to 1861. These spaces were designed to exhibit 360-degree scenes that the spectator viewed from a central point. This format had developed at the end of the eighteenth century and was a logical extension of the growing interest in topographic views and maps. Large trompe l'oeil wall paintings had graced a number of aristocratic homes of the period, and in 1787 an artist named Robert Barker patented a scheme he had conceived for overcoming the perspectival problems inherent in painting a circular, 360-degree landscape painting. Sir Joshua Reynolds, who had initially expressed skepticism at his efforts, admired the panorama eventually presented by Robert and his son Henry Barker in 1791, "Panorama of London from the Albion Mill, Southwark." Over the years, the city of London would prove a surprisingly popular subject for panoramas in London itself, suggesting that the vantage point afforded by panoramas was distinctive enough to be valued even by those with ready access to the real scene. The anonymous watercolor panels that comprise the circa 1810 "Rhinebeck panorama of London," now at the Museum of London, convey a sense of the extraordinary detail and attention to perspective that were typical of the genre.

The London panorama was followed by the even more successful "Grand Fleet at Spithead" in the same year, one of many panoramas that functioned as a kind of *reportage*. The naval theme proved popular, and in 1795 Barker's panorama "Lord Howe's Victory and the Glorious First of June," depicting a victory of the previous year, would establish the value of panoramas as newsreel-like depictions of virtually current events. As Stephan Oettermann notes, "The panorama ceased to be just one form of entertainment among others in the mind of the British public; it succeeded in linking itself with patriotism and national pride" (107). Panoramas depicting battles, natural disasters, and other newsworthy events would continue to be popular, and even panoramas that were primarily scenic in nature would make every effort to be au courant. Burford's 1848 Panorama of Paris, for example, coincided with the height of interest in revolutionary events in France, an advantage noted by the *Illustrated London News*, which described it as a "well-timed addition to the sights of the metropolis" that represented "that focus of Republican excitement, the Place de la Revolution," as well as "vast processions" moving toward the Chamber of Deputies ("Burford's Panorama of Paris," June 1848, 373). Only a few weeks earlier, the *Illustrated London News* had produced its own scenic depiction of the Revolution, a fold-out view of the Hall of the National Assembly and the "Proclamation of the Republic" (*ILN* 12, May 1848, 309–10).

Panoramas were also seen as a source of useful information about other countries, which suggests that after a century of Grand Tours, "knowing" another country was generally understood to mean seeing the major sights of its major cities. The degree of contemporary interest in specific places can be charted by enumeration of the foreign capitals and historic cities featured in panoramas. Although mountain and river views were popular subjects of moving panoramas, cities were by far the favorite subject of static representations. The experience of standing in the center of a 360-degree picture was perhaps more comparable to the real experience of surveying a city skyline than that of viewing a mountain or river prospect; most natural landscapes would generally be viewed from a lower angle, and would probably present a "better" view from a single direction. The experience of surveying an entire city, in all directions, however, was well suited to circular representation, and created a parallel between the immersive experience of the panorama and the actual experience of being in the city itself. A partial list of cities featured in panoramas (in many cases, more than one) in London over the century, as reflected in surviving programs and advertisements, includes London, Paris, Cairo, Vienna, Hong Kong, Damascus, Benares, Cabul, Edinburgh, Rome, Berlin, Constantinople, Moscow, Delhi, Venice, Canton, Messina, Naples, Jerusalem, Nimrod, Calcutta, Florence, Geneva, Bombay, New York, Lima, Antwerp, and Dublin.[6] As we will see, viewers seem to have enjoyed the totalizing perspective of the panorama, its capacity to make vast urban spaces seem "knowable."

Although panoramas provided access to exotic or unknown locations, paradoxically, one of the most popular panoramas ever shown in London was a panorama of the city itself. This panorama, which opened at the Colosseum in 1829, though it was not fully completed until 1832, resulted from the unique opportunity presented by renovations to the spire of St. Paul's earlier in the decade. An artist, Thomas Horner, secured permission to climb the construction scaffolding at the very top of the spire for the purpose of completing a series of sketches of London. The meticulous detail of the 2,000 sketches he ultimately produced formed the basis for a painting that took years, and many hands, to complete. Though not a financial success, it was an enormous popular success, and a standard sight to visit in the metropolis for many years. Strong public interest in the mechanics of producing such a massive painting is evident in the popular series of lithographs of the project produced by the same print seller who printed tickets and other advertising materials for the exhibition. Ackermann's five prints, "The Colosseum: The panorama of London seen from a painter's platform," document the gradual process of erecting the platforms needed to access the enormous wall space of the painting, as well as the painting process itself. The final print depicts the panorama and the viewing platform as they appeared just before the panorama opened.[7]

A permanent viewing platform was erected in the center of the building, so that visitors could see the panorama from a central vantage point, on two levels. This control of the viewer's visual access would become a hallmark of stationary panoramas, which often attempted to reproduce a specific viewing environment. The platform of the London panorama was in part a replica of the actual painter's scaffold that Thomas Horner had used for his sketches in 1821, so that viewers looked out from behind railings and ropes that created the illusion of being perched atop the spire of St. Paul's.

This sort of foreground scenery was often used to help create a transition from the actual space of the viewer to the imaginary space of the panorama. As late as 1881, such faux terrain was satirized in a *Punch* cartoon that depicted viewers of the "Charge at Baladash" panorama in Leicester Square commenting on the lifelike figure of a man in the foreground—who is in fact another spectator who has leapt over the railing to retrieve his hat (Hyde, 174).

Sometimes, foreground scenery turned into a complete stage set. The most successful panorama exhibitions tried to create an "authentic" environment around the display of the panorama itself. Albert Smith was a master at manufacturing ambience intended to reinforce his audience's sense of entering a foreign land. For "Ascent of Mont Blanc" (1851–56), Smith converted the Egyptian Hall into a Swiss scene that included a full-scale chalet exterior; a pool of water, surrounded by rocks and plants and containing live fish; miscellaneous baskets, knapsacks, and other items strewn picturesquely about the hall; and vines and creepers hanging from the rafters. In his second season, Smith added ten Saint Bernards, who would trot about the auditorium delivering packets of chocolate to children. A subsequent show, "Mont Blanc to China," required audiences to enter through an Oriental foyer where they could purchase souvenirs like willow-pattern plates with Smith's picture. The chalet was replaced with a Chinese pagoda (Altick, 475–77).

Jonathan Crary, commenting on Richard Wagner's capacity for "illusion-making" in his productions at Bayreuth, suggests that Wagner's strategies resembled those of the diorama, "which was based on a . . . disruption of an intelligible distance between viewer and illusory scene." Crary notes that "numerous firsthand accounts [of dioramas] stressed the visual disorientation that confounded conventional pictorial cues about the relative proximity of near and far objects" (1999, 252). The same might be said of panoramas, which also attempted to disorient the viewer's "real" perception so as to situate him or her more firmly in the illusory space of the panorama. Crary emphasizes the difference between such a "process of optical disorientation" and conventional theatrical distance, which does not involve the same kind of "perspectival breakdown" and does not compel the viewer's attention to the same hypnotic degree (253–54). Even the most vivid theatrical dramatizations took place on a raised stage, carefully framed by the proscenium, so that the audience understood themselves to be at a safe remove from the action. Panoramas, however, sought to erase the distance between audience and representation, fully immersing the viewer in the scene before him or her.

The panorama "Paris by Night" featured in the Colosseum in 1848 was notable for the success with which it synthesized foreground and background perspectives into a complete illusion of place. The perspective of the panorama assumed that the viewer was hovering over the Tuileries in a balloon, and a typical review in the *Illustrated London News* noted that "the illusion is admirably carried out, even down to the cords supposed to dome from the netting of the balloon between which the spectator looks at the view." The reviewer praises the elevated perspective itself, noting that "by this novel plan a much better coup d'oeil is obtained than by sketching the localities from the summit of a building, by which means the principal feature in a city is always lost." The reviewer concludes, "Nothing can be more perfectly deceptive nor minutely correct than this view" ("The Colosseum," 1848, 312). Another viewer, the visiting American William Wells Brown, agreed: "Nothing can surpass the uniformity of appearance which every spire, and house, and wood, and river—yes, which every shop-window, ornamented, presented. All seemed natural, from the twinkling of the stars above us, to the monkey of the organ-man in the market-place below" (quoted in Altick, 157). These two commentaries encapsulate many of the characteristics that made panoramas satisfying: coherence, uniformity, distance, and the creation of an imaginary space for the viewer to occupy.

Thus we see that a key characteristic of panoramic exhibitions was their attempt to create a complete immersive experience, a mediated space that would attempt to blur the boundaries separating reproduction from reality. This attention to transitional spaces and theatrical effort to evoke ambience would eventually be transferred to other forms of exhibitions and museum displays, both in England and on the Continent. In London, panoramas were used to created realistic backgrounds at such varied venues as the Exeter Change menagerie, the Egyptian Hall, and the London Museum (Oettermann, 127). In *Colonizing Egypt*, Timothy Mitchell notes that the Paris World Exhibition of 1889 included a block-long reproduction of a Cairo street for the viewer to stroll through, complete with donkeys, realistic buildings, and deliberately worn and dirtied wall paint. Mitchell describes the bemusement of a set of Egyptian visitors who passed through the facade of a mosque to find, not a space for contemplation, but an "Egyptian cafe" featuring dancing girls and whirling dervishes (4–5).

The anthropologist Franz Boas, in his capacity as curator of the anthropological collections of the American Museum of Natural History in the 1890s, described the specific visual qualities needed to create a successful illusion in a museum display. He emphasized the importance of introducing a darkened setting and organizing material around a single, central perspective, then concluded, "The only place from which such an effect can be had is in a Panorama Building" (Jacknis, 102; quoted in Dias, 172). Boas's interest in importing some of the illusory qualities of the panorama into the world of the museum demonstrates the extent to which the panoramic perspective had infiltrated not just the world of public entertainment but the intellectual culture of the nineteenth century.

Anne McClintock has pointed out the Victorian middle class's "peculiarly intense preoccupation with boundaries," and suggests that "as colonials travelled back and forth across the threshold of their known world, crisis and boundary confusion were warded off by fetishes, absolution rituals, and liminal scenes" (133). One way of enhancing the realism of the panorama experience was to create imaginary boundaries that would need to be crossed by the viewer, so that the panorama itself became a kind of liminal space in which one dwells temporarily, secure in the knowledge that the journey back to the known world will not be an arduous one.

It is worth noting in this context that the Colosseum introduced the first passenger elevator in London, an "ascending room" that would whisk visitors to the upper level of the two-story viewing platform. The sudden disorientation of finding oneself instantly transported to a strange place no doubt reinforced the magical quality of the panoramic illusion awaiting one at the top. It is tempting to compare the probable reaction of a Victorian riding such a contraption for the first time to Fredric Jameson's late twentieth-century description of an elevator ride in the lobby of the Bonaventura Hotel in Los Angeles. Jameson describes elevators as being less a form of movement than "reflexive signs and emblems of movement proper," in which the "narrative stroll has been underscored, symbolized, reified, and replaced by a transportation machine which becomes the allegorical signifier of that promenade we are no longer allowed to conduct on our own" (42). The passenger is denied the power to control his own movements or, ultimately, the scene that awaits him. Jameson's elevator lands him "in one of those revolving cocktail lounges, in which, seated, you are again passively rotated about and offered a contemplative spectacle of the city itself, now transformed into its own image by the glass windows through which you view it" (43). Los Angeles as seen from the Bonaventura, like the panorama of London as seen from the upper gallery of the Colosseum, becomes a representation of itself. Homi Bhabha describes Jameson's anecdote as "the *mise-en-scène* of the subject's relation to an unrepresentable social totality," an image of the "postmodern panopticon" in which "you lose your bearings entirely" (1984, 217), but this form of disorientation and displacement does not seem distinctively postmodern compared with the Victorian experience. As we will see, the panoramic perspective provided a temporary means of projecting oneself into another space and adopting a new perspective on either a scene you thought was familiar or a place that you were "seeing" for the first time.

2. THE PASSING SCENE: MOVING PANORAMAS

In addition to circular panoramas, the nineteenth century saw the development of an entirely new form of representation, the moving panorama. Panoramas painted on linear canvas that could be unrolled slowly while viewed from a stationary seat, usually presented in conjunction with music, commentary, or some combination of the two, developed first as backdrops to theatrical productions. In 1823, for example, a Covent Garden pantomime featured as scenery a cloth "representing bird's-eye views of London and Paris supposed to be seen from a balloon" (Altick, 199). As we will see, this "balloon's-eye view" would continue to be a popular format for panoramas. Eventually, moving backdrops supplanted the plays they had once supplemented, and took center stage themselves.

Albert Smith's "Ascent of Mont Blanc" and his second major monologue program "Journey on the Overland Mail" were typical of this genre, in which a traveller-showman narrated of his journey to the sights being viewed behind him. A review of another such display, reprinted in "An Illustrated Description of the Diorama of the Ganges" (1850; JJ Coll, Dioramas 1), compared it to Smith's performances, stating that "the mode of exhibition adopted is the same as that of the overland journey, the canvas being in continual motion, and seen through a circular opening. . . . In other like exhibitions, we have particular spots selected; but here we have the whole length of the view as it would really be seen if passing up the river." These displays seem generally to have aimed for a close to real-time pace of presentation that allowed the viewer to visually travel the landscape along with the lecturer.

The transitional stage-setting seen in relation to stationary panoramas assumed an even more detailed form in the case of moving panoramas, which often attempted to reproduce a specific form of travel. River journeys and rail journeys were among the most popular formats, and some panoramas included replicas of excursion boats (Altick, 203) or other conveyances. This continued to be a very popular feature of panoramas; as late as 1900, at the Exposition Universelle in Paris, spectators of the "Trip from Moscow to Pekin on the Trans-Siberian Railway" sat in "luxurious" real railway carriages, looking through real windows at a scene in which "four successive layers of landscape moved at different speeds," simulating the effect of looking at both near and distant scenery (Comment, 74). This effect would soon be perfected and popularized in America in conjunction with moving pictures, when George C. Hale began offering "Hale's Tours": an "illusion ride" in which spectators of ten-minute films of various "Scenes of the World" sat inside a rocking railway carriage while painted scenery passed by the windows.

Among the most popular subjects of moving panoramas were river journeys that provided a sense of access to foreign lands by allowing the viewer to "travel" down the Nile, the Rhine, or the Mississippi. The river journey, I will suggest in Part Two, became a powerful metaphor for the movement of British culture abroad. Rivers, after all, frequently mark political boundaries; the traveller has equal access to either side, but moves inexorably toward a predetermined goal that shapes his perceptions of what he sees along the way. From a practical point of view, river journeys provided a way of linking a disparate series of scenes into a seamless continuum, so that the viewer's experience of them is naturalized as the experience of a real-time journey through an identifiable landscape. A review of the 1850 "Diorama of the Ganges" sees the continuity of the viewing experience as a crucial element of the experience: "The mode of exhibition adopted is the same as that of the view of the overland journey. . . . the course is taken up the Ganges, and the wild and wondrous regions afford ample scope for the artist's power. . . . In other like exhibitions, we have particular spots selected; but here we have the whole length of the view as it would really be seen if passing up the river" (JJ Coll, Dioramas 1).

This form of almost maplike representation, in which a long stretch of a river is presented in great detail, would have been familiar to Victorians who had seen the many foldout topographical views or "panoramas" of rivers that were published from the late eighteenth century and throughout the nineteenth century. Guidebooks to the Thames, Rhine, and other rivers would often include a detailed foldout view; later, these became freestanding novelties on their own. An 1830 advertisement for an engraved "Panorama of the Maine" alludes to the popularity of the genre: "Unlike . . . the Panorama of the Thames from London to Richmond, recently published by Mr. Leigh, the panorama of the Maine is a bird's-eye view, representing the meanderings of the river" (JJ Coll, Dioramas 1). Small souvenir panoramas that either folded out or unscrolled from a box were popular throughout the century, and in addition to rivers, often featured processions, such as the Duke of Wellington's funeral and the coronation processions of George IV and Queen Victoria. Among the available panoramas of Queen Victoria's coronation were two twenty-foot panoramas, Tyas's and Robins's, and Fores's sixty-foot "Correct Representation of the State Procession," the title and length of which are indicative of the comprehensiveness of the genre.[8] (This use of popular media would be echoed near the end of Victoria's reign by moving film footage, currently on display at the Victoria and Albert Museum, of the Queen in her carriage during the 1897 Diamond Jubilee procession.) Many panorama exhibitions sold foldout replicas to serve as guides and souvenirs.

The popularity of panorama prints is seen in the decision of the founders of the *Illustrated London News* to offer, as a special bonus to its initial subscribers in 1843, an engraving of the "Colosseum Print of London." Initially issued as two long views on a single sheet, it was later sold separately in a continuous print that was wound onto a roller with an elegant buckram cover (Hyde, Ill. 201). It was, as Peter Sinnema (22–24) points out, an extraordinarily ambitious engraving project, occupying three artists and eighteen engravers full-time for more than two months. The view was taken, as the *Illustrated London News* announcement proudly informs its readers, from a daguerreotype atop the York Column, and "its perfect likeness cannot be disputed." The announcement goes into great detail about both the daguerreotype process and the engraving process, even specifying the type, size, origin (Turkey), and characteristics of the wood blocks used ("Key to the Colosseum Print," December 21, 1842, 545). The Victorian love of printed panorama strips suggests that whatever the format, a crucial source of appeal in any panorama was its comprehensiveness and detailed accuracy, which satisfied the quasi-scientific impulse toward cataloging and enumeration that was so characteristic of the period.

While they do not, of course, embody all of the characteristics of painted panoramas, these printed panoramas do manifest qualities of continuity and comprehensiveness that are critical aspects of the panorama's appeal. A description of the Rhine that appears in a pamphlet printed by Burford in connection with his panorama of 1843 demonstrates the appeal of the panorama's connection of one scene with the next, so that the viewer experiences the exhibition of scenes as a kind of journey: "[The Rhine's] banks throughout present a series of the most enchanting views, which develop themselves and arrest the imagination in one perpetual and ever changing chain of beauty and grandeur" (ML, Dioramas, Panoramas A1, Burford 7). The fact that these "views" are both singular and part of a series, both "perpetual" and also "ever changing," underlines the importance of the continuous format of the panorama. A river like the Rhine, which passes through so many well-known cities, served as its own itinerary. The 1859 advertising bill for the Great Globe, Leicester Square's "Grand Moving Diorama of a Tour up the Rhine, Embracing every feature of Interest, from Rotterdam to St. Gotthard" (ML, Dioramas, Panoramas, A3) has a geographical specificity that seems designed to assure viewers that this tour is all-inclusive.

Over the course of the century, London saw panoramas of the Thames, the Nile, the Ganges, the Rhine, the Seine, and other rivers, but the locus classicus of the river panorama was an American import, Banvard's Panorama of the Mississippi. Brought to England in 1848 after tremendous success in America,[9] it was an immediate sensation and inspired many imitators. Dickens, who had seen the Mississippi in 1842 and written about it in *American Notes*, reviewed "Banvard's Geographical Panorama of the Mississippi and Missouri Rivers" in the *Examiner*. Dickens begins his commentary in typically forthright fashion: "It may be well to say what the panorama is *not*." He goes on to enumerate its deficiencies: "It is not a refined work of art. . . . it is not remarkable for accuracy of drawing, or for brilliancy of color, or for subtle effects of light and shade." In short, its value is not in any sense aesthetic.

> But it is a picture three miles long, which occupies two hours in its passage before the audience. It is a picture of one of the greatest streams in the known world, whose course it follows for upwards of three thousand miles. It is a picture irresistibly impressing the spectator with a conviction of its plain and simple truthfulness. . . . It is an easy means of travelling, night and day, without

any inconvenience from climate, steamboat company, or fatigue . . . and seeing every town and settlement upon the river's banks. . . . To see this painting is, in a word, to have a thorough understanding of what the great American river is. (Slater, 135–36)

The popularity of Banvard's panorama clearly owed something to British interest in an American scene that was much less familiar than the banks of the Rhine or the Seine. But Banvard was also a canny showman whose instinct for publicity allowed him to generate considerable interest in a format that was not, after all, new to the British public in 1848. Banvard's charismatic Yankee persona was central to the performance, and his own account of his production of the panorama paints him as a classic American success story. Dickens's review repeats with admiration the moving tale of a painter who though "poor, untaught, wholly unassisted . . . conceives the idea—a truly American idea—of painting 'the largest picture in the world'" (Slater, 136).

Dickens, with his keen instinct for showmanship, understood that the sheer magnitude of the undertaking—it's three miles long! it takes two hours to see it!—contributed to its value to the public. The tendency of many panorama exhibitors to rely heavily on that form of recommendation had already became a subject for satire. A "Comical Christmas Chronicle" supplement to the *Illustrated London News* that appeared in 1848, the year of Banvard's panorama, contains, among other fictitious advertisements: "MR. LONGCHALK'S moving PANORAMA of THE GREAT WALL OF CHINA, ten miles long. Equal to six-and-eight-pence worth of cab-hire; and all for a shilling. Begins at 10 a.m., and finishes at 11 p.m. Refreshments provided. Luncheon, dinner, &tc." (*ILN* Vol. 13, December 23, 1848, 414). "An Old Question Settled at Last," a *Punch* joke from 1850 (69), reads, "Who is Miles' Boy? Mr. Banvard, Mr. Bonomi, and Mr. Brees are clearly 'Three Miles' Boys' from the fact of their Panoramas all running that distance."

The popularity of panoramas also made them a useful vehicle for satire on other subjects. A *Punch* notice of 1850 reads: "PANORAMA OF THE BRITISH CONSTITUTION. Panoramas are the fashion—Lord John Russell, with the wisdom of a Whig, proposes to avail himself of this mode; and during the recess to superintend a very moving display of his one pet subject—his subject produced on the floor of the House on all occasions, namely, the British Constitution, with the very best Whig designs. . . . the Panorama will give the flight of JAMES THE SECOND, the Battle of the Boyne, the accession of WILLIAM AND MARY, and so on; the whole to conclude with the advent to office of LORD JOHN RUSSELL amid a shower of fireworks" ("Panorama of the British Constitution," 1850, 70). Here, the author equates Russell's predictable, inflated rhetoric with the aggrandizing overview provided by a panorama.

Dickens himself, though he spoke approvingly of the instructional qualities of panoramas, would later satirize their educational pretensions in his essay "Mr. Barlow." In his imaginary portrait of that "instructive monomaniac," for whom "knowledge is the power to bore," he writes: "Knowing Mr. Barlow to have invested largely in the moving panorama trade, and having on various occasions identified him in the dark with a long wand in his hand, holding forth in the old way . . . I systematically shun pictorial entertainment on rollers" (*The Uncommercial Traveller*, 338–40). Nevertheless, it is clearly the case that, as with so many other forms of Victorian entertainment, the claim to educational merit enhanced the value of this form of enjoyment. John Ruskin claimed that Burford's Panorama in Leicester Square was "an educational institution of the highest and purest value, and ought to have been supported by the government as one of the most beneficial school instruments in London" (quoted in Comment, 118).

The success of Banvard's Mississippi panorama led not only to the rapid development of other river panoramas that boasted of their similarity or superiority to Banvard's, but even to competing panoramas of the Mississippi, including one that appeared at the same time as Banvard's and compared itself explicitly to Banvard's production. A Mississippi panorama by Risley and Smith came to London in the winter of 1848, provoking the usual war of advertisements, with claims of "spurious copies" countered by claims of superior accuracy (Oettermann, 330). The idea of multiple Mississippis flowing into London at the same time, each claiming that the others were mere "copies" of their own copy of the real river, may be humorous, but it suggests the extent to which these exhibitions strove for and jealously preserved whatever degree of Benjaminian "aura" they could generate.

The accuracy, reliability and up-to-dateness of panoramas was always a talking point for advertisers and reviewers. A guidebook for the new Colosseum, reopened after extensive renovation in 1845, says of the newly refurbished Panorama of London: "Histories, descriptions, maps, and prints, are all imperfect and defective, when compared with this immense Panorama—they are scraps and mere touches of the pen and pencil—whilst this imparts at a glance, a Cyclopedia of information—a concentrated history—a focal topography, of the largest and most influential city in the world" ("Description of the Colosseum," 8). Reviewers tended to focus less on intrinsically aesthetic qualities of a panorama than on its accuracy as a representation of how a specific vista actually looked, from a single vantage point, at that very moment. Success was entirely dependent on the quality of the illusion, the degree to which the panorama could substitute for the place itself.

3. WISH YOU WERE HERE: MARKETING THE EXPERIENCE

Most panorama exhibitors included in their advertisements lengthy testimonials from appropriate individuals: mariners, well-known travellers, eminent figures such as Dickens, people associated with the depicted scene who could vouch for its faithfulness to the "original." The souvenir pamphlet that Banvard produced to accompany his panorama concludes with laudatory letters from engineers and steamboat captains (as well as the text of a resolution by the Massachusetts Senate and House of Representatives, praising the painting). In this way, spectators were invited to become part of an experiential loop in which the experience of others validated the simulacrum that would in turn substitute for their own experience. This validation was often reinforced through emphasis on the difficulties involved in obtaining the on-site sketches needed to produce the panorama. A description of a hundred-foot painting of Jerusalem, for example, notes "the perilous circumstances under which the drawings for this view were executed," suggesting that "those who have travelled in the Holy Land are well aware that the Turks, its fanatic masters, esteem the city sacred; and, that any attempt of this kind, if unhappily detected, would have been punished according to their laws with a cruel and ignominious death" (JJ Coll, Dioramas 1). An experience so fraught with difficulty and danger embodies enough reality, it seems, to spare some to its secondhand incarnation. The viewer could scarcely be blamed for preferring the method of travel described in a competing advertisement: "Many have long desired to visit the Holy Land, but now, through Mr. NEIL's magnificent display, Palestine has come to them for some 5s" (JJ Coll, Dioramas 1).

Because the realism of the scene depicted depended in part on the recognition that *someone* had actually seen and experienced it, the presence of a lecturer as a kind of "tour guide" was an indispensable component of the most successful panoramas. The authenticity of the representation seemed to be validated by the presence of an eyewitness who could bear testimony to its accuracy. Banvard's panorama of the Mississippi was able to capitalize on this sense of authenticity because it was presented by the painter, Banvard himself. Dickens said of this panorama, "These three miles of canvas have been painted by one man, and there he is, present, pointing out what he deems most worthy of notice. This is his history" (Slater, 135–36). As a writer who was always anxious to, in Jay Clayton's words, expand the "cultural bandwidth" (200) of his work, Dickens created a valuable authorial persona through public readings, and he understood the way in which physical presentation of a work can reinforce its sense of authenticity. Panorama lecturers came to be called "cicerones," in imitation of real tour guides (Hyde, 133).[10]

The claim that panoramas could be regarded as a substitute for real travel experience was a strategic element of the publicity created by panorama exhibitors. A scenic view of a Swiss waterfall incorporating "the various changes of the day" is said, in an 1831 advertising handbill, to produce so "enchanting" an effect that spectators "cannot help fancying themselves imperceptibly transported into the very interior of the province of Switzerland; and that they are viewing in reality, the very identical spot, on which their admiration is so intensely fixed" (JJ Coll, Dioramas 3). An advertisement for a panorama of Niagara Falls pretends that there is no distinction between the image and the reality: "Have You Seen Niagara Falls? If not, go now to Niagara Hall" (JJ Coll, Dioramas 2) (fig. 3). The famous Panorama of London by Night, exhibited in the Colosseum after interest in the Grand Panorama of London had waned, is given this testimonial in a souvenir guide to the reopened Colosseum: "We confidently state, that it is next to impossible, that any person can lean over the balustrade for five or six minutes, and mark the fleecy clouds sailing steadily along, lighted as they come within the influence of the halo-encircled moon . . . [and] recall themselves immediately to the conviction that the scene before them is nothing but an illusion" ("Description of the Colosseum," 22).

Promotional materials for these exhibits insist so forcefully on the analogy between panorama viewing and real travel that they quickly become self-consciously facetious. An advertisement for "Mr. Washington Friend's Grand Tour of Five Thousand Miles in Canada and the United States of America" dryly notes that travel to Canada and the United States "is expensive, requires time, involves the chances of shipwreck . . . whereas by visiting MR. FRIEND, you are placed at once on the other side of the Atlantic by payment of One Shilling" (Guidebook, 6). Although jokes about how cheap and easy such a journey could be acknowledge the difference between a real trip and armchair travel, they also suggest that exhibitors used these texts to mediate the distance between the two.

The guidebook for "Mr. Friend's" exhibition suggests that this mode of travel has practical applicability, too, for the "intending emigrant" to Canada or the United States, who will receive "a complete account of the principal cities,

Have you seen Niagara Falls?

If not, go now to

NIAGARA HALL

Where the finest Panorama ever painted is on view.

ST. JAMES' PARK STATION
YORK STREET, WESTMINSTER
(Two minutes' walk from Westminster Abbey).

ST. JAMES' PARK STATION
YORK STREET, WESTMINSTER
(Two minutes' walk from Westminster Abbey).

If you have, then revive your memories of the sublime picture of Nature by visiting Niagara Hall, and see them clothed in their beautiful Winter garments.

DAILY, 10 to 10.   ADMISSION, ONE SHILLING.

Fig. 3. "Have You Seen Niagara Falls?" Handbill, n.d. Reprinted courtesy of the Bodleian Libraries, University of Oxford.

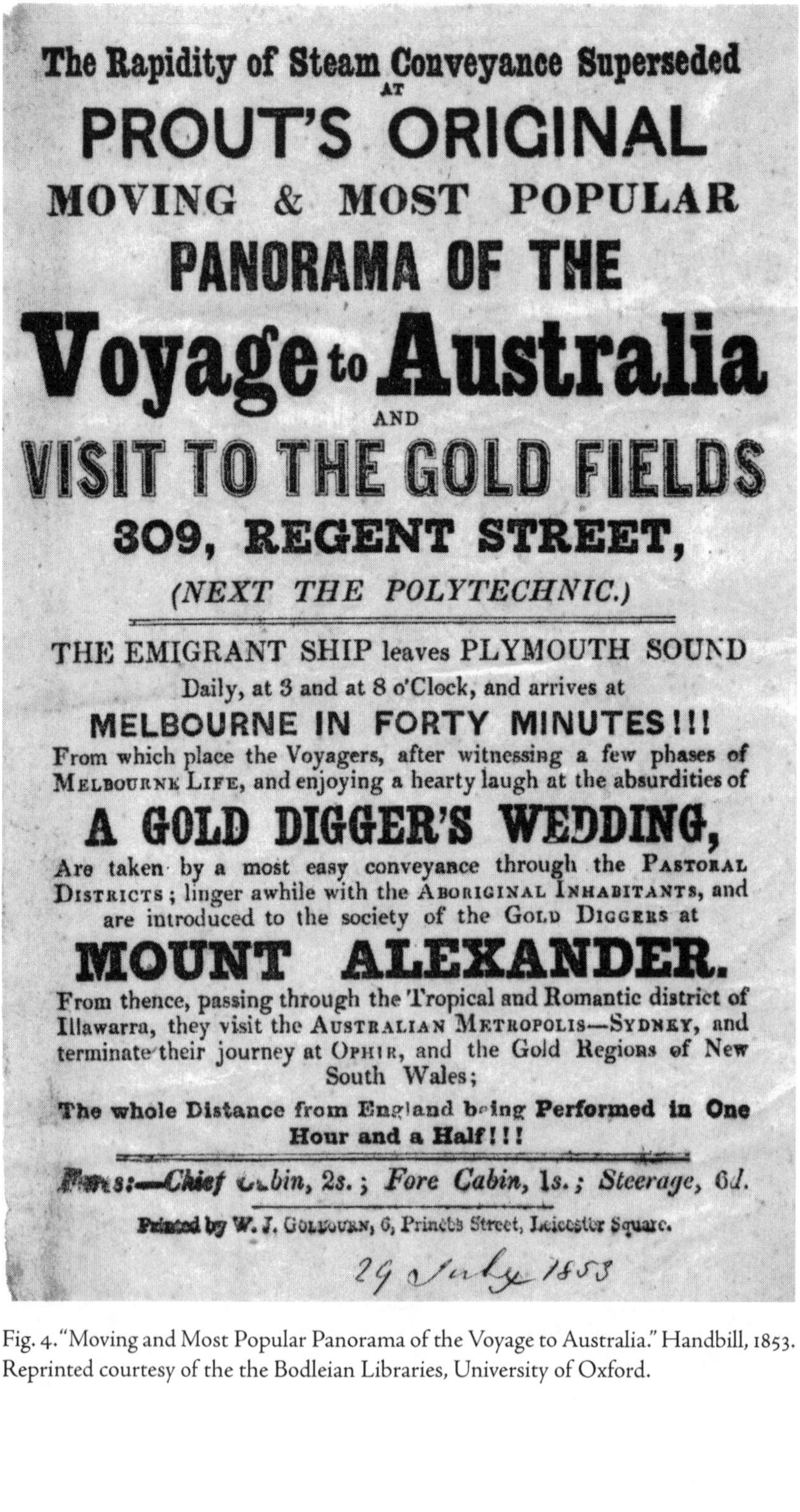

The Rapidity of Steam Conveyance Superseded
AT

PROUT'S ORIGINAL

MOVING & MOST POPULAR

PANORAMA OF THE

Voyage to Australia

AND

VISIT TO THE GOLD FIELDS

309, REGENT STREET,

(NEXT THE POLYTECHNIC.)

THE EMIGRANT SHIP leaves PLYMOUTH SOUND

Daily, at 3 and at 8 o'Clock, and arrives at

MELBOURNE IN FORTY MINUTES!!!

From which place the Voyagers, after witnessing a few phases of
MELBOURNE LIFE, and enjoying a hearty laugh at the absurdities of

A GOLD DIGGER'S WEDDING,

Are taken by a most easy conveyance through the PASTORAL
DISTRICTS; linger awhile with the ABORIGINAL INHABITANTS, and
are introduced to the society of the GOLD DIGGERS at

MOUNT ALEXANDER.

From thence, passing through the Tropical and Romantic district of
Illawarra, they visit the AUSTRALIAN METROPOLIS—SYDNEY, and
terminate their journey at OPHIR, and the Gold Regions of New
South Wales;

The whole Distance from England being **Performed in One
Hour and a Half!!!**

Fares:—Chief Cabin, 2s.; Fore Cabin, 1s.; Steerage, 6d.

Printed by W. J. GOLBOURN, 6, Princes Street, Leicester Square.

29 July 1853

Fig. 4. "Moving and Most Popular Panorama of the Voyage to Australia." Handbill, 1853.
Reprinted courtesy of the the Bodleian Libraries, University of Oxford.

rivers, and lakes of this wonderful continent" as well as learn "the cheapest and best mode of getting there" (*Guidebook*, 3). Similar motives might have been expected to encourage spectators to see the "Moving Panorama of a Voyage to Australia, with descriptive lecture by Mr. Prout," advertised in a handbill of 1853, which claims that "the rapidity of steam conveyance [is] superseded" by the voyage of this "emigrant ship" (JJ Coll, Dioramas 1) (fig. 4). Such panoramas address themselves specifically to viewers in search of concrete information about colonies to which they may be considering moving. These advertisements do not seem to expect the viewer to feel apologetic about taking the easy route to their destination; another handbill is headed: "A TRAVELLER in Spite of Yourself," and promises to satisfy the "rage for Emigration, and the speculative desire of individuals to visit all parts of the globe," by presenting "the enterprising traveller" with "a variety of the most interesting places in the world to select from" (JJ Coll, Dioramas 3). The viewer can become an "enterprising" traveller merely by allowing a sampling of scenes to be presented for his or her inspection.

A Leicester Square panorama was even more explicit about its practical utility: "COLONIZATION! THE EMIGRATION PANORAMA, NEW ZEALAND. If you are desirous of escaping the miseries of this country, and improving your condition in life, SEE THIS PANORAMA! With Mr. Brees' information, you will be better acquainted with the subject than those who have been to the Colonies." Adding a further twist to the class-based appeal of this handbill, the ad continues, "To the NOBILITY & GENTRY who unfortunately cannot leave England the Panorama affords a perfect exposition of Colonial Life" (ML, Dioramas, Panoramas A1). By presenting the prospect of emigration as a privilege denied those unfortunate enough to be tied to England by hereditary landownership, the exhibitors intensify the viewer's identification of this panorama with escape from English society and in particular its class stratification.

Even the advertisements that were inserted into the longer panorama brochures seem to bear out the assumption that the target audience included potential travellers to the place depicted. An 1850 guidebook for a "New Oriental Diorama" of "Life and Scenes in India" includes ads for Thresher's Regulation Overland Trunk ("authorised by all the Companies connected with the various Overland Routes to India"), Pears's Genuine Transparent Soap ("Especially Adapted for the Indian Climate"), and a Hand-Book of India that promises to provide the traveller with all the information needed for his or her journey (JJ Coll, Dioramas 1). Or the viewer might have recently returned from abroad with a taste for the local food: the "Diorama of the Ganges" guidebook includes ads for curry powders, chutneys, and mulligatawny paste (JJ Coll, Dioramas 1).

It is impossible to say, of course, whether these ads accurately reflect the target audience, or whether their inclusion in these brochures is partly atmospheric, like the steamer trunks and field glasses scattered around a Banana Republic boutique.

The implied parallel between real travel or emigration and the imaginary journey taken by way of the panorama suggests that the marketers of these exhibitions understood the complex, even contradictory, reasons for their appeal. They offered a mode of casual exploration that did not require the inconvenience, even danger, of real travel, and that did not require the "traveller" to fully invest himself or herself in the journey. Far from a confrontation with the Other, the panoramic journey was a colonization of the other, a way of incorporating new territory into one's own world and worldview. The correlation between this kind of imaginative possession of a foreign place and the literal colonization of other parts of the world seems implicit in the description of a panorama of the Rhine from 1853. This panorama presented a tour from Dover to Naples, or Naples to Dover, alternating with each performance as the scene was unscrolled and then reversed. The "Descriptive Book of the Tour of Europe" that accompanied the exhibition of this "immense Moving Diorama" makes an explicit connection between the work of the panorama artist and the work of European culture: "The telegraph, the rail-way, and the Steam-Boat have been making great changes and doing their utmost to bring about a Brotherhood of Nations;—may not also the Pencil of the Artist claim its share of this great work; here we have the Exploration of a Continent showing in pictorial form the energies of past ages and in the present civilized and intellectual world" ("Descriptive Book," 51).

What is perhaps more surprising than these inflated claims by promoters is the degree to which they were echoed in the reviews of these exhibitions that appeared not only in the popular press but in more refined venues as well. In part, this similarity may reflect the generally murky boundary between advertisement and "review" in a period when unsigned reviews often depended heavily on information and accounts provided by the theaters or exhibitors themselves. Nevertheless, even writers like Thackeray and Dickens were willing to entertain, with greater or lesser degrees of facetiousness, the hypothesis that the experience of panorama viewing was in some ways comparable to real travel. An unsigned *Punch* essay by Thackeray in 1850, for example, mockingly describes the dramatic realism of panoramas as a source of fear and anguish during the supposed author's sightseeing visit to London.

Having been assured that he could "view some scenes at least of foreign countries without the danger and fatigue of personal travel," he encounters, he says, a "view of Mount Ararat . . . so dreadful, so lonely, so like nature that it was all I could do to prevent myself from dashing down the peak and plunging into the valley below." After visiting a representation of the Lisbon Earthquake that he finds equally terrifying, he finishes up at a panorama of Ross's arctic exploration at Leicester Square, where he refuses to allow his children to see "the icy picture of eternal snow—the livid northern lights, the killing glitter of the stars; the wretched mariners groping about in the snow round the ship." He concludes on the comic note with which he began: "I beseech all people who *have nerves* to pause ere they go sight-seeing at the present day" ("The Sights of London," 132). But the vividness of his descriptions belies his comic tone by suggesting that these sights did have a powerful effect on his imagination. Thackeray seems to admit the power of these panoramas to draw him into the scene, much as his own novels work to engage the reader not only through realistic depictions but through a mode of rhetoric that attributes specific points of view to implicit or intended readers.[11]

Dickens, too, seems ambivalent in his attitude toward the idea of panoramic travel. His review of Banvard, as we have seen, has a satiric edge when referring to the panorama as "an easy means of travelling . . . without any inconvenience from climate," and so forth, but generally affirms the power of this "indisputably true and faithful representation of a wonderful region" to convey "a thorough understanding of what the great American river is" (Slater, 136–37). He praises the panorama's "incidental revelations of the different states of society" and enumerates the wide range of different people and scenes it conveys. He concludes by suggesting, "It would be well to have a panorama, three miles long, of England. There might be places in it worth looking at, a little closer than we see them now; and worth the thinking of, a little more profoundly" (137). Here, the imagined panorama becomes an image of what Dickens tries to accomplish in his own fiction: a portrayal of England that forces the reader to stand back and view familiar scenes with the critical objectivity of a traveller from elsewhere.

Dickens often used the persona of a "traveller-narrator" himself in his essays, of course, most notably in *The Uncommercial Traveller*, and it may be that he recognized in the secondary or displaced travel experience of the panorama something similar to the insights generated in his own literary travels.[12] An overtly comic approach to the subject, Dickens's "Some Account of an Extraordinary Traveller," digs more deeply into the question of what motivates the panoramic traveller and how his view of an exhibition differs from the real experience. Though inspired, according to a letter Dickens wrote to Charles Knight, by watching a globe-maker and imagining him as a kind of mental traveller, Dickens used the presence of numerous panoramas and dioramas in London to create a similar imaginary universe for his character, Mr. Booley. As Michael

Slater points out, all of the places mentioned in the course of Dickens's description of Mr. Booley's travels reflect current or recent exhibitions: Banvard's panoramas of the Mississippi and Ohio rivers; Brees's "Colonial Panorama" of New Zealand; a panorama of the Queen's visit to Ireland; a "transparency" of the Nile; the famous "Overland Route to India" panorama; and, finally, Burford's Arctic panorama (commented on by Thackeray above) (Slater, 201–2).

Dickens's essay describes the "extraordinary amount of travel" Mr. Booley has managed to accomplish, and the ease with which it has been performed, involving as it has no change in dress, no departure from English customs, no understanding of any language other than English. "Mr. Booley's powers of endurance are wonderful," Dickens writes. "All climates are alike to him. . . . he has travelled alone, and unattended. Though remarkable for personal cleanliness, he has carried no luggage; and his diet has been of the simplest kind. He has often found a biscuit, or a bun, sufficient for his support over a vast tract of country" (Slater, 203). The essay describes the scenes "visited" by Mr. Booley in terms that could apply equally to real scenery or to a panoramic representation, but that are generally closer to a view of actual landscape, so that for brief moments it is possible to forget that this is not a real travelogue. Dickens's description of the river as "a winding thread through the enormous range of country, unrolling itself before the wanderer like the magic skein in the story" may remind us that we are talking about a canvas on rollers; but his list of the canoes, steamboats, and flat-bottomed boats on the river conveys a sense that his account is recording the observations of a traveller who has really shared this "moving highway" with other boats (204). Dickens plays on the conventional use of pictorial language to describe landscape by imagining Mr. Booley himself characterizing the overland journey to India as both "'a beautiful piece of scenery'" and "'a perfect picture'" (209).

The description of Mr. Booley's travels to the Arctic follows the same pattern of alternating broad satire with evocations that are as gripping as many a real travelogue. Dickens paints a vivid picture of ice, snow, and frozen ships, "shrouded in gloom and darkness," before noting in a sprightly tone: "And yet the desolate sublimity of this astounding spectacle was broken in a pleasant and surprising manner." Amidst this "remote solitude," Mr. Booley encounters "two Scotch gardeners; several English compositors, accompanied by their wives . . . two coach-painters . . . and several other working-people from sundry parts of Great Britain" (210). Again, however, Dickens immediately plunges into a paragraph-long description in which faint traces of satire are overwhelmed by the intensity of the scene.

The "working-people" noted above are among the most improbable components of the scene, and this important difference between real and fictive travel is not only satirized but also, to some degree, applauded. Mr. Booley is quoted as saying that this kind of travel—"the gigantic moving-panorama or diorama mode of conveyance, which I have principally adopted"—is a "delightful characteristic of these times . . . new and cheap means are continually being devised for conveying the results of actual experience to those who are unable to obtain such experiences for themselves; and to bring them within reach of the people—emphatically of the people; for it is they at large who are addressed in these endeavours, and not exclusive audiences." His tone is serious as he adds, "New worlds open out to them, beyond their little worlds, and widen their range of reflection, information, sympathy, and interest. The more man knows of man, the better for the common brotherhood among us all" (211). By allowing the perspective to oscillate between the satiric view of the author and the more naive view of Mr. Booley, Dickens allows the reader to sketch out a middle ground in which some of Mr. Booley's appreciation for the "moving-panorama or diorama mode of conveyance" is legitimated. The "little world" of the panorama may not be the real world, but it is a different world from the one usually inhabited by these working-people.

However much we might laugh at the idea of their imbibing "the results of actual experience" secondhand, Dickens suggests that even this mediated experience has some value to those for whom this "new and cheap" mode of travel offers an imaginative entry into a larger world. He sees the panorama as offering the same kind of broad access that he hoped to provide in his own novels, and in particular in his public readings. While critics may dispute the claim that Dickens's readings in fact drew large numbers of working-class audience members, there is little doubt that Dickens believed that he was helping to "redefine the experience of culture" by creating a "unified experience" of his fiction.[13] Dickens's appreciation of the value of a public, shared experience of literature offers an important counterbalance to the interiority of reading.

4. WATCHING THE GRAND TOUR

The popular, if playfully exaggerated, sense of panorama viewing as a form of virtual travel reflects both the wide range of distant places to which panoramas offered access and the sense of mobility generated by the panorama experience. Paradoxically, panoramas were not used to created imaginary landscapes that could not be seen any other way; they were used to represent real places that already existed. One explanation for this interest in re-creating the already-there is perhaps the likelihood that viewers of a known place would feel a stronger sense of its reality. However, this does not fully explain the success of many panoramas of familiar locations. Descriptions of the panorama-viewing experience show that the viewer's sense of the realism of the pictured location derived not only from the familiarity or accuracy of the details rendered but from its success in stimulating a physical sensation of mobility in the viewer.

The extremely miscellaneous nature of Mr. Booley's itinerary is a key component of Dickens's satire, and he was not the only commentator struck by a sense of geographic discontinuity when reviewing the many distant places that were concurrently represented by competing panoramas. Panoramic London seems to manifest what Foucault describes as the third basic principle of the "heterotopia": it is "capable of juxtaposing in a single real place several spaces, several sites that are in themselves incompatible" (1986, 25). Foucault's heterotopia is "a kind of effectively enacted utopia in which the real sites, all the other real sites that can be found within the culture, are simultaneously represented, contested, and inverted." The heterotopia is like a mirror, making the space one occupies while viewing it "at once absolutely real, connected with all the space that surrounds it, and absolutely unreal, since in order to be perceived it has to pass through this virtual point which is over there" (24). The panorama is itself both real (as an object) and unreal (as an illusory depiction of a place it is not). More important, however, it alters the spectator's sense of his or her own relation to reality by creating an imaginary projection of the spectator who is transported elsewhere.

To imaginatively "leave" London and travel to a strange place was itself an event; the realization that London itself offered numerous portals into alternate universes was both exhilarating and destabilizing. It made the process of imagining oneself elsewhere seem almost routine, like catching one of several trains at the station. One satirist wrote, "Geography now-a-days is fearfully outraged, in the distribution of the different quarters of the habitable globe, for we find Calcutta within five minutes' walk of the Nile; and the Arctic Regions next door but six to New Zealand, which is separated from Australia by a narrow rack of cab-stands" ("'There Be Land Pirates,'" 1850, 163). Such satiric comments do bespeak a kind of nostalgia for a sense of the distance, difficulty, individuality, and foreignness of travel. Perhaps this form of experience was unearned, and worth less than real travel.

On the other hand, Victorian publicists pointed out, it cost less as well. Analysis of the monetary value of the experience panoramas offered was a recurrent, even obsessive theme in advertisements and reviews. As we saw in "Mr. Washington Friend's" advertisement and others, panoramic travel was praised as an inexpensive alternative to real travel, a comparison that simultaneously highlighted and challenged the immateriality of panoramic travel. Such comparisons were often overtly satiric, as in a brief poem complaining about the fees charged visitors to the London panorama taken from St. Paul's Cathedral.

> *There's India, the Nile, New Zealand, and Australia,*
> *America, Niagara, and other wondrous falls,*
> *May be seen for a shilling; but five times the money*
> *Is demanded of the traveller all round St. Paul's.*
> ("All Round St. Paul's," 1850, 179)

Though made in jest, such claims were repeated often enough to give the impression that fictive travel was entering into direct competition with real travel, and that the cheap imitation was beginning to devalue the original product. An anonymous reviewer of Allom's panorama of Constantinople alternates, like Dickens, between satire and genuine admiration, but seems authentic in his claim that "there is nothing so delightful as this kind of walking." He provides a detailed rendering of the almost hypnotic experience of imaginatively projecting oneself into the scene.

> You choose some dark corner of the room, and there unseen by everyone, and seeing no one, you leave England, and all thoughts of duns and debtors and household cares, far behind you. The next minute you open your eyes, and find yourself wandering in the streets of some foreign capital. You have no necessity to leave your seat; only give yourself up to the pictorial influence of the scene, and let your eyes walk instead of your legs. It is more amusing, less fatiguing, and does not wear out the shoe-leather. ("Constantinople Removed to Regent Street," 1850, 97)

The reviewer later notes that Albert Smith provided a detailed itemization of his travel expenses in his performance "Two Months at Constantinople," and does a mock tally for his own "trip" to the same region, concluding that his calculations leave, "over the sum which Albert Smith spent in the same journey, a balance in our favour of £59 16s. 3d." ("Constantinople," 97). Whereas Smith had sought to authenticate his exhibition by reference to the real travail and expenses he incurred in gaining the experience it represented, audiences were now ready to reverse the process and authenticate the representation by reference to the sums that were *not* expended in experiencing the re-creation.

The above passage is also remarkable in its unapologetic appreciation for the passive nature of the experience. The only effort needed, apparently, is the negative effort of erasing one's mind of distracting reality. Beyond that, your eyes substitute for your other sensory organs and remove any need for physical exertion. In this sense, panoramic travel is similar to Curtis and Pajaczkow-ska's description of actual tourism. According to their definition, tourism is a "negotiated interface" that substitutes the "privileged distance of the onlooker or spectator" for the "'moral stakes' of reality." This distance is "guaranteed by maintaining a primarily visual relationship to reality." Tourists are "deprived of effective dialogue with the human, cultural, or natural environment, remaining pleasurably stranded on the insularity of the body" (209). The panorama provided just such an interface, encouraging spectators to read their primarily visual perception as a complete, multisensory experience.

This image of pleasurable passivity and pure spectatorship is similarly manifested in another characteristically Victorian experience that was frequently, one might even say invariably, compared to panorama viewing: travelling by hot-air balloon. As we have seen, several popular panoramas were presented from the perspective of an imaginary balloon traveller (a trend that continued through the end of the century, when the "Cineorama Air Balloon Panorama" at the 1900 Paris Exhibition used ten simultaneous projections of an actual balloon voyage to create a 360-degree cinematographic view of a balloon ascent and descent from the Tuileries [De Vries, 126]). Even panoramas that did not explicitly claim to replicate the experience of balloon travel capitalized on the public's increased familiarity with a bird's-eye perspective of their world that was unimaginable a few decades earlier. A brief look at several popular accounts of balloon travel shows that the panoramic perspective embodied in ballooning narratives, like the experience offered by panoramas themselves, reinforced the development of a new sense of the spectator's relation to the world.[14] Hovering above the all-encompassing view, visually immersed in it, and yet physically detached from it, the spectator perceives the landscape topographically rather than experientially. The landscape below becomes like the map in the Borges story, "On Rigor in Science," so detailed that it completely covers and replicates the territory it was intended to represent. The viewer is neither an inhabitant nor a mere spectator of the scene below. He or she is a consumer, able to analyze its constituent parts from a safe distance and develop a contingent relation to an image of the world that does not simply represent, but temporarily replaces, reality.

5. MOVING PICTURES:
THE VIEW FROM A BALLOON

While the experience of ballooning was unusual, and the views it provided unique, balloonists were not, as it turned out, at a loss for words to describe it. Virtually every balloonist who wrote about his or her experiences compared the landscape passing below to a panorama. James Glaisher, whose book *Travels in the Air* is the most comprehensive account of ballooning experiences from this period, describes the view as "like a grand natural panorama" (20); G. Tissandier, in an account included in Glaisher's book, refers to "the splendid panorama which unrolls itself before our eyes" (287); and as early as 1853 an anonymous writer in *Ainsworth's Magazine* says apologetically, "I need not describe the effect of this bird's-eye panorama—it has already been 'done' by abler pens than mine" ("Mr. William Johnson's Grand Balloon Ascent," 349). Perhaps he was thinking of Henry Mayhew's account of a balloon journey, published just eight months earlier in the *Illustrated London News*.

> The earth, as the aeronautic vessel glided over it, seemed positively to consist of a continuous series of scenes which were being drawn along underneath us, as if it were some diorama laid flat upon the ground, and almost gave one the notion that the world was an endless landscape stretched up on rollers, which some invisible sprites below were busy revolving for our especial amusement. (Mayhew 1852, 265)

This description is remarkable for the confidence with which it absorbs the visible scene into a conception of "the earth," which here appears as an independent geographical entity, separate from and larger than man-made political boundaries. The writer's familiarity with the panoramic perspective gives him a context in which this previously impossible view seems to make sense.

Balloon voyage and panorama descriptions share an emphasis on the viewer's passivity that complicates questions of agency in these narratives. In both cases, the experience seems to produce a kind of proprioccentric disorientation that leads viewers to rely exclusively on their sense of vision. One of the most remarked-upon aspects of the balloon journey was the unexpected ease with which the balloon ascended and then proceeded horizontally. Margaret Burgoyne, in an unsigned review in *Bentley's Miscellany*, marveled at the "total absence of any sensible motion," asserting that the travellers felt themselves to be "perfectly stationary." She notes the "want of feeling as regarded our bodies, of any wind or current of air; unlike the effect of all other kinds of locomotion, we were carried *along with* the wind, and at the same pace, instead of being conveyed *through* it" (530). Although the eye confirmed that movement had taken place, the body did not feel it, resulting in an impression that the landscape itself was moving.

The *Ainsworth's Magazine* writer begins his description of the ascent by saying, "The earth rapidly left us. I say advisedly the earth *left us*, for nothing would have induced me to believe that, for the first few minutes, the balloon moved at all." Like Burgoyne, he is surprised by the physical feeling, or rather lack of feeling, associated with this form of travel. "I did not feel the least giddy, nor, strange to say, at all nervous; in fact, I completely forgot my situation in the enjoyment of the wonderful landscape stretched out beneath me" ("Mr. William Johnson's Grand Balloon Ascent," 349). The pleasure of the ride seems to depend not simply on the novel visual perspective provided, but on the way in which that visual effect was augmented by the absence of other physical sensations. Glaisher makes the same connection: "Journeying in this way was delightful; all motion seemed transferred to the landscape itself, which appeared when looking one way to be rising and coming toward us, and when looking another as receding from us" (62–63). The movement of the ground below allows the balloon traveller to become the central axis against which the movement of the world is defined. Rolling and unrolling itself like a panorama, the landscape is no longer regarded as an inhabitable place. Instead, it becomes an image of a place that is comprehensive yet more comprehensible to the viewer above.

Glaisher notes that from a balloon, the scenery below seemed flattened, its "surface dwarfed to a level plane, and the whole country appears like a prodigious map spread out beneath [one's] feet" (5). When viewing London, for example, he is able to see simultaneously "every large building" but also, more important, the overall shape and layout of the city: "The suburbs were . . . very distinct, with their lines of detached villas, imbedded as it were in a mass of shrubs; beyond, the country was like a garden, its fields, well marked, becoming smaller and smaller as the eye wandered farther. . . . there was the Thames, throughout its whole length . . . dotted over its winding course with innumerable ships and steamboats. . . . the southern shore of the mouth of the Thames was not so clear, but the sea beyond was seen for many miles; when at a higher elevation, I looked for the coast of France" (99–100). This broad, topographic perspective allows him to see the relationship between the center of the city and the suburbs, the city and the country, this country and its neighbor across the channel. Many of the illustrations included in Glaisher's volume reflect his desire for geographic specificity in depicting his travels. "Path of the Balloon over London (Night)," for example, is one of several that chart the actual path of the balloon by superimposing a graph of elevation reached over a depiction of the landscape below.

Other balloon travellers also described London as being like a vast map or model, its constituent parts visible for the first time. Writing anonymously in *Bentley's Miscellany,* Margaret Burgoyne says of her 1851 journey: "We looked down on the country as we passed rapidly over it; first, the suburbs of London, and then, in succession, villages, woods, fields, and houses . . . having before us, as it were, a varying animated map" (531). Henry Mayhew, writing in 1852, calls the "peculiar panoramic effect" of balloon travel an "exquisite visual delight," and his description conveys a sense that this delight derived from his ability to see and understand the landscape below from a structural perspective that was new to him. The overall shape and pattern of things is suddenly comprehensible, as seen in Mayhew's comparison of various aspects of the vast scene to familiar, even cozily domestic, objects.

> Far beneath . . . lay the suburban fields; and here the earth, with its tiny hills and plains and streams, assumed the appearance of the little coloured plaster models of countries. The roadways striping the land were like narrow brown ribbons. . . . The bridges over the Thames were positively like planks; and tiny black barges, as they floated along the stream, seemed no bigger than summer insects on the water. The largest meadows were about the size of green-baize table covers; and across these we could just trace the line of the South-Western Railway, with the little whiff of white steam issuing from some passing engine, and no greater in volume than the jet of vapour from an ordinary tea-kettle. (265)

This simple, childlike vision of the vast metropolis is very different from the street-level view of Mayhew's *London Labour and the London Poor,* which had recently appeared in its preliminary form as a series of articles in the *Morning Chronicle* (1849–50). *London Labour and the London Poor* is notable for its extraordinary geographical specificity, precise street locations of particular trades being among the wealth of details Mayhew provides about London's workers. "The many courts in Ray-street, Turnmill-street, Cow-cross, and other parts of Clerkenwell," for example, "are full of street-sellers, especially costermongers, some of those costermongers being also drovers. . . . The many who use the Brill as their place of street-traffic, reside in Brill-row, in Ossulton-street, Wilstead-street, Chapel-street, and the many small intersecting lanes and alleys connect-

ed with those streets, and in other part of Somers-town" (145). Mayhew's ability
to map London's less well-known sights contributes to the authentic texture
and materiality of what Regenia Gagnier has characterized as his "humanistic"
portrayal of working-class subjectivity (92). During his balloon ride, however,
Mayhew seems comforted by the broad generality of the view, which allows him
to see London as a distant object, rather than a setting for intimate scenes of
human misery.

Similarly, the French balloonist M. C. Flammarion described the "panorama
of Paris" as spreading itself out gradually, so that "you can soon see it entirely . . .
its thousands of roofs, its domes and cupoles, its gardens, its boulevards, and its
surrounding landscape." The "whole town of Paris is reduced, after a little while,
to the size of one of those maps in relief which we see in the museum of the
Invalides" (Glaisher, 125–26). Glaisher describes cities viewed from a balloon
as like "models in motion" (99), and this sense of the landscape as constituting
a complete, miniature world of its own appears in virtually every balloonist's
account. "The earth appeared as one immense plane, decorated in many-varied
colors, like a beautiful miniature," writes Flammarion (Glaisher, 126). Margaret
Burgoyne says of the "diminutive" objects below, "Giving way to the illusion of
the moment, we almost felt a desire to have the tiny things in our own hand,
and examine them through a microscope" (531). Tissandier, too, sees a "cloud of
microscopic spectators" below as being like "a family of ants" (Glaisher, 297). The
sense of distance and shift in scale experienced by the viewer allowed him or
her to view familiar objects with scientific detachment, and also to feel himself
or herself to be in a superior, almost godlike position. The pleasure of such a
perspective finds contemporary expression in the popularity of the video game
SimCity, which allows the user to construct and populate an entire world. In
the words of one critic, "*SimCity* is a cultural artefact that satisfies a specifically
human need: the desire to miniaturize the real, to redefine it in microscopic
form, to make the mundane, urban experience intelligible" (Bittanti, 34). The
panoramic view from the balloon, like the screen of a *SimCity* player, reduces a
complex landscape to the status of a toy.

The toylike perception of the world found in these balloonists' accounts may
remind us of Thackeray's famous image of his "puppets" being shut back in their
box at the end of *Vanity Fair*, and as we will see, the panoramic perspective
provides an important analogue to the omniscient narrative perspective that
characterizes many Victorian novels. The sense of Olympian detachment that
pervades the balloon accounts offers a possible model for the famous passage
in Hardy's *Tess of the D'Urbervilles* that compares Tess to a fly. At the end of
a description of Tess's descent into the Valley of Froom, Hardy writes, "Not

quite sure of her direction Tess stood still upon the hemmed expanse of verdant flatness, like a fly on a billiard-table of indefinite length, and of no more consequence to the surroundings than that fly" (Phase the Third: XVI, 136). The idea of humans seeming like flies to greater powers is not new, of course. In the preface to later editions of *Tess*, Hardy uses the Shakespearean quotation "As flies to wanton boys are we to the gods; / They kill us for their sport" (xix) to illuminate his controversial closing statement to the novel, that "The President of the Immortals" had "ended his sport with Tess." Hardy's image has a specifically visual quality, however, that seems indebted to the aerial perspectives that had become familiar to himself and his readers. The reader is forced to move from the "bird's-eye perspective before [Tess]" (Phase the Third: XVI, 133) to a bird's-eye perspective that includes Tess, thus positioning himself or herself somewhere above the action of the novel.

The anonymous balloonist's account from *Bentley's Miscellany* that has been attributed to Margaret A. Burgoyne also uses the image of a fly to emphasize the disjunction of the author's perspective, but in a way that demonstrates the extent to which this disjunction affects the subject as well as the object of the gaze. The author describes the excitement of the crowd as the balloon ascended and, recognizing her own secondary status as a mere guest on the journey, adds, "Though but the fly on the Lord Mayor's state coach . . . I fancied myself like a great hero in a crowd of his admiring countrymen, with the advantage, however . . . of being able to retire into the humble unnoticed individual, and not remain an unnecessary spectacle for the popular gaze" (530). This statement shows a fascinating oscillation between an embrace of the role of masculine adventurer, and a desire to remain quietly in the background.

Burgoyne's ambivalence about her role is evident in the ambiguous narrative voice she assumes in her account, an ambiguity that echoes the broader indeterminacy of the balloonist's suspended position. Though the piece is titled "The Balloon. An 'Excursion Trip,' but not by Railway, by a Lady," the author seems anxious to disguise her gender. After beginning with a languid claim to being "overcome with *ennui*" during the month of September, and a reference to "the unseasonable society the club affords at such a period" (528), she soon finds occasion to comment unfavorably on the presence of two other women whom she refers to as "my fair companions": "I was surprised to observe, two ladies . . . I must confess that my first impression on perceiving this ingredient in our party, was anything but one of gallantry. . . . [I feared] our attention would be occupied in 'taking care of the ladies'" (529). It may be that Burgoyne assumed her anonymity would allow her to maintain a masculine persona, while her editor added a title that assumed her gender would lend a certain cachet to an other-

wise increasingly common genre. But the effect in any case is to highlight the extent to which the experience was valued because of the disorientation it created,
the shift in perspective that could lead to shifts in the viewer's own subjectivity.

The narrative cross-dressing and ambivalence about heroism seen in Burgoyne's nonfiction account is strikingly paralleled in a well-known passage from
Charlotte Brontë's *Villette*, published less than two years later, in which Brontë's
famously retiring heroine, Lucy Snowe, talks about the effect of her assuming a
masculine role in the school vaudeville. Lucy has not only performed the male
part with relish, she has followed her performance by extraordinarily bold remarks in a discussion with her friend Dr. John.

> For the second time that night I was going beyond myself—venturing out of
> what I looked on as my natural habits. . . . On rising that morning, had I antici-
> pated that before night I should have acted the part of a gay lover in a vaudeville;
> and an hour after, frankly discussed with Dr. John the question of his hapless
> suit, and rallied him on his illusions? I had no more presaged such feats than I
> had looked forward to an ascent in a balloon, or a voyage to Cape Horn. (Vol.
> I, Ch. XIV, 211)

Lucy, like Margaret Burgoyne, has generally preferred the role of spectator to
that of spectacle, yet she takes pleasure in having this role temporarily inverted.
Like Burgoyne, who enjoys playing the "great hero" but then returns to being
a humble, unnoticed individual—that is, a female—Lucy ultimately chooses
to become herself again the following day. Brontë uses the image of a balloon
ascent to symbolize a temporary, hypothetical broadening of Lucy's perspective
and sphere of action. Brontë's use of this metaphor underscores the hybridity of
the image: it is a kind of travel, but uncontrolled travel to nowhere in particular;
it provides a unique viewpoint, but not one that can be realistically sustained;
it leaves one hovering above the landscape, unable to engage the scene below.

The difficulty of sustaining a wholly detached perspective and the challenge
of conveying it to a third party are reflected in some of the illustrations that
accompany *Travels in the Air*. While the written accounts stress the uniqueness
of the aerial view achieved by the balloonist, the illustrations do not attempt
to reproduce the view as actually seen by the travellers but instead depict each
scene as it would appear to another observer, were it possible for another observer to be stationed in midair. Most dramatically, a picture like "Mr. Glaisher
Insensible at the Height of Seven Miles" focuses on the balloonists themselves;
but even "The Seine and the Marne as Seen from the Car in Mr. Flammarion's
Second Ascent," although it claims to show the view from the balloon, instead

locates the balloon car in the center of the picture, as if the viewer were travelling in a second balloon. Without some trace of humanity to provide a context, the unanchored view would be difficult to assimilate. Like the stage sets and *faux terrain* of the panorama exhibitions, the representation of the balloon itself frames a transitional space for viewers of the illustration to occupy.

The panoramic language used to describe ballooning was, as we have seen, so quickly standardized that a few common tropes reappear in nearly every description. By the time Jules Verne wrote his novella *Six Weeks in A Balloon* (1863), inspired by his friendship with the French balloonist-photographer Nadar, it was possible for him to compose a description of balloon travel that reads like a compendium of all of the accounts above. His balloonist is a British gentleman who sets off, with two companions, in a balloon they respectfully dedicate as the *Victoria*. The view as they travel over Africa has a familiar ring.

> What a magnificent panorama unrolled itself before the eyes of the explorers! The island of Zanzibar was displayed in its entirety, its deeper colour causing it to stand out as though on a huge relief map; the fields looked like samples of various coloured stuffs, and the forests and jungles like small clumps of trees. The inhabitants of the island had the appearance of insects. (206)

Here, as in descriptions of actual panoramas, the landscape is flattened into a map that invites spectatorship rather than entry. The people who live there are no more than insects to the observers above. They, in turn, admire the aesthetic effect of having this lovely canvas unrolled beneath their feet. Even the simple servant Joe marvels, "You don't feel as if you were moving and the scenery slides along under you to be looked at" (207). The experience resembles film-watching more than travel, and the panoramic perspective of the travellers in this case involves a detachment from and, at times, condescension toward the places and peoples they view on their journey.

The aestheticized view of these ballooning narratives turns the landscape into a panorama, as if the scenery were a representation of itself. In this sense, the bird's-eye view, like an actual panorama, becomes what Baudrillard (1994) would call a "simulacrum" of the reality below. It manifests the "hallucinatory resemblance of the real to itself" that is the mark of the "hyperreal" (23). Baudrillard sees contemporary culture as part of an "era of simulation" in which representation does not involve "imitation, nor duplication, nor even parody" of the real. Instead, simulation "substitut[es] the signs of the real for the real," thus calling reality itself into question (2). Simulation, he suggests, is different from mere "dissimulation," or pretending, in which the distinction between real and unreal is "always clear . . . [but] simply masked." Simulation "threatens the difference between the 'true' and the 'false', the 'real' and the 'imaginary'" (3). The panoramic perspective of the nineteenth century seems to perform a similarly destabilizing gesture. It pulls the rug out from beneath the viewer, erasing the boundary between here and there, real and unreal. This moment of hovering in midair is a transition, a vacation rather than a permanent retreat from ontological security. Nevertheless, the Victorian predilection for visiting this no-man's-land between reality and illusion may represent an early step toward what Baudrillard describes as a world in which "the image can no longer imagine the real, because it is the real" (1996, 4).

6. SURVEYING THE SCENE: THE PANORAMIC GAZE

Balloon travel, like panorama viewing, produced a dramatic shift in perspective that allowed the viewer to take a comprehensive overview of a place he or she had previously seen only in pieces, transforming the way in which Victorians viewed the landscape as a whole. The preceding passages suggest that balloon travellers, and readers of their accounts, became more aware of the shape of a city like London: the infrastructure reflected in its rivers, canals, and railways, the way in which it blended into suburbs and finally countryside, and the sense in which it was a home not just for individuals like themselves but for a large and diverse population. Benjamin noted the irony of the urban panorama viewer's interest in rural landscapes: "The city dweller, whose political supremacy over the provinces is demonstrated many times in the course of the century, attempts to bring the countryside into town. In panoramas, the city opens out to landscapes—as it will do later, in subtler fashion, for the flâneurs" ("Exposé of 1935," *Arcades*, 6). By "opening out" the city, the panoramic perspective gives an air of knowability to the vast expanse that allows the viewer to feel he or she has grasped it as an organic whole. Like Bentham's proposed panopticon, the panorama places the subject at the center of an all-encompassing view.[15] I would argue, however, that it does not constitute the viewer as the kind of invisible observer described by Foucault in *Discipline and Punish*. On the contrary, part of the viewer's enjoyment of the panoramic perspective derives from his or her own visibility. The sight, description, or self-conscious awareness of a "traveller" viewing the scene is an integral part of the spectacle.

As suggested earlier, the capacity of the panoramic perspective to provide a comprehensive view seems to have reinforced an already present sense of mastery and appropriation of landscape generally associated with imperialism. As an effort to synthesize and contain the increasingly complex geography of the world, the panorama resembles the many rituals and spectacles through which, according to David Cannadine, the British "created their imperial society, bound it together, comprehended it and imagined it" (122). Faced with "a global phenomenon of unrivalled spaciousness and amplitude" (121), the British "exported and projected vernacular sociological visions from the metropolis to the periphery, and they imported and analogized them from the empire back to Britain, thereby constructing comforting and familiar resemblance and equivalencies and affinities" (122). This self-referential process of mutual replication finds its parallel in the panorama's attempt to capture a world that had grown too large to be understood, even as the world itself began to look like a panorama.

In this sense, the panorama seems to represent an exaggerated manifestation of a crucial impulse underlying real travel in the nineteenth century, according to James Buzard (1993): the effort to grasp "the essence of 'whole' places," to derive from fragmentary experiences an authentic sense of what "places essentially were," in their totality (10). While the tourist recognizes that he or she has only a partial knowledge of the places visited, he or she seeks the authentic, culturally "saturated" (185) experience that will synecdochically represent the country as a whole. The panorama takes that impulse one step further. It does not claim to convey the people, language, customs, or culture of a place. Instead, it presents a visual synthesis of its landscape and architecture that is defined as the essence of London, Paris, Cairo, or the Mississippi River. To define such a perspective as equivalent to "being there" is, of course, to risk writing culture out of one's definition of what makes a place distinctive. This form of travel requires no engagement with foreign people or ideas. A broad vista of a city's skyline, with all its churches, mansions, warehouses, and railway stations meticulously included, tells you all you need to know.

The all-encompassing visual reach of the panorama is reflected in its frequent use as a metaphor for broad overviews, particularly those suggesting mastery or dominion, in other contexts (a definition of *panorama* that survives today in many languages). William Wells Brown, a black American abolitionist and fugitive slave who visited England in 1851, uses the word in ways that had already become conventional and yet seem surprising given his own experiences and position. Brown's account of seeing the panorama "Paris by Night," cited earlier, may have inspired his use of the term *panorama* throughout his travelogue. For example, he says of a nighttime view of York, "The moon, the stars, and the innumerable gas-lights, gave the city a panoramic appearance" (137), a description that echoes contemporary accounts of the Paris panorama's effective use of back-illuminated pinholes to create tiny, glittering lights.

But an extended description of the Crystal Palace, which Brown greatly admired, perfectly conveys the more conceptual meaning of *panorama*, a privileged sense of seeing the total picture that enhances the viewer's own stature.

> He who takes his station in the gallery, at either end, and looks upon that wondrous nave, or who surveys the matchless panorama around him . . . may be said, without presumption or exaggeration, to see all the kingdoms of this world and the glory of them. He sees not only a greater collection of fine articles, but also a greater as well as more varied assemblage of the human race, than ever before was gathered under one roof. (171)

The extraordinary number of superlatives that suffuse this account reflect Brown's perception that he is seeing the best, the most complete representation of the world possible. The people who attend the Exhibition form part of that representation. Contemporary commentators on the Great Exhibition frequently lauded its supposed democratization of Victorian society, the unique opportunity it provided for people of all classes and races to stand side by side and share this entertaining and educational experience. More recent critics have been struck by the extent to which spectators themselves, particularly members of the working class and foreigners, became part of the spectacle. Jeffrey Auerbach notes that "fear of foreigners" who were expected to come for the Exhibition was "rampant during the months preceding the opening" (180). George Eliot's passing comment on the Exhibition seems to reflect a moderate version of this reaction. She wrote to Sophia Hennell, "Carlyle was very amusing the other morning to Mr. Chapman about the Ex[hibition]. He has no patience with the Prince and 'that Cole' [Henry Cole] assembling Sawneys from all parts of the land till you can't get along Piccadilly" (*Letters* I: 369 [13 October 1851]).

Auerbach compares the numerous representations of foreigners in pictures of the Exhibition to factual data that appear to suggest that there were in fact relatively few foreign visitors. He suggests that these illustrations reflect "the ideological purpose of the exhibition" as a "celebration of humanity as one happy family" rather than the actual numbers of foreigners present. If that is the case, then Brown, too, seems to have mentally exaggerated the number of foreigners he saw at the Crystal Palace. Or perhaps this assemblage seemed unimaginably varied only by comparison to the usual population of London.

In Brown's description, the objects and the people blend into a view that is striking in its miscellaneous completeness. It is a collection of people and objects, a synthesis of items that create a miniature world, with "all its kingdoms" laid out for Brown to assimilate and admire. Andrew Miller has described the world of the Exhibition as a "depthless, abstract space" (53) that "juxtaposed goods from all parts of the world" (51) to create a "total representation of the world, a copy placed at a distance from the original" (52 n.5). In this sense, it resembles a panorama of the entire globe that allows the visitor to view the peaks of industrial achievement in the same way that he or she might view an Alpine landscape. Thomas Richards has described the Exhibition as teaching "the dominant system of spectacular representation" to advertisers, noting that, "like a modern shopping mall, the Crystal Palace set up an elaborate traffic pattern for channeling people around things," so that everyone could become "a leisured flâneur" (1990, 4–5).

The idea of the Exhibition as a panorama of commodity culture is reinforced by the foldout "Grand Panorama of the Great Exhibition," consisting of four parts published in two issues, with a total of twelve 18-inch panels, printed in the *Illustrated London News* of November and December 1851, which depicts the Exhibition as an endless procession of people pausing before countless tables and displays.

The common view of the Great Exhibition as a comprehensive survey of foreign cultures that would bring all men closer together is satirized by Douglas Jerrold in a short piece in the *Illustrated London News* featuring a "simple traveller" to the Exhibition. The traveller describes his perambulations through the hall as a tour through many countries ("Leaving China, I travelled through Switzerland . . ."). He finally writes home to his wife: "Burn all my books of travel . . . I have seen the world; have judged for myself; and the upshot is this: I love the world and all that's in it" (738). Like the panorama, the exhibition does your travelling for you, collecting diverse scenes into a common space that allows you to view and compare them from a single vantage point.

This vantage point, of course, places one country at the center. A picture of Brown's perspective might resemble the classic *New Yorker* cartoon showing "The New Yorker's View of the World," with Manhattan in the center, outer boroughs a bit smaller, the United States absorbing most of the remaining landscape, and the rest of the world's nations shrinking to interchangeable blobs at the periphery. A synthesizing representation of the world as seen through the eyes of imperial Britain, Brown's view is a true panorama. Brown's account of his travels was first published in England in 1852 under a title, *Three Years in Europe: or Places I Have Seen and People I Have Met*, that seems to present his own story as a kind of panoramic miscellany, a collection of people and places that have passed before his eyes during a specified period. The fact that Brown, who was not only an American but a fugitive slave, could to some extent absorb the colonizer's perspective speaks to the power of these exhibitions to shape the viewer's perceptions.[16] The panoramic perspective is not, however, a fully realized "imperial gaze," with the confidence and stability that term implies. The panoramic traveller is a temporary tourist who knows his visa may expire at any moment. The illusion will dissipate, and he will once again be standing in the Egyptian Hall, or the Colosseum, staring at a canvas on a wall.

7. THE HYPOTHETICAL TOURIST

Having outlined the development of the panoramic perspective and its cultivation of a sense of virtual travel on the part of the spectator, I turn now to an analysis of the way in which this visual effect is translated into fiction. Nonfictional attempts to replicate the panoramic perspective, such as the panorama guides and journalistic accounts examined earlier, play a crucial mediating role in this process. They construct the rhetorical strategies of inclusion that are then adopted by the novelists. When this interactive strategy is embedded in a fictional work, as we will see, it serves to enhance the realism of the narrative world.

The frontispiece to Dickens's *Sketches by Boz* (1836), which depicts a balloon ascending into the air while the crowd below looks up in admiration, suggests that the author intends to present a kind of panoramic overview of the London scene. Cruikshank's drawing portrays Boz as a lofty presence surveying a world that cannot be viewed in its entirety by those who compose it. This image provides a concrete personification of the omniscient narrative voice of the nineteenth-century novel. The type of visual perspective embodied in accounts of panoramas and balloon journeys finds its parallel in the characteristic narrative perspective of Victorian fiction. The narratologist David Herman (2002) has suggested that, within Gérard Genette's scheme of classifying narratives into "internally focalized narratives, externally focalized narratives, and nonfocalized narratives, that is, narratives with zero focalization" (304), a passage such as the famous foggy opening of *Bleak House* seems to approximate "zero focalization" in that it is "narrated in a manner that does seem to transcend the limits of space and time, the constraints of an individualized point of view" (305). This destabilized, floating, unidentifiable point of view reflects in part an increased experience within Victorian culture of the kind of generalized perspective embodied in panoramas.

In the landscape of the nineteenth-century novel, I will argue, we see a specific form of visual representation transformed into a narrative strategy that literalizes the idea of "point of view" in order to complicate our understanding of the interplay between subjective and objective perspectives. The duality of the panoramic perspective, its imaginary instantiation of an alternative self who is an actual traveller, is reflected in the Victorian novelist's penchant for creating an imaginary onlooker whose perspective is used to characterize a scene or vista. We have already seen that descriptions of panoramas attempt, whether for serious or comic effect, to blur the boundaries between fiction and reality, subjective experience and objective view. Panorama guidebooks reinforce that confusion by addressing themselves to a reader who is simultaneously the viewer of a panorama and an imaginary traveller through the place depicted. The rhetorical effect is similar to that created in the many novels that present key scenes from the point of view of a generalized onlooker, observer, or traveller: the reader is offered a choice of positions to occupy in relation to the scene described. The language of the panoramic accounts like those discussed above may in fact have influenced the development of this mode of landscape description.

Most panoramas offered for purchase a companion or key to the exhibition that was usually written in the form of a guidebook, as if the reader was being led through a tour of the actual location. Some "real" guidebooks also used inclusive, present-tense narration, but when the represented tour is of a represented place, the reader is placed at a further remove from the actual scene. This format neatly elides the difference between being a real traveller and being the potential traveller imagined by a tourist guide. In "An Illustrated Description of the Diorama of the Ganges," for example, the author offers to conduct "the stay-at-home traveller" to the places "where every enterprising traveller should go" (4). The scenes visited by the person who describes them become identical to the scenes unfolded to the viewer. "On leaving Calcutta to proceed up the country, the traveller may . . . travel by dawk to Benares, a distance of 480 miles. . . . The traveller is now supposed to land from his boats . . . at sunset, to enjoy a stroll on its banks. . . . In the present instance he joins a party of pilgrims proceeding towards Benash" (27). The party of pilgrims is depicted resting under a banyan tree, a scene singled out by a *King's College Magazine* reviewer as particularly realistic: "We almost fancied we were enjoying the quiet repose of the place" ("Diorama of the Ganges," inside cover).

Ali Behdad has suggested that the literary form of the "travelogue" was replaced in mid-nineteenth-century orientalist writing by a different form of travel writing, the "tourist guide." What distinguishes the two genres, he argues, is the "situation of the speaking subject" (39). Travelogues emphasize the role of the author-explorer, whose personal experiences provide "discursive justification and legitimization" (40). Tourist guides, on the other hand, often fail to identify their author at all, appearing instead under the aegis of an editor or publisher. When they do name an author, they provide little personal information about him. The "disappearance of the author" changes the text's relation to the reader. The travelogue "produces its first-person subject ('I') as the site of an act of interpretation—'making sense' of the orient—and as someone who is authorized to *make* meaning. The centrality and discursive authority of the first-person subject in turn imply exclusion, separating the orientalist [traveller] from the reader, whose desire for exoticism can be satisfied only as a displacement of or identification with the enunciative subject's desire." The tourist guide, however, "constructs the reading subject as a *potential traveller* and presupposes the realization of its addressee's desire" to travel (41). The "discourse of tourism" manifests an "obsessive desire to include, to incorporate every kind of traveller in its implied domain" (41).

The typical panorama description quoted above seems to construct this sort of touristic relation between text and reader. Its goal is not to convey an author's unique experience to a reader who has not had, perhaps never will have, the opportunity to experience the places described. Instead, it works on the assumption that the experience they describe is common to both author and reader. It treats the journey and the spectator's viewing of the journey as if they were identical processes. The reader becomes the traveller who visits the scene, thus partaking of the expertise of the "real" traveller. This may explain why so many of the advertisements for panoramas either allude to reasons why the viewer might be planning to visit the place described, or maintain the polite fiction that many viewers have probably seen these sights themselves and will be in a position to confirm their accuracy. Panorama proprietors understood that audiences wanted not simply to watch a representation of travel but to assume the persona of a traveller.

This popular rhetorical strategy, I argue, may have inspired a narrative trope that is common in nineteenth-century novels and fundamental to their efforts at realism. As we will see, novels by Eliot, Hardy, and Dickens frequently describe unfamiliar landscapes or panoramic vistas not, as one might expect, by describing a major character's response to them, but by describing the typical response that might be felt by any traveller or viewer who happened to stumble on the scene. Such descriptive passages seem to belong to a category of narrative that Herman classifies as "hypothetically focalized," in that they "explicitly appeal to a hypothetical witness" (2002, 311). While one might expect that a stronger thematic point could be made by showing the scene's effect on a central character, Victorian authors chose instead to present a generalized response that allows the viewer to imaginatively substitute himself or herself for the anonymous viewer. The hypothetical traveller becomes a proxy or avatar for the reader, whose immersion in the scene contributes to the perceived realism of the fiction. At the same time, the novelists often criticize or qualify this partial view, emphasizing the need for the reader to ultimately move beyond the traveller's superficial perspective. In George Eliot, the traveller's perspective is not inaccurate, yet it seems to anticipate the limited vision of characters, like Arthur Donnithorne or Rosamond Vincy, who see the world around them as a distant backdrop to their own desires. For Hardy, an emphasis on the distant, visual elements of the scene reinforces the reader's sense of the world's objective there-ness and its indifference to human agency. And in Dickens, the panoramic perspective mirrors the omniscience of the narrative voice, as we are invited to see the world from a viewpoint that rises above the subjective view of any individual character.

Adam Bede, for example, introduces an early scene by describing at length the way it appeared to "a traveller" who rides up on horseback and looks down on the town green below. Like a panorama, the view from this vantage point is comprehensive: "From his station near the Green he had before him in one view nearly all the . . . typical features of this pleasant land" (chap. II, 22). He looks across at the "picture," methodically surveying its constituent parts, from the horizon, with its undulating hills, below which "the eye rested on a more advanced line of hanging woods," to the valley below, beyond which "our traveller" saw a "foreground which was just as lovely" as the mansion that lay hidden behind the meadow (chap. II, 22–23). While this sort of picturesque description is not new, what is noteworthy is the description's reliance on the broad impressions of the anonymous traveller (who reappears briefly at the end of the novel). The scene could as easily be described from the omniscient narrator's point of view or, conversely, that of a major character. But Eliot wants to evoke an objective, almost touristic response that mimics what the reader might see if he or she actually travelled to this spot. This objective view of the landscape mirrors the reader's initial response to the action taking place in the town below.

The anonymous traveller in this scene is generally categorized by critics as a somewhat clumsy framing device used to present a charmingly picturesque view of the town. One might well ask, however, why it was important to isolate this view not only from the narrator but also from the major characters in the novel. By creating the anonymous traveller and then jettisoning him as soon as his descriptive task has been performed, Eliot reinforces a sense that his perspective is specifically a *traveller's* perspective, the view of someone who stops briefly, makes judgments, and then moves on. It is a perspective that is available and accessible to the reader, which the reader may even be tempted to adopt. But though this perspective may seem adequate at this early stage of the story, it will be important for the reader to move beyond this superficial level of perception and enter the community in order to understand it. It is a limited and contingent perspective that will be amplified and corrected as the reader travels more deeply into the fictional world of the novel.

Mary Louise Pratt has noted that "promontory descriptions" like the passage cited above are common in many kinds of nineteenth-century writing, and in exploration literature function as way of rendering "momentously significant, what is, especially from a narrative point of view, practically a non-event": the "discovery" of a scene that is new to the viewer but not, of course, unknown to others (202). The "act of discovery" consists of "a purely passive experience—that of seeing" (204). In fact, as noted earlier, nineteenth-century landscape paintings often included a spectator in the foreground whose presence on a promontory mirrors the viewer's own relationship to the scene. Eliot's inclusion of an anonymous traveller seems designed to evoke a sense of discovery in relation to a scene that would have been familiar to characters already present in the novel; the point is not simply to describe what the place is like, but what the place seems like to someone discovering it for the first time, as we are.

Similarly, Hardy's *The Mayor of Casterbridge* begins with a description of what "a casual observer" (35) might have noticed about two figures walking along a country road. Rather than specifying the relationship between them, Hardy has us follow the deductions of the imaginary spectator.[17] Again, this mechanism seems intended to distance us from the protagonists and view them as part of a scene to be visually deconstructed. Hardy's description of the Vale of Blackmoor, in *Tess of the D'Urbervilles*, begins by noting that it is "an engirdled and secluded region, for the most part untrodden as yet by tourist or landscape-painter," yet Hardy goes on to present the view as it might appear to precisely those two genres of spectator.

> The traveller from the coast, who, after plodding northward for a score of miles over calcareous downs and corn-lands, suddenly reaches the verge of one of these escarpments, is surprised and delighted to behold, extended like a map beneath him, a country differing absolutely from that which he has passed through. . . . The atmosphere beneath is langorous, and is so tinged with azure that what artists call the middle distance partakes also of that hue, while the horizon beyond is the deepest ultramarine. (39)

This description sounds remarkably similar to a ballooning narrative in its emphasis on the sudden appearance of the scene beneath the traveller, the maplike appearance of the country when seen from this height, and the appearance of the atmosphere itself.

One function of the figure of the traveller may be to add a time dimension to an otherwise static picture. By situating this scene in the context of the journey that preceded it, Hardy emphasizes the dynamism of the viewing figure, who pauses to look at a scene that is only one stop on his journey. This sudden opening up of the narrative frame is similar to the illusion of movement created by the unrolling of a panorama.

An imagined traveller also opens Hardy's *The Woodlanders:* "The rambler who, for old association's sake, should trace the forsaken coach-road running almost in a meridional line from Bristol to the south shore of England, would find himself . . . in the vicinity of some wood-lands" (chap. I, 1). This hypothetical view is described in some detail before Hardy explains that "at this spot, on the louring evening of a bygone winter's day, there stood a man who had thus indirectly entered upon the scene" (chap. I, 2). The hypothetical viewer is completely unnecessary, given that an actual viewer immediately appears and occupies the precise vantage point described. Hardy's point in creating the hypothetical viewer would appear, then, to be the fact that he is hypothetical, that he allows the reader to imaginatively substitute herself for him.

Even when, in *Jude the Obscure,* Hardy presents the boy Jude's view of Christminster, he gradually leaches the personal perspective from the scene, emphasizing the purely visual qualities of a sunset landscape that transforms itself like a diorama.

> Some way within the limits of the stretch of landscape, points of light like the topaz gleamed. The air increased in transparency with the lapse of minutes, till the topaz points showed themselves to be the vanes, windows, wet roof slates, and other shining spots upon the spires, domes, freestone-work, and varied outlines that were faintly revealed. It was Christminster, unquestionably; either directly seen, or miraged in the peculiar atmosphere.
>
> The spectator gazed on and on. . . . the vague city became veiled in mist. Turning to the west, he saw that the sun had disappeared. The foreground of the scene had grown funereally dark, and near objects put on the hues and shapes of chimeras. (41)

Jude has become "the spectator," and his view has become so suffused with his dreams that the city appears to embody, objectively, his own idealized perspective. Though it is not clear whether he is seeing the reality or a mirage, the narrator seems to make no distinction between the two, insisting that in either case, "it was Christminster, unquestionably." Just as a panorama is considered equivalent to the real place it represents, the mirage of Christminster becomes Christminster itself in the eyes of a spectator who is simultaneously Jude, an objective observer, and the reader.

Like the twinkling panorama of Paris, Christminster as outlined by lights seems to reveal every detail of its structure. The gradual revelation of the scene resembles the light effects of certain panoramas and more specifically the dioramas of Daguerre and others, which used a combination of altered lights and transparent scrims to create the illusion of movement and change in the panoramic scenes they portrayed. A similar transformation is described in *Bleak House*, when Esther looks out the window of her new home on her first morning at Bleak House.

> It was interesting when I dressed myself before daylight, to peep out of the window, where my candles were reflected in the black panes like two beacons, and finding all beyond still enshrouded in the indistinctness of last night, to watch how it turned out when the day came on. As the prospect gradually revealed itself, and disclosed the scene over which the wind had wandered in the dark, like the memory over my life, I had a pleasure in discovering the unknown objects that had been around me. . . . At first they were faintly discernible in the mist, and above them the later stars still glimmered. That pale interval over, the picture began to enlarge and fill up so fast, that, at every new peep, I could have found enough to look at for an hour. . . . the dark places in my room all melted away, and the day shone bright upon a cheerful landscape, prominent in which the old Abbey Church, with its massive tower, threw a softer train of shadow on the view than seemed compatible with its rugged character. (92)

Like the Hardy passage cited above, this passage presents a perspective that is positioned somewhere outside the character's mind, yet seems to mirror the vantage point of the character. Unlike more frankly subjective landscape descriptions, these passages use the landscape, not as a reflection of a character's feelings, but as a kind of filter through which Jude's and Esther's responses pass in the process of being formulated in their own minds.[18] As the scene becomes clearer and more distinct, their inchoate feelings are clarified and simplified. Esther's tentative "peeps" out the window are like the framed views of a stereoscope, as the broad view comes slowly into focus. The contrast between Esther's immediate surroundings, the "dark places" of her room, and the brightly lit scene outside recalls both aspects of the ideal panorama setting described earlier: a central, darkened viewing space from which one views a brightly illuminated panorama.

The use of a "traveller" or more loosely articulated hypothetical observer in these novels creates a triangulation of perspective in which another point of view can be panoramically exhibited, imaginatively entered, and eventually adopted or discarded. In addition, many of the conventionally objective landscape descriptions in novels that are often described as picturesque or cinematic can be characterized more specifically as panoramic: natural scenes and cityscapes are presented through a broad, overarching perspective that would be impossible for a single individual to achieve under normal circumstances. In *The Mayor of Casterbridge*, for example, Hardy describes the urban landscape this way:

> To birds of the more soaring kind, Casterbridge must have appeared on this fine evening as a mosaic-work of subdued reds, browns, greys, and crystals, held together by a rectangular frame of deep green. To the level eye of humanity it stood as an indistinct mass behind a dense stockade of lines and chestnuts, set in the midst of miles of rotund down and concave field. The mass became gradually dissected by the vision into towers, gables, chimneys, and casements, the highest glazings shining bleared and bloodshot with the coppery fire they caught from the belt of sunlit cloud in the west. (IV, 30)

By beginning with a bird's-eye view, and then dropping down to "the level of humanity," and finally zooming in on specific details, Hardy insists on a perspective that transcends the point of view of specific characters.

Hardy's description of the Valley of Froom, referred to earlier, begins with Tess standing on a "distant elevation" and looking down at a scene that is more like a surveyor's map than a place to live: "The world was drawn to a larger pattern here. The enclosures numbered fifty acres instead of ten, the farmsteads were more extended. . . . These myriads of cows stretching under her eyes from the far east to the far west outnumbered any she had seen at one glance before. The green lea was speckled as thickly with them as a canvas by Van Alsloot or Salaert with burghers" (III: XVI, 133). This description, though triggered by Tess's presence on the ridge, does not really register Tess's point of view (she is unlikely to be familiar with the paintings of Van Alsloot or Salaert). Instead, it presents a panoramic perspective of the valley that allows the reader to survey the scene in a detached, comprehensive, analytic manner that is quite different from what we might expect Tess's own response to be. Hardy's frequent use of this broad, godlike perspective in his novels prepares the reader for the global ironies and twists of fate that remain invisible to the characters themselves.

Unlike Hardy, Dickens is not generally associated with landscape description, but Sambudha Sen has suggested that Dickens's novels in general present the city in a "panoramic" manner, which he defines as a sequence in which
the various scenes are "locked in their linearity" and related only by "contiguity"
(489). This structural sense of the word *panoramic* has occasionally been applied to Thackeray's *Vanity Fair*, too, presumably to convey that it consists of
varied scenes, in many different locations, somewhat loosely strung together.
But while Thackeray covers a lot of territory, he usually stays very close to the
ground. In *Vanity Fair* a new setting is generally introduced not by sweeping
overviews but by people stepping in and out of carriages, as when we are told
that "the London lamps flashed as the stage rolled into Piccadilly" (chap. XLI,
378). Dickens, of course, was unsurpassed in his ability to give a personality to
specific neighborhoods and streets. As J. Hillis Miller notes, "Dickens's characters are surrounded and circumscribed by roads, buildings, bridges . . . public
and private interiors" (105–6). However, Dickens often connects his disparate
scenes by allowing the narrative voice to rise above the action of individual characters in order to characterize the life of London as a whole.

Dickens begins chapter 33 of *Dombey and Son* by stating, "Turn we our eyes
upon two homes; not lying side by side, but wide apart, though both within easy
range and reach of the great city of London" (553). He then provides an overview
of each home and its surroundings that recalls the panoramic surveys of balloon
travellers. The second home is in a neighborhood that is "neither of the town
nor of the country. The former, like the giant in his travelling boots, has made
a stride and passed it, and has set his brick-and-mortar heel a long way in advance; but the intermediate space between the giant's feet, as yet, is only blighted
country, and not town" (555). Later in the novel, this sort of expansive, bird's-eye
view is equated with breadth of moral feeling in an impassioned diatribe about
disease and contagion, both real and metaphoric, in London. The narrator concludes, "Oh for a good spirit who would take the house-tops off, with a more potent and benignant hand than the lame demon in the tale, and show a Christian
people what dark shapes issue from amidst their homes, to swell the retinue of
the Destroying Angel. . . . For only one night's view of the pale phantoms rising from the scenes of our too-long neglect." Such a scene would be "blest," for
"rousing some who never have looked out upon the world of human life around
them, to a knowledge of their own relation to it" (chap. 47, 738–39).

A description from *Our Mutual Friend* resembles the balloon accounts
even more closely in the distant perspective that makes the world below seem
small: the suburbs on the Surrey side of the Thames are said to look like "a toy
neighborhood taken in blocks out of a box by a child of particularly incoherent

mind" (218). This type of broadly topographic perspective might not occur to an author, or be visualizable to his readers, were it not for the panoramic views of London that had become familiar through visual displays and written accounts. Audrey Jaffe has suggested that the omniscience of Dickens's narrators represents "a fantasy of unlimited knowledge and mobility; of transcending the boundaries imposed by physical being and by an ideology of unitary identity" (6). While this might be a fantasy, it was one shared by readers who had also seen it played out in panorama exhibition halls.

In addition to providing a descriptive framework, the panoramic perspective can be used thematically within the novel to define a particular way of looking at the world. Although, as we have seen, George Eliot uses some panoramic techniques in her own landscape descriptions, she also critiques the detachment and unreality associated with panoramas. In *Adam Bede*, Eliot uses the image of the panorama to convey the dreamlike unreality of Arthur's vision of his own life. As Arthur returns to his home, unaware of the tragedy unfolding in his absence, he thinks contentedly of the various ways in which he will play the role of the "first-rate landlord." He does not know that Hetty Poyser, the dairymaid he has seduced, is at that very moment imprisoned for the crime of murdering her baby. "Arthur's Return" is a very unusual chapter in the novel, being composed entirely of a present-tense interior monologue in which Arthur's thoughts pass quickly over past mistakes and dwell instead on the good things he will do in the future. Eliot likens her survey of his happy thoughts to a series of "scenes in a long, long panorama, full of colour, and of detail, and of life" (II: XLIV, 228). The chapter mingles Arthur's immediate perceptions of the world around him with his idealized picture of the future.

> Pleasant the crack of the post-boy's whip! Pleasant the sense of being hurried along in swift ease through English scenes, so like those around his own home, only not quite so charming. Here was a market-town—very much like Treddleston . . . then more fields and hedges. . . . What a much prettier village Hayslope was! And it should not be neglected like this place: vigorous repairs should go on everywhere among farm-buildings and cottages, and travellers in post-chaises . . . should do nothing but admire as they went. And Adam Bede should superintend all the repairs.

His view of the landscape resembles his view of himself in that the scene before him is never as pleasant as the scene he imagines. Just as he pictures his family's neglected estate transformed into a picturesque landmark that draws the admiring eyes of passing travellers, so he creates a happy ending to his illicit romance

with Hetty in imagining her safely married to the faithful Adam. When Eliot
notes dryly, "You perceive what sort of picture Adam and Hetty made in the
panorama of Arthur's thoughts" (II: XLIV, 229), she reinforces the fact that this
passing parade of pleasant scenes bears no relation to reality. Arthur can look at
these scenes, but he can't bring them about, because they are already rendered
impossible by his earlier conduct.

   Arthur's perspective is described throughout the novel in pictorial terms.
Earlier, Eliot had noted that "all his pictures of the future, when he should come
into the estate, were made up of a prosperous, contented tenantry, adoring their
landlord, who would be the model of an English gentleman" (I: XII, 184). Specific references to illusory forms of visual art such as panoramas and magic lantern shows help convey the way in which Arthur imagines that the world will
shape itself around his own self-centered perspective. Early in the novel, when
Arthur tries and fails to confess to the rector, Mr. Irwine, that he is heading
down a dangerous path, Mr. Irwine inadvertently diverts the conversation by
noting that at Arthur's colonel's birthday fete "there were some transparencies
that made a great effect in honour of Britannia, and Pitt, and the Loamshire
Militia, and above all, the 'generous youth,' the hero of the day" (I: XVI, xx).
Ironically, he suggests Arthur should help him to "get up something of the same
sort to astonish our weak minds," unaware that Arthur himself is far from being
a young hero and has already begun to furnish Hetty's mind with dream-images
of its own. The future has the magical quality of a panorama or diorama to him;
he fails to see that his flawed actions will lead to a very different outcome from
the one he has pictured.

   Eliot's familiarity with panorama displays and performances like Albert
Smith's "Ascent of Mont Blanc" is suggested by her publisher John Blackwood's
casual reference in a letter to G. H. Lewes (and his friend "G. E.") in 1858, during
Eliot's composition of *Adam Bede*, to recent encounters with several authors including Thackeray, Bulwer, and Albert Smith: "The indefatigable Albert seems
pretty well done at present, and no wonder. Fancy playing on that confounded
horn and telling the same stories for two thousand nights. He will be greatly the
better of his trip to China and I doubt not he will popularise China and give the
public a clearer idea of the Chinese than we have hitherto derived from the Tea
Chests and three fellows in pigtails crossing the bridge on the old blue plates"
(*Letters* II: 458–59 [23 May 1858]). Blackwood's remark displays condescension
toward this genre of presentation but also recognition of its educational function and popular appeal. Eliot had enough respect for author-showman Smith
to put him on the list of nine individuals—a list that included Dickens, Froude,
Thackeray, Tennyson, Ruskin, and Mrs. Carlyle—to whom she asked Black-

wood to send complimentary copies of her first book, *Scenes of Clerical Life*, in 1857 (Haight, 246).[19] Eliot evidently understood the nature of the panorama well enough to see it as a powerful metaphor for an all-too-human readiness to confuse products of the imagination with reality itself.

In both its descriptive and thematic fictional incarnations, then, the panoramic perspective signals a bifurcation of viewpoint that allows the novelist to create a hypothetical or transitional space that parallels the imaginary destination created by the panorama. In the passage above, Arthur's mental panorama allows him to immerse himself in an idealized vision of the future even as his physical self performs actions that will make that future impossible. In the descriptive passages cited earlier, the panoramic perspective mediates between the various points of view associated with the narrator, individual characters, and even the reader. It creates a generic response that functions like the "reasonable person" test in a court case, defining a baseline against which other viewpoints are measured. It is the response that, the novelist implies, you would have if you were there.

This does not, of course, make it the "correct" response. On the contrary, it is often a perspective that must be deepened and corrected by the more nuanced understanding that the novel undertakes to develop. Most of the descriptive examples cited earlier are located either at a novel's opening or at a moment of transition into a new setting. The sense of invitation offered by such scenes is still recognized by filmmakers and video-game designers. King and Kryzywinska explain the "panorama of global scale" found at the start of the game *Age of Mythologies* by noting, "Many games include large-scale 'vista' shots in their expositional cut-scenes, partly to establish a sense of space in the player's mind, but also often as an enticement to explore the game-world" (54). Like a visual panorama, verbal panoramas offer to transport the reader to a new place and provide an overview of its most important features. While the Victorian novel famously contains many rhetorical devices designed to engage the reader, the panoramic perspective offered a unique strategy. It allows the novelist to present a scene, shape a possible response to it, invite the reader to share that response, and yet also signal its provisional nature by framing it as the impressions of a "traveller."

As we have seen, the "panoramic perspective" was employed by an astonishingly wide range of nineteenth-century artists, showmen, journalists, commentators, and novelists. At a time when real travel seemed to offer unlimited opportunities for both personal enrichment and imperialist expansion, virtual travel nevertheless held a powerful appeal for the Victorians. How does this form of imaginary travel differ from the real thing, and in what sense could it be preferable? The accounts examined above clearly demonstrate that audiences were not disappointed or frustrated by the partial, contingent nature of their panoramic journeys; on the contrary, that was an important source of their appeal. Victorian audiences reveled in the panorama illusion, the sensation of being poised between two places. The panorama was valued not as an object but as a space, a passageway to a new perspective. An important aspect of this passageway, however, was that it allowed you to come back. The return journey was as easy as the voyage out.

The Victorian willingness, even eagerness, to grasp at this kind of *faux* experience can be seen as an early sign of the incipient commodification of reality described by Benjamin. Anne Friedberg has suggested that the transition from modernity to postmodernity is marked by "the increasing cultural centrality of an integral feature of both cinematic and televisual apparatuses: *a mobilized 'virtual' gaze*," first created through "protocinematic" forms like the panorama and diorama, that "travels in an imaginary *flânerie* through an imaginary elsewhere and an imaginary elsewhen" (1993, 2). Friedberg's flâneur, like Benjamin's, is first and foremost a consumer.

But Victorian spectators and readers were not simply sampling potential objects of consumption. They were testing the capacity of art to create realistic facsimiles of the world they knew, and developing their own capacity to become immersed in these worlds. Their experimentation with the representational limits of different forms of art, and blurring of the boundaries between these forms, would set the stage for the development of contemporary media that push these boundaries even further, creating powerful sensory experiences that attempt to complicate the line between representation and reality. Through their adaptation of descriptive techniques borrowed from the culture of panoramas, Victorian novelists were an important part of this ongoing experiment.

Part Two

TOTAL IMMERSION

Navigating the Thames

> Picture yourself, your family and your friends in a boat, floating gently down
> the beautiful River Thames. . . . Drift past peaceful water meadows rich in
> wildlife. Visit the world of "Wind in the Willows" and "Three Men in a Boat"
> or explore the history and pageantry of Hampton Court Palace and Wind-
> sor Castle. Wherever you choose to start your journey you will encounter
> constantly changing scenery and discover fascinating delights. No stress, no
> hassle—just complete relaxation.
>
> —www.visitthames.co.uk, 2002

If you visit the Thames through the "visitthames" website, you won't need a life
jacket or sweater. The site recommends that you take a virtual tour by clicking
on individual segments of a map of the Thames and reading a detailed description of the sights you would see during a trip along that portion of the river's
path. The website, like the nineteenth-century guidebooks from which it is de-
scended, invites the reader to experience the river as a nostalgic, relaxing alternative to more hectic forms of travel. But its present-tense narrative also invites
the reader to experience the descriptions it provides as a potential replacement
for the actual journey. Similarly, descriptions of the mobile app "London: River
Thames Guide & Audio 1.0" (Way2GoGuides) emphasize that it is not a map
but a "perfect companion to experiencing the River Thames," an "encounter" that
"begins well before arriving and can be continued long after leaving" ("London:
River Thames Guide"). Except for the electronic mode of access, these contemporary forms of virtual travel are virtually indistinguishable from Victorian versions of the Thames experience.

   In fact, nineteenth-century accounts of travel on the Thames depict an experience that seems strangely familiar to twenty-first-century readers accus-

tomed to web-surfing through travel sites. River travellers would hook into a
network of rivers and canals that allowed them to get off or on anywhere along
the route, moving quickly past some areas, and stopping to linger at other sites
or towns along the way. Rather than spending a lot of time at a single destination, travellers on these journeys enjoyed sampling a wide array of sights and
then moving on. Sometimes they would merely read a guidebook description
of a site while passing it in their boats. Sometimes they would skip the trip altogether, immersing themselves instead in detailed and vivid accounts of other
travellers' journeys.

As we will see, this lack of particularity, this emphasis on experience rather than place, is an important source of the enduring appeal of travel on the
Thames in British culture. A form of travel that emphasizes the sensations of
being on a journey while simultaneously erasing the importance of a specific
destination, Thames travel creates the same paradoxical mixture of suspension
and control that we associate with the virtual. We saw in Part One that rivers
were among the most popular subjects of representation for moving panoramas.
While circular panoramas often represented famous cities as seen from a particular vantage point, moving panoramas generally adopted the fiction of some
sort of journey—by coach, railway, or river—to organize the perspective presented. River scenes were appealing in part because the existence of important
towns along major waterways provided a useful alternation between pastoral
and urban scenes. More important, however, the linearity of the river paralleled
the linearity of the panorama medium itself. The river provided a sense of connection between the various scenes, allowing them to flow together into a kind
of narrative, and creating a sense of mobility and immersion that was central to
the panorama experience, as it would later be central to the experience of films,
video games, amusement park rides, and virtual reality environments.[1]

The unique characteristics of river travel, as described by the Victorians,
render it analogous to the kind of virtual travel experienced through panoramas
and through contemporary media. As we will see, the river itself functions as
itinerary, guide, and motive force, relieving the traveller or spectator of responsibility for directing the journey. As in the balloon journeys described in Part
One, the impression of a moving landscape passing before one's eyes encourages
the viewer to see the landscape as a kind of show, prefiguring a mode of experience that would be provided even more vividly a few decades later by early
cinema. The riverbank scenes form, in the words of one writer on the Thames,
a "pageant" that displays characteristic scenes in a manner and at a pace that
makes them appealing and comprehensible. At the same time, the viewer's phys-

ical movement through these scenes creates a greater sense of immersion in this landscape than a static visual experience would provide.

This part of my study will explore the extraordinary popularity of journeys along the river Thames in the nineteenth century, and the reasons for the immense appeal of this form of virtual travel. The Thames journey became such a standard pastime that it spawned an entire subgenre of elaborately illustrated guidebooks, minor topographical poems, and anecdotal personal accounts. In addition, a journey up the Thames provides the central organizing principle for two novel-length prose works: Jerome K. Jerome's enormously popular *Three Men in a Boat* (1889) and William Morris's utopian fantasy *News from Nowhere* (1890). Looking at the characteristics associated with the Thames in these more descriptive or expository works will prepare us to understand the vision of the Thames presented, in a different register, in some major works of Victorian realist fiction. We will see many of the descriptive and rhetorical tropes of these earlier forms used to ironic effect in Dickens's *Our Mutual Friend* and *Great Expectations*. In *Daniel Deronda*, the sense of the Thames as a familiar and comforting image of British nationalism is inverted in Eliot's depiction of the river as the natural environment of the alien and alienated.

In Part One, we confronted a central paradox in the panorama experience: why were the Victorians so attracted to the idea of seeing panoramas of real places, even when the places themselves were easier to visit than ever before? Here, too, we will ask: what made the experience of travelling on the Thames so compelling that it was repeated over and over again, in a variety of genres?

As we will see, a trip up the Thames becomes a timeless journey into the heart of England, an exploration of an already-familiar landscape. Like a panorama, a trip up the Thames allows the traveller, viewer, or reader to experience the sensations of travel without really going anywhere. The point of such journeys is not getting to a destination, or even acquiring knowledge of new places along the way. The point is the journey itself, and the opportunities it provides for experiencing the sense of freedom associated with mobility and spectatorship—within a carefully delineated route that may offer the illusion of agency, but follows a preprogrammed path.

The Thames journey is presented as a form of exploration, similar in overall structure to the journeys taken by travellers to more exotic locations. Here, however, the subject of ethnographic interest is Britain itself. In a sense, the Thames journey is already a virtual tour: a replication of a different kind of journey. A trip up the Thames may resemble such common touristic jaunts as a trip up the Rhine, but Victorian writers about the Thames create a deliberate contrast with the foreign tours to which their audiences were accustomed. The Thames journey mimics these popular forms of travel but presents itself as a more authentic, real experience.

The Thames river has always functioned as a kind of representation, an image that mirrors broader cultural currents. Over the past two centuries, the Thames has been valorized as the wellspring of early British mercantile success, derided as a source of industrial pollution and decay, and appreciated with renewed vigor as a site of leisure and recreation. Its geography makes visible the interdependence of England's constituent parts. As a river that runs the length of the London metropolis and far into the surrounding countryside, the Thames represents the possibility of transition between urban and rural spaces, providing important reassurance to city dwellers that escape to the countryside is still possible, while also reminding those in the country of their continuing connection to the vibrant center of British life, culture, and industry. At the same time, it emblematizes Britain's connection to the outside world through the great port of London, and the degree to which her imperial vision depended on maintaining and fostering that connection.

In the literary journeys we will examine, the Thames presents a fluid picture that reflects the tensions and transitions common to Victorian culture as a whole. The massive docklands development that took place early in the nineteenth century reaffirmed the river's status as an engine of industry and conduit of trade. From the early 1800s till past midcentury, the Thames was primarily a "working river," crowded with every kind of craft, from enormous sailing ships full of overseas cargo, to small skiffs and wherries that ferried passengers up and down the river. As the developing railway system began to supersede the country's network of rivers and canals as a means of transporting people and goods, however, the Thames's role as both water source and sewer for the city of London became more prominent. By midcentury, it was not the backbone of British industry, it was a public health crisis, and the repository of both legitimate sanitation concerns and more generalized fears about the effects of industrialization. The cleaning up of the Thames in the 1860s and 1870s paved the way for its reemergence as a site of leisure and recreation at the end of the century.

Even those Thames accounts that stress the pastoral beauty of its upriver portions, or the grandeur and historical importance of the London river, contain a subcurrent of awareness of the river's darker side. But in all of these representations, the Thames is presented as a route into some essential but generalized aspect of England itself—a route that transcends the specific geography of the landscape traversed, and becomes a journey into the past, into the future, or into an idealized England that can only exist in the form of passing scenes that are as distant as those of a panorama. The fact that the Thames has always been seen as a kind of metaphor allows it to function within these texts as a mode of imaginative transport, a conduit to a place that is different and yet feels strangely familiar. A trip on the Thames embodies the same suspension between here and there that we saw in the virtual travel experience offered by panoramas. It is a trip into the heart of England, a tour of a place that is already known, a journey with no fixed destination that takes you back to the place where you began. It is a journey to nowhere.

I. NO PLACE LIKE HOME:
THE THAMES AS ENGLAND

Charting the many turns in the Thames's literary course throughout the period allows us to map the shift from a picturesque romanticism to a new realism, as we see the England symbolized by the Thames begin to acknowledge the gritty realities of Victorian life. The Victorian obsession with describing and redescribing the familiar journey up and down the Thames demonstrates the high value that was placed on these travelogues as representations. Long after such accounts could add any new insights or information about the landscape, they offered a replication of the travel experience that functioned, like the panorama viewings examined in Part One, as a form of virtual travel.

To travel the Thames was, at the beginning of the nineteenth century, to connect oneself to an enduring symbol of British success. It is difficult to overstate the crucial role played by the river itself in the development of British trade and industry. London's ability to serve both as a major port for ships arriving from other countries and a major artery into the heart of England was responsible for its leading position in England and in the world for several centuries. In the words of an anonymous writer in 1869, the Thames was both "the main street of the town" and "the great highway that connected the town with the country" ("The Thames," 309). The easy movement of goods and people up and down the river was a primary reason for Britain's economic dominance from the sixteenth century onward, and any understanding of the symbolic importance of the Thames must begin with an acknowledgment of its original status as a primarily mercantile environment. Even the idyllic and allegorical visions of the Thames that appear in the poetry of Drayton, Spenser, and Pope are dependent on an identification of the Thames with English economic and political power.

The centrality of the Thames to British culture is evident in the long tradition of river poetry in British literature, a heritage that embraces Song XV of Michael Drayton's *Poly-Olbion*; Milton's *Comus*; Spenser's *Epithalamion* and the marriage pageant of the Thames and the Medway in *Faerie Queene* IV.xi; William Camden's *Britannia*; John Taylor's *Thames-Isis* (1632); the anonymous Latin poem *De Connubio Tamae et Isis* (trans. 1695), also attributed to Camden; and Pope's *Windsor-Forest* (1713), which includes a passionate declamation by Father Thames. Later, James Thomson's *The Seasons* (1746) would continue to present the Thames as a symbol of "Happy Britannia!" while Thomas Love Peacock's *The Genius of the Thames* (1810) lists, among the themes announced in the First Canto, "Acknowledged superiority of the Thames ... View of some of the principal rivers of Europe, Asia, Africa, and America ... Pre-eminence of the Thames."

Simon Schama has pointed out that the popular theme of river-marriages in English poetry served to enhance the political status of the "royal river-road." As various tributaries merged upstream, the "confluence of waters, moving irresistably to the sea, seems to embody both the natural harmony of the English landscape and an end to the strife that for centuries had torn the realm" (330). The Thames represents a merging of fertile waters that gives birth to "the awesome embryo of the British Empire" (Schama, 330). In many of these works, the Thames served as the focus for nationalistic and patriotic themes, and "a standard motif of river poetry was the challenge to foreign waters to provide an equal" (Rogers, 295), a theme we will later see repeated in prose accounts of the Thames. By outdoing the Ganges, Rhine, Tyber, and Nile, the Thames could reinforce England's claim to political dominance in the period.

The Thames continued to inspire poetry throughout the nineteenth century, though it no longer inspired great poetry. Single-volume poetic descriptions of the Thames include Thomas Hartree Cornish's *The Thames: A Descriptive Poem* (1842); Richard Hippisley Domenichetti's Newdigate prize poem, *The Thames* (1885); *The Thames: A Poem*, by John Stapleton (1878); H. G. Hooper's *Poetical Sketch of the Thames from the Seven Springs to the Nore* (1885); and *Thames Sonnets and Semblances*, by M. Armour (1897). But in addition to these minor poetic continuations of the river poetry tradition, we can also see some of its tropes and themes reflected in Victorian prose accounts of river journeys, which both reflect and satirize the traditional understanding of the Thames as a symbol of England at its best.

One nineteenth-century prose writer, Charles Mackay, notes the poetic heritage and romance associated with the Rhine, Danube, Rhone, and Seine, then begins his own account by asking plaintively: "'And what has been done for these, shall none be found to do for thee, O Thames?'" (366). This question exemplifies a recurrent paradox in these accounts: at the same time that the Thames is lauded for its important place in British history and culture, it is also presented as undervalued or taken for granted. The anonymous author of an 1869 article in *Saint Paul's* begins by claiming, "Few people in the present day have meditated on the advantages of a great river. Yet there is no country in the world where those advantages are as conspicuous as our own" ("The Thames," 306). His purpose is to give a history of the river, "not its banks" (318), meaning that he is more concerned with the Thames's role as a waterway than with the picturesque and historic sights that may be seen while travelling on it. The Thames represents the real rather than the ideal.

John Murray attempts a similar distinction between streams that "owe much of their reputation to their banks—as men rise in the world by the interest of patrons" and Father Thames, "who owes everything to himself." Who is this self? Murray admits that "his banks are nowhere sublime, and although in the greater part of his career beautiful, yet it is a quiet beauty." The value of the Thames, he claims, is "the gently gliding character of the stream itself . . . its transparent waters and silvery surface, its copiousness without profusion" (64). In contrast to the showier scenes offered by the great rivers of Europe, the Thames offers a humbler beauty, more in keeping with the English character. The representational power of this beauty is so strong that it is ascribed an actual identity. This sense of the Thames as representing the essence of England gives permanence but also fluidity to that sense of identity and allows each generation of writers to mirror a different England in its waters.

Many Victorian writers strove to establish the superiority of the English river through head-to-head comparison of the Thames with another favorite travel destination, the Rhine. In part, comparisons of the Thames to other rivers may reflect the general indebtedness of the emerging genre of naturalistic prose description to earlier loco-descriptive poetry. But the frequency of such comparisons suggests that aesthetic competition masked underlying political competitiveness. By the mid-nineteenth century, the superiority of the Thames was not as indisputable as it had seemed to the poets of earlier centuries, and the political point to be made through such comparisons had become more complicated. The Rhine symbolized the picturesque river par excellence. In this sense, it also represented the supposed superiority of European culture. In suggesting the Thames as an alternative, British writers were challenging the definition of aesthetic and cultural merit that seemed to assign these qualities to places in proportion to their remoteness. The Thames was seen as symbolic of England as a whole, and defense of its scenery constituted defense of the realm.

In the "Prefatory Remarks" to his 1842 poem *The Thames*, Thomas Cornish notes, "The Thames, it is quite true, is unequal to his brother the Rhine in many respects. . . . No mountainous scenery, no lofty towers stand forth in majesty supreme—but sylvan landscapes, luxuriant meadows" are the scenes the Thames has to offer (vi). His actual poem makes even larger claims for the English river.

> Old Rhine, himself, seems dull compared with thee,
> River of charms unsung; for far and wide,
> Like a dear child of darling Liberty,
> Rolls in wild splendour thy imperial tide. (18)

The anonymous 1849 prose work *The Tour of the Thames* begins with an invocation to the Thames, and the alliterative admission that "thou art not so long as lazy as the Rhine, or so rushing and rough as the Rhone . . . so sunny and slow as the Ganges . . . or so might and miry as the Mississippi" (3) suggests that this is prose aspiring to the condition of poetry, just as the Thames itself aspires to the prestige of the great continental rivers. Many other writers quote Pope, Spenser, Denham's lines from "Cooper's Hill," or other poems to lend their accounts a literary quality. The obligatory comparison to the Rhine, then, can be seen as in part an attempt to establish a literary pedigree for these prose narratives. But it also reveals a kind of nationalistic competitiveness and uncertainty about the value of visiting something that is not simply close to home, but *is* home. The Thames represents the epitome of Englishness but, at the same time, must be viewed as if it were a foreign river in order to seem worth seeing.

While Renaissance and eighteenth-century poets were unstinting in their lyric praise of the river, Victorian writers often have a slightly defensive tone that reveals their uneasy recognition of its essential ordinariness. Margaret Oliphant begins her 1870 narrative of a journey on the Thames with an assertion of the Thames's equality to her European cousin. She claims that "the Rhine is far from the delight which it was once supposed to be" (460). Calling the reader's attention instead to the "historic stream connected with a thousand memories at once more homely and more dear," she promises the mild delights of "beautiful scenery, quiet, fine air, and, in proportion to the pleasure, little fatigue." Admitting that "English rivers are not gigantic in their extent, like the American, nor are they magnificent volumes of water, like the Rhine and the Danube," she nevertheless boldly asserts that she is "by no means sure that the traveller of fine taste and poetic eye would not find attractions as great in the lovely woods and silvery reaches of the Thames, as in the more famous windings of the great German river which has this year exchanged tourists for soldiers" (1870, 460).

The double negatives of this statement tend to qualify Oliphant's endorsement, and her emphasis on the Thames as a "homely," peaceful refuge from political traumas elsewhere reinforces the impression that she is defending England as much as describing the river.

As we saw in Part One, the Rhine, like the Mississippi, the Nile, and other large rivers, was frequently reproduced in panoramas, and it was associated with a romantic, picturesque, Grand-Touristic sense of Europe that contrasts sharply with the pleasant, domestic associations generated by representations of the Thames. The Rhine embodies a picturesque natural beauty that unfolds itself before the educated traveller. George Eliot's 1860 novel *The Mill on the Floss* alludes nostalgically to the Rhine's emblematic status as the most romantic of rivers, comparing it to the less picturesque Rhone.

> Journeying down the Rhone on a summer's day, you have perhaps felt the sunshine made dreary by those ruined villages which stud the banks . . . telling how the swift river once rose, like an angry, destroying god, sweeping down the generations. . . . Strange contrast, you may have thought, between the effect produced on us by these dismal remnants of commonplace houses . . . and the effect produced by those ruins on the castled Rhine, which have crumbled and mellowed into such harmony with the green and rocky steeps . . . that was a day of romance! . . . Therefore it is that these Rhine castles thrill me with a sense of poetry: they belong to the grand historic life of humanity, and raise up for me the vision of an epoch. But these dead-tinted, hollow-eyed, angular skeletons of villages on the Rhone oppress me with the feeling that human life . . . is a narrow, grovelling existence, which even calamity does not elevate. (237–38)

Eliot's description characteristically mingles her own response with what her reader "may have thought," admitting the general human tendency to prefer the ideal to the real. But she goes on to compare this response to the way she imagines her readers might feel while "watching this old-fashioned family life on the banks of the Floss" (238), a phrase that conflates the stream of her narrative with the river at the center of the novel. She admits that the lives she portrays are narrow and ordinary, but insists on the importance of understanding them nevertheless. Eliot's metaphoric association of a reader's journey through her book with a traveller's voyage down a famous river suggests that she recognizes that the familiar touristic perspective of the outsider encourages one to passively critique the text passing before one's eyes rather than emotionally engage it. Her goal is to overcome this distant attitude and force her readers to "feel . . . [the] sense of oppressive narrowness" that shapes the lives of her characters (30).

Eliot may have been influenced here by a passage in Ruskin's *Modern Paint-*

ers (1843–60) that describes the valley of the Rhone with a similar emphasis on the contrast between idealism and realism. Ruskin vividly captures the sense of gradual disillusionment a traveller may feel when he gets closer to the picturesque scene he admires.[2] Eliot's and Ruskin's contrast between the gritty reality of the Rhone and the idealized, touristic view associated with the Rhine shows the extent to which the Rhine is seen to embody a particular kind of scenery that is the projection of a specific aesthetic perspective: that of the picturesque. Comparisons between the Rhine and the Thames, therefore, often function as an implied comparison between the picturesque perspective and the new mode of realism that was emerging as a dominant strain in literature and visual art in the nineteenth century.

In many Victorian novels, a journey up the Rhine had already become a touristic cliché that reveals how passé the "picturesque tour" had become. Trollope asks rhetorically, "where is the man who can tell his wife and daughters that it is quite unnecessary that they should go up the Rhine?" Thackeray, who knew the Rhine well, having travelled it first as a young man in 1830, used it as a setting for fashionable travel in several of his novels. *Vanity Fair*, of course, contains the "Am Rhein" chapter that describes the progress of Amelia, Jos, Georgy, and Dobbin through the Rhineland, where Amelia sketches, Jos drinks, Georgy orders the servants about, and Dobbin carries the bags. *The Newcomes*, too, includes a Rhineland trip during which Clive sketches the scenery but finds Ethel even more picturesque. Thackeray wrote an entire novella, *The Kickleburys on the Rhine* (1850), satirizing the pretensions of British travellers along the great river. Written after Thackeray's own 1848 trip up the Rhine, it is peopled with ambitious socialites, flirtatious daughters, bored husbands, and assorted characters who conspicuously fail to enjoy, or even notice, any of the river's fabled sights. At Bonn, the narrator looks at the hotel register and notes, "Why, everybody is on the Rhine! Here are the names of half one's acquaintance" (1850, 33), confirming that the main purpose of the trip is to perform what has become a standard social ritual.

Throughout *The Kickleburys on the Rhine*, Thackeray emphasizes the way in which the travellers' experience of the river is conditioned by the social and logistical challenges of the trip, rather than appreciation of the picturesque sights to be seen. Thackeray's account contrasts the idealized scenery around them with the mundane preoccupations of the travellers, deftly mixing conventional lyric description with immediate deflation of his own elevated language.

> And so we pass by tower and town, and float up the Rhine. We don't describe the river. Who does not know it? How you see people asleep in the cabins at the

most picturesque parts, and angry to be awakened. . . . It is as familar to numbers of people as Greenwich; and we know the merits of the inns along the road
as if they were the Trafalgar or the Star and Garter. (43)

The standard rhetorical question of guidebook descriptions, "Who does not
know it?" is generally used to highlight the deserved fame of a picturesque destination. Here, Thackeray answers the question, and the answer—no-one—
suggests that familiarity has bred contempt of the river.

The fault is not with the scenery, but with the jaded viewer, Thackeray implies: "How stale everything grows! If we were to live in a garden of Eden now,
and the gate were open, we should go out, and tramp forward, and push on,
and get up early in the morning, and push on again—anything to keep moving,
anything to get a change, anything but quiet for the restless children of Cain"
(43). Here, as in *The Tour of the Thames*, where all "hope of novelty" has been
exhausted, we see change valued for its own sake, and travel characterized as
the impulse to go somewhere, anywhere, so long as it is new. At the same time,
it cannot be too new: one must expect to find "half one's acquaintance" there.

Thackeray satirizes the idea of choosing a destination simply because it is
elsewhere, rather than because it is preferable, asking, "How much further shall
we extend our holiday ground?" and speculating that "ere long we shall be going
to Saratoga Springs, and the Americans coming to Margate for the summer"
(44). The idea of British and American tourists changing places to visit equally
bourgeois spots on opposite sides of the ocean conveys the arbitrariness of these
alternatives. A traveller making such a meaningless choice is essentially going
nowhere. At the end of *Kickleburys on the Rhine*, the narrator bids a ceremonial
farewell to one river as he returns to the other: "Farewell to holiday and sun-
shine . . . kindly sports and pleasant leisure! Let us say goodbye to the Rhine,
friend. Fogs, and cares, and labours are awaiting us by the Thames; and a kind
face or two looking out for us to cheer and bid us welcome" (87). The contrast is
not between two physical locations but between two states of mind. The Rhine
represents holiday and leisure; the Thames, the workaday world of labor, but
also the familiar comforts of home. The Thames would become a popular alternative to the Rhine when it became possible for travellers to feel that it simulated the "travel elsewhere" experience, and yet within the context of English,
rather than foreign, culture.

Thames narratives, it seems, embody a mode of realism that ascribes aesthetic and moral value to the ability to appreciate the familiar with the same dis-
cernment as one applies to things foreign. Many writers emphasize the degree
to which their journey, though it might cover known territory, allowed them

to see things anew. By contrast, Thackeray's disparagement of the tourist who travels up the Rhine without really seeing it found a specific target in two earlier reviews for the *Foreign Quarterly*. In reviews of two books on the Rhine that appeared in 1842, Thackeray is contemptuous of both authors' claims to have arrived at a superior understanding of Germany and Germans. In "*The Rhine*, by Victor Hugo," Thackeray notes that "there are very few people who read the *Foreign Quarterly Review* who have not gone over every inch of the ground that M. Hugo describes, who have not seen Champagne with their own eyes, Eperney and Rheims" (1842, 376). He raises a question that is central to every travel narrative that covers accessible, perhaps even familiar, territory: what is the value of an author's description of a place, when the place itself is there to be seen? Why prefer the virtual to the real?

The obsessive contrasting of the Thames with the Rhine seen in these accounts did not simply reenact the traditional Anglo-French rivalry. Such comparisons evoked an idealized image of picturesque journeys through well-known scenes, implying that this is what one might expect from a journey on a British river as well. At the same time, comparisons to the Rhine appealed to national pride by suggesting that it was not really necessary to step outside of England to experience the aesthetic pleasure and cultural education associated with travelling the world's great rivers. A trip on the Thames represented a domesticated version of the once-exotic travel experience. It offered an opportunity to experience the sensation of travelling into new territory and seeing interesting things—but in a much more limited period of time, on a much more convenient scale, and without really going anyplace unfamiliar. This homely, familiar form of travel, as it turned out, would precisely suit nineteenth-century tastes. The Victorians were happy to replace their exotic Rhine wine with ordinary Thames water.

The landscape of the Thames became the backdrop for a nostalgic appreciation of the beauty of the English countryside, and in particular of the kind of pastoral scenery that seemed to be rapidly disappearing during this period. Like the "scenic corridors" of tree plantings along contemporary highways that create the illusion one is driving through a forest, the strip of landscape along the Thames allowed boaters to feel a sense of access to a large swath of British countryside without their having to delve more deeply into the environment through which they passed. They enjoyed passing through the landscape, but the emphasis of the experience was on the sensation of passage, not the complex reality of the landscape itself.

Travel on the Thames did not provide access to new scenes but simply reinforced one's appreciation of the familiar. Paradoxically, familiarity seems to be the most valued aspect of the landscape. Far from apologizing for the ordinariness of the Thames, Victorian writers praised the river for offering travellers the pretty, undramatic scenery they saw as typical of the English countryside at its best. There is an oddly circular quality to the descriptions of Thames enthusiasts, because the most frequent compliment the English river receives is that it is thoroughly English. Perhaps the commonest adjective in all of these nineteenth-century river narratives is *characteristic*. One village is praised for being particularly "characteristic of the upper Thames" (Pennell, 71), while Edmund Ollier leaves Battersea Reach saying "farewell to the characteristic scenery of the River Thames" (*Royal River*, 257). A continuous line of woods prompts the comment that this kind of repetition is frequently found in "true Thames scenery," being as "characteristic of the country as are the church-towers in the background" (Oliphant, 466).

The "sameness" (6) of landscape that makes it possible for James Thorne to generalize about Thames scenery leads Cornish to refer to the "*sameness of prospect* peculiar to our river . . . which contradistinguishes the scenery of the Thames from that of the romantic Rhine." Cornish admits that long stretches are "without any striking objects to vary the picturesque" (vii). David Hill has noted that several of J. M. W. Turner's many hundreds of sketches of Thames scenery evince a quality of sameness in their repetition of landscape features. An 1805 drawing of "nothing in particular," just "ordinary river-bank" without any specific landmarks, suggests that Turner was interested not just in the most picturesque or striking scenes along the river but in registering what the experience of viewing it continuously was actually like (Hill, 29).

The area around Abingdon, we are told by one writer, admittedly has "somewhat of the foreign aspect" but also includes many "scenes that are very English" (Bonney, *Royal River*, 68). Thames scenery as a whole is praised for many scenes that are "freshly, strongly, characteristically English" (Turner, *Royal River*, 161). The Thames is valued, it seems, for its forthright Englishness, its resemblance to itself.

Andrew Wynter, viewing a picturesque scene at Maidenhead bridge, exclaims, "There's old England for you . . . !" But as a train shoots by, he adds enthusiastically, "And this is 'Young England'!" (64). The inherent contradictions of his attitude are evident as he approvingly quotes Tennyson's lines "Let the great world spin for ever down / the ringing grooves of change" but then bemoans the fact that "we seem to get further from nature every day" (64). The movement toward change, however highly valued, is recognized as a move away from nature, from "old England." Wynter's trip on the Thames is an attempt to get back to nature. But it ends, of course, with him getting back on the train.

Within this construct, *Englishness* refers to a particular dimension of English character and experience, a rural or pastoral dimension that was imperilled by the growth of cities and expansion of rail networks. The fact that the Thames Valley was not only the setting for river idylls such as the ones discussed here, but also, as Patrick Parrinder has pointed out, a number of late nineteenth-century "catastrophe fictions" (including H. G. Wells's *War of the Worlds* [1898] and *The Time Machine* [1895]; Richard Jeffries's *After London* [1885]; and Grant Allen's "The Thames Valley Catastrophe" [1897]), is indicative of "the threat that suburbanization posed to the countryside, and, more specifically, the growth of the modern transport network which turned the river above London into a leisure resource for the capital" (Parrinder, 59).

What experience did urban writers seek as they travelled up the Thames? As early as 1839, Charles Mackay describes himself as a "dweller among the smoke" (374) who invites us to "go in search of wisdom and of health along the banks of the Thames, and drink its pure water from its very fountain-head among the hills of Gloucestershire" (373). His description of the trip as a "pilgrimage" reinforces his characterization of the journey as a kind of mythic quest for the original spring from whence the river flows. By making his goal the "fountain-head" itself, Mackay aligns himself with a tradition, reaching far back into antiquity, of seeing the origin of a river as symbolic of the wellsprings of human thought. In a wide variety of texts and cultures, the pure flowing water of a river is associated "with the divine element and the origin of all things," as W. H. Herendeen notes (110). While Mackay's account may not reach any level of philosophical profundity, his characterization of the journey as a search for "wisdom and . . . health" does suggest that it is a trip aimed more at recreation and self-development than at discovery of new scenes.

The Thames is often seen as a source of imaginative energy, a spring from which to replenish one's creative juices. Wynter's 1847 narrative begins with a description of writer's block on a hot and sunny afternoon: "It was the influence of the weather, I suppose: nibbing my pen would do no good. I had gazed at a well-known spot on the ceiling without drawing any inspiration from it . . . the heat was intense." There is only one solution. "'I'll have a day upon the Thames,' said I, 'and lounge upon the pure crystal!' The thought itself was cooler than one of Gunter's ices" (62). He jumps impulsively onto a Great Western cab, and from thence onto a train, which soon takes him to Maidenhead. While the informal, down-to-earth tone of this prose account may seem far from Spenser's "Sweet Themmes, run softly, till I end my song," Wynter was following a long line of British poets in seeking inspiration from a river. In Wordsworth's *Prelude*, the river Derwent symbolizes the power of nature to create a music that, combined with the Aeolian stirrings of the "correspondent breeze," helps to generate Wordsworth's own song. In addition to describing the panoramic prospect of the Thames from Westminster Bridge in one of his most famous poems, Wordsworth also composed a poem from Richmond Bridge that directs the Thames: "Glide gently, thus for ever glide, / O Thames! That other bards may see/ As lovely visions by thy side / As now fair river come to me." Wynter's sly appropriation of this poetic trope legitimates his choice of topic and aligns his own up-to-date narrative voice with the voice of literary tradition. One of the nonexistent "places" to which the Thames transports the traveller is the depths of his or her own imagination.

2. JOURNEY TO THE INTERIOR

A trip on the Thames was an escape from a particular kind of reality: a modern, urban, technological reality. A journey into the heart of England might, it was hoped, allow the modern traveller to cultivate a more relaxed, introspective attitude. Most accounts of a journey on the Thames begin, like Wynter's, by contrasting the frantic urban existence of the narrator-traveller with the pastoral recreation represented by a trip on the river. James Thorne praises the river for removing the traveller from the city, so that "for a brief space the busy working-world, with all its cares and duties, is to him a distant thing" (128). The author of *Up the River from Westminster to Windsor* (1876) asks:

> What Londoner, choked with the dust of streets, and deafened by the noise of traffic, has not often looked with wistful eyes at the one dustless and noiseless thoroughfare of the city, "Old Father Thames"? . . . with what longing do we think of the grassy banks a few miles up the river, where there is sunlight and fresh air . . . we look up the stream, and pine for the atmosphere of old-world tranquillity which yet hangs around the villas and villages upon its banks. (2)

He notes that "there is a special attraction for all Londoners in going 'up stream'" (2), and most accounts emphasize the categoric distinction between journeying through the city itself and travelling up the river into the pastoral landscape above London. As in most of these accounts, Thorne's journey is not simply a trip out of the city and into the country, it is a trip into the mythic and historic heart of England, a trip into the "old-world tranquillity" that has long disappeared from urban life.

Just as it begins with a train ride, so Andrew Wynter's account ends with an abrupt transition between the hypnotic beauty of the river and the faster-paced world to which he must return.

> We pushed off the boat to cross to the other side. . . . A footpath through two or three corn-fields leads to the station. I was but barely in time for the up-train from Exeter. . . . In less than half-an-hour the beautiful spire of the new church at Paddington came to view—the station was gained—and then, like a rocket which has reached its greatest altitude, and bursts into a thousand balls of fire, the doors were thrown open, and the multitude of travellers (I among the number) were in a moment dispersed in every direction. (67)

Wynter stresses the leisurely pace, the picturesque beauty, and the sense of contrast through which, for example, "all the sensations of early day to a townsman in the country are delightful" (64). But his phrasing implies a recognition that being awakened early by the singing of birds might be less enjoyable if it were less of a novelty, and he seems not simply resigned but happy to return to London at the end of his brief sojourn. The fact that his account is framed at both ends by a railway journey marks it as an interlude in his life, an interlude that is in fact made possible by the modern technology he wishes to escape.

The picturesque tour taken by John Murray is presented as a similarly spontaneous rejection of the city and its stresses. He, too, sits contemplating a sunny morning and describes feelings he presumes are universal: "Desire for the country asserts itself like an instinct . . . we feel as prisoners in a dungeon." The voice of a nightingale proves too much, and, still speaking in the voice of generalized experience, he asserts, "We can stand it no longer. Seizing our hat, stick, and sandwich-box, we rush distractedly to Hungerford or Queenhithe, and without a moment's consideration, enter for the day on board a Richmond steamer!" (4). Throughout his account, "we" travel with him, his collective pronoun creating a sense that he is not only describing, but also providing for his reader, the "pleasurable sensations of escape" (63) that motivate his own tour. This sensation of escape can be entirely perceptual. Murray's virtual tour makes it unnecessary for the reader to go far.

An 1849 guidebook, *The Tour of the Thames; or, the Sights and Songs of the King of Rivers*, though anonymously authored, begins with a personal characterization of this particular tour as an escape from the steaming miasma of London.

> Never was there such a summer on this side of the Tropics . . . London a vast

cauldron—the few people left in its habitable parts resembling stewed fish . . . (3)

At length, in a pause of the conversation, someone asked where somebody else was going, for the dog-days . . . every Englishman of the party had been everywhere already—Cairo, Constantinople, Calcutta, Cape Horn . . . There was not a corner of the world, where they had not drunk tea, smoked cigars, anathematized the country, the climate, the constitution. . . . The great globe itself was a lump of ennui. There was no hope of novelty, except in an Artesian perforation to the centre, or a voyage to the moon.

At last an . . . old personage, with a nondescript visage . . . asked, Had any one at table seen the Thames? . . .

I determined to *see* the Thames. (5)

The Londoners "stewing" like a cauldron of fish seem to experience a kind of stagnant entrapment that might require the pull of novelty to escape. But assuming that the author is likely to have seen at least parts of the Thames before, his emphasis here on "seeing" the Thames suggests that he is drawing a contrast between the banal travel experiences of his companions, who have gone abroad but in effect seen nothing, and his own effort to understand something about his homeland by seeing it with new eyes. In their endless quest for novelty, these travellers feel they have exhausted all the sights the earth has to offer. The author, however, feels he can make a journey up the Thames as novel as a "voyage to the moon" if he is willing to take it in the proper spirit. The ordinary old gentleman who gently reminds them all of the beauty they are overlooking might almost be Father Thames himself, an embodiment of the essential British heritage that these Englishmen have ignored. In a statement reminiscent of Dickens's suggestion that "it would be well to have a panorama, three miles long, of England," the author takes up the old man's challenge to take a good look at what his own country has to offer. The main point of such a journey is the imaginative effort involved, not the actual landscape surveyed.

The direction of the journey is itself significant. Because it made an easier journey for anyone rowing, travelling downstream was generally the more popular option. Going upstream, therefore, marks a more decisive break from ordinary routine. Charles Dickens the Younger's *Dickens' Dictionary of the Thames* makes a point of saying in the Preface that "the favourite excursion from Oxford to London will be found fully dealt with," noting that "of late years the journey has become one of the regular things to do" (253). The railways made it easy to travel to a town upstream and rent a boat for the journey back. The largest and most successful boating company on the river, Salter's of Oxford, offered boats, camping equipment, and other supplies to be rented in Oxford and returned on arrival in London. This is how Joseph and Elizabeth Pennell made the journey recounted in their 1891 account, which begins with a description of the men at Salter's boathouse.

Jerome K. Jerome satirizes the smugness of the rower who distinguishes himself by flouting popular taste and going upstream.

> Among folk too constitutionally weak, or too constitutionally lazy . . . to relish up-stream work, it is a common practice to get a boat at Oxford, and row down. For the energetic, however, the up-stream journey is certainly to be preferred. It does not seem good to be always going with the current. There is more satisfaction in squaring one's back, and fighting against it, and winning one's way forward in spite of it—at least, so I feel, when Harris and George are sculling and I am steering. (152)

D. G. Wilson notes that because "excursions between Lechlade and Oxford and London were generally taken in the downstream direction . . . traditionally, with a few exceptions, descriptions of the river have been from source to sea" (xviii). But while this is true of the basic guidebooks that limit themselves to "describing scenery and giving potted histories of riverside churches, mansions, villages, and towns" (Wilson, xi), most of the best narratives take the more adventurous approach—a journey upstream, against the current. This is the direction of Jerome's trip, and the direction taken by the narrator of *News from Nowhere*. In both of these narratives, as we will see, the journey upstream is a journey away from London, from civilization, from the present, into a fantasy world of the narrator's own making. For Jerome, it is fantasy constantly satirized, challenged, and deflated. For Morris, it is a dream to be cherished and, he hopes, realized.

Going upstream psychologically reinforces the sense of escape from London that is central to many of these narratives, as George D. Leslie observes.

> If time allows, the journey up the river is for many reasons preferable to the down one; in the down-stream journey the beauty and wildness of the scenery keep lessening as you near the metropolis, producing with me always a rather sad feeling. Each mile-post at the locks reminds me that I am returning to town . . . and that my journey is only of a temporary character—in fact, a Saturday to Monday sort of affair; whereas in making an up journey, hopes are kept up by the sense of exploration. . . . [and] the delightful feeling of getting farther from man, town work, and smoke. (245)

The sense of exploration associated with going upriver allowed the traveller to feel that he or she was penetrating into unfamiliar, if not unknown, territory. This redefinition of rural England as uncharted territory reflects the growing estrangement of the city-dweller from the countryside and his or her nostalgia for that lost world.

In fact, a number of these accounts use a rhetoric of exploration that seems clearly exaggerated in relation to the actual proximity of the landscape being explored. By invoking the tropes of exploration that had become familiar from the accounts of travellers to far more exotic places, these writers created a parallel between the journeys of arctic, alpine, or jungle explorers and their own more modest expeditions. The purpose of these comparisons is not necessarily self-aggrandizement—in fact, these writers are often ironic and self-deprecating about their own roles. Rather, they attempt to inflate the value of the landscape they are "discovering" anew: the landscape of home. Their accounts replicate on a smaller scale the sense of discovery associated with "real" travel to genuinely unfamiliar destinations.

Susanne Strobel has noted that in nineteenth-century travel literature, "the theme of the river journey is closely associated with the exploration of the interior of Africa by men like Burton, Baker, or Stanley, who were searching for the sources of the Nile, Niger, or Congo" (71–72), and travellers on the Thames often appropriate the sense of adventure attached to the idea of travelling upriver. William Senior seems to cast himself in an adventurer's role through his description of "the varied and interesting voyage upon which we are embarked" (*Royal River*, 10). He mentions the search for the source of the Thames as a particularly difficult aspect of the trip, noting that "the explorer" can expect to "experience failure in his endeavour to find, with any satisfactory clearness, either Old Father Thames or his oozy bed" (5). His language evokes travel accounts of the kind Strobel has in mind, and creates a parallel between his "voyage" and heroic journeys into more remote locations.

Margaret Oliphant, too, seems to regard her journey up the Thames as akin to a voyage into alien territory. She begins her account by describing English "boating men" as if they were a foreign race: these knowledgeable "mermen," often "half-naked," seem like "aborigines of the Thames, more natives than the bargees themselves" (1870, 461). She notes that they seem the sole inhabitants of the river upstream of the more popular Oxford to Windsor or London routes. When Oliphant writes that "very rare and few between are the explorers who venture into the silence" (462) of this area, she might be describing the darkest reaches of the Amazon rather than simply the Thames between Oxford and

Henley. Her description of "dark, unknown, undecipherable windings" (462)
makes it easy to forget that every inch of the river had been surveyed in numerous guidebooks and maps that gave precise distances to every town and lock,
as well as providing the names of the friendliest lockkeepers, and best inns and
pubs.

Oliphant adds a tinge of adventure to her narrative by pointing out a number of supposed hazards. There is the "grand danger" of "the weather, which
can at once convert the expedition into something difficult and disagreeable,"
though she notes that this is a "risk" to all forms of travel (462). Even the locks
are full of "rushing and foaming" water that "might whirl our tiny boat about,
if not as wildly, at least as dangerously as any Niagara" (463). This alarming
picture is contradicted by most accounts, however, which characterize the locks
as oases of civilization along the route, pleasant and sociable stopping-points
where travellers often smoked, chatted, or stretched their legs while waiting for
their boats to go through. Popular locks, such as Boulter's Lock or Mapledur-
ham Lock, could become quite crowded at times, not only with travellers but
with refreshment sellers, casual entertainers, and "speculative photographers" of
the kind Jerome encounters at the Hampton Court lock (146), who, establishing
a tradition still followed at amusement parks and ski resorts, would take random pictures in the hope that lighthearted holidaymakers could be persuaded
to buy them. A well-known 1886 illustration from the *Illustrated London News*
depicting boaters stopping at Boulter's Lock on their way to Henley Regatta is
described by text that notes, "Even the brief detention at one of the locks . . . is
rather amusing when they have plenty of time to spare" (10); another *Illustrated
London News* picture from 1872 shows a similarly relaxed scene in which boaters
waiting at a lock smoke, flirt, and chat sociably with each other (fig. 5). These
depictions suggest that the obligatory pause at a lock was seen as emblematic of
the leisurely pace and carefree nature of the expedition. In this context, Oliphant needs to use highly dramatic language in order to invest an upstream lock
with an aura of danger.

Oliphant also worries about getting lost in canals or backwaters, and notes
that sticking to the towing-path can be an important "shield and defence" against
this particular threat (463). Clearly, Oliphant values the way in which the upriver journey creates the *sensation* of adventure and exploration. She writes,
"When we are sure of our towing-path, and when every new winding brings before us a new scene of ever softer and more tranquil beauty, we know no gentle
civilised adventure which is so fascinating" (463). This statement highlights the
contradictions inherent in her perspective. She casts herself in the role of adventurer, yet she wants a clear, predetermined path to follow. She likes the windings

Fig. 5. "Boating On the River Thames." *Illustrated London News*, 1872. Reprinted courtesy of the Mary Evans Picture Library.

that create new views, but she knows in advance what she wants to see. Where a conventional narrative of exploration describes a landscape that grows progressively more alien as the explorer penetrates further into it, the scenes that present themselves to Oliphant ideally grow ever more soft and tranquil. When she writes that the experience "is as new as if we were the first explorers who ever steered a boat into those undiscovered waters," she reveals the hypothetical nature of the experience: it is not genuinely new, but "as new as if" they were explorers. She likes to feel "as if" she were going somewhere but has no real goal beyond enjoyment of this simulated, "civilised," adventure.

The parallel created in many of these texts between a journey up the Thames and a journey into a more remote interior would find its most memorable evocation in 1898, in Joseph Conrad's *Heart of Darkness*. Conrad describes the "great spirit of the past" embodied in the lower reaches of the Thames, writing, "What greatness had not flowed on the ebb of that river into the mystery of an unknown earth! . . . The dreams of men, the seed of commonwealths, the germs of empires." But Marlow's comment, "This also . . . has been one of the dark places of the earth" (5), connects the Thames with its downriver destination, the ocean into which it flows, and the other river that Marlow will follow up into the African interior. Thus a link is established between the heart of the English countryside and Conrad's heart of darkness. A trip on the Thames was an imitation of the more dangerous and exotic journey, and functioned as a virtual voyage to the interior, immersing the traveller in the sensations of discovery while reassuring him that no place was more worth discovering than his own country.

3. YOU ARE HERE:
THE GUIDED TOUR

If a trip up the Thames seemed to happen in a space located somewhere between real and simulated experience, then it is not surprising that the Victorians craved texts that would help them to orient themselves in this amorphous space. Over the course of the century, guidebooks were instrumental in negotiating the boundaries between real and imagined landscapes. Guidebooks to panorama exhibitions, as we saw in Part One, often imitated the format of "real" guidebooks—that is, guidebooks describing a real location. Guidebooks to the Thames are perfect examples of this peculiarly nineteenth-century form of narrative, as they are typical in their rhetoric—so typical, in fact, that they are not just clichéd but at times almost parodic in their close adherence to the standards of the guidebook genre. While guidebooks of all kinds strove to establish a sense of companionship with the reader, guidebooks describing close-to-home locations have a particular rhetorical intimacy. The journey is described, not as a trip taken by the author and then recounted to the reader, but as if it were being enjoyed by both author and reader at the same time. This format is used in guidebooks of all kinds, but it is particularly pronounced in guidebooks to the Thames and, as we will see in Part Three, the emerging genre of railway guides.

All three forms of guidebooks—panorama exhibition guides, river guides, and railway guides—work hard to create the illusion of a trip that is experienced simultaneously by the author who describes it and the reader who follows the author's narrative. Accounts of foreign journeys often presented themselves either as records of the author's extraordinary, unrepeatable experiences or as preparatory aids to those who planned to take such trips themselves. Guides to English journeys, however, present themselves as versions of the travel experience itself.

The writer drags the reader along as he or she moves from place to place, suggesting, for example, that we "proceed upon *our* voyage of some two hundred miles from source to Nore" (*Royal River*, 3, Senior; emphasis added). In another account, the anonymous author pretends to direct the reader's gaze, so that we may feel that we are seeing the scene rather than merely reading about it: "From where we start on our river expedition, instead of fields or grassy banks, we see, as our eye follows the course of the stream, the traces of the rapid growth of the mighty city" (*Up the River*, 2). William Senior choreographs our response even more specifically, using a second-person "you" that has the force of a command: "After pausing on the shoulder of Charlton Hill, and admiring—as who can fail to do?—the magnificent panorama of hill and valley receding into the mist of distance north and north-east, you proceed from Cheltenham" (*Royal River*, 6). This delicately poised mode of address, halfway between description and instruction, in some ways resembles the "walkthroughs" of contemporary video-game manuals. It leads you, step by step, not simply through the scenery but through the action. (The fact that one noted author of video-game strategy guides, David Hodgson of Prima Games, began his career by writing from "a German fishing trawler floating on the River Thames" [2009, 1] tempts one to imagine that some familiarity with the river guidebook genre may even have influenced his work.)[3]

The reader becomes almost a character in these texts, playing a role similar to that of the "hypothetical traveller" of Victorian novels discussed in Part One. The "you" of the text is an avatar for the reader, a virtual representation of ourselves. While an avatar has the capacity to act as an agent, as the addressed reader does not, the traveller evoked here is more than an "implied reader": he is an imaginary companion to the author. The role of what Garrett Stewart calls the "designated reading agent," the "dear reader" so often addressed in Victorian realist fiction (5), is here conceived as a physical presence within a specific spatial location. The reader is encouraged to feel that he or she is collaborating in the process of lifting the journey off the page and placing it within a three-dimensional framework.

To translate these descriptions into visual terms, this gesture of inclusion resembles the way in which first-person perspective video games have evolved to include portions of a player's body—a hand, for example—in the depicted space, so as to create "a stronger experiential homology between the fictional world of the game and the real world, where virtual space begins to seem continuous with the player's space" (Lahti, 61). Seeing a represented portion of ourselves in the "other" world bridges the gap between here and there. Using second-person rhetoric to create a surrogate reader within a guidebook can be seen as a textual equivalent to that kind of bridge. It, too, has the effect of creating a more immersive reading experience.

These authors appeal to the power of the reader's imagination to make the journey with them: "We return to Richmond, either by the magic of imagination in a moment, or by the more prosaic and practical method of the railway, and pass at once from the atmosphere of busy life . . . back again to the tranquillity of the river scenes" (*Up the River*, 24). Here, the imaginative leap of the reader is akin to the magical power of the railway to whisk the traveller to a new location before he or she has fully adjusted to being somewhere else. Charles Mackay prepares us for our trip with explicit instructions: "And now, reader, thou hast only to fancy thyself at London Bridge, on board the Richmond steam-boat, awaiting the bell to ring as a signal for starting . . ." (374). Mackay creates a parallel between our imaginative journey and the journey he describes in his narrative, which in turn is a replication of the actual trip. The persistence of this sort of rhetoric suggests that authors expected their readers to enjoy the self-conscious vicariousness of this form of travel. These texts emphasized, rather than disguising, the degree to which they were presenting a highly mediated "travel" experience.

Such authorial directives are common to other kinds of guidebooks, of course, but here they reinforce the sense of passivity already associated with the river traveller's perspective. Whether driven by steam, borne along by the movement of the current, or more actively engaged in rowing, river travellers experience a kind of relief at allowing the river to take charge of their journey. An 1843 account of a voyage on the Rhine claims that the "singular charm" of this means of travel is "that it is perpetually moving one onward from scene to scene, whether one chooses it or not" (Quin, 15). W. Senior comments on the "indescribably soothing influence exercised by a river in a soft mood which characterizes the Thames throughout," concluding, "How pleasant it is to be simply moving with the current, which does so much and is heard so little" (*Royal River*, 17). As James Thorne notes, the traveller allows the Thames itself to be his guide: "His river, as he follows it from its source to the ocean, leads him through many of the gentler and grander scenes of nature" (127). The traveller can focus on and enjoy the role of spectator because he or she does not have to act as director of the journey. He is more like the viewer of a film that is unfolding in front of him.

The power and independent agency of the Thames is reinforced by a longstanding tradition by which it is frequently personified as "Old Father Thames," invoked ("O Thames . . ." [Mackay, 366]) and apostrophized ("Thames, broad, bright, and beautiful!" [*Tour of the Thames*, 3]). The Thames takes on a life of its own, and the traveller has nothing to do except go with the flow. The sense of passivity associated with river travel helps to explain why many of the personal narratives and fictional representations sited on the Thames use the river to represent a kind of control that sweeps the traveller along a current of emotion, reverie, or destiny.

At times, the rhetorical pretense of author and reader travelling together reaches absurd heights of artificiality, as when John Murray pauses his account by noting, "Rest and refreshment demand the attention of the reader. . . . While dinner is getting ready, we may bestow a word or two on the picturesque of the Thames from London to Richmond" (Murray, 63). But such awkward gestures simply underscore the author's anxiety to create a sense that the reader's imaginative journey is virtually equivalent to the experience of genuine travel.

The term *panorama*, as used above by W. Senior, appears so frequently in such guides that it inevitably evokes the specific context most analogous to the visual experience offered by the river ride: the moving panorama. Another account makes this subtle connection even clearer: "The next scene in our shifting panorama of the gentle river will be the fair stretch of bank and stream which extends from picturesque Maidenhead to the winding shore . . . of Royal Windsor" (*Royal River*, Wilson, 143). For another author, Waterloo Bridge is the focal point of a scene that is reminiscent of the London panoramas described in Part One.

> Any one who wishes to enjoy a panoramic view unequalled of its kind in Europe, has only to proceed thither, just at the first faint peep of dawn, and he will be gratified. A more lovely prospect of the city it is impossible to imagine. . . . Scores of tall spires, unseen during the day, are distinctly seen at that hour. (Mackay, 378)

Mackay's description recalls both the Christminster passage from Hardy's *Jude the Obscure* and the passage from Dickens's *Bleak House* that conveys the slowly dawning view seen from the window of Bleak House on Esther's first morning there. Mackay adds that Somerset House and St. Paul's are the most elegant buildings "in all the panorama" (378). Charles Dickens Jr.'s *Dictionary of the Thames* cites a gloomy description of the Thames from the French poet Auguste Barbier but adds that "this powerful description, if it does not owe its inspiration to indigestion, must have been due to the mingled influences of rain and fog and wintry weather," for "if the poet had stood on London Bridge in the early hours of a clear summer morning he would have beheld a panorama of surpassing loveliness" (200).

As in a painted panorama, the aesthetic quality of the river landscape seems to be enhanced by the continuity of the vision, the way in which one scene melds into another to create a sense of immersion on the part of the viewer. In attempting to characterize the "pure beauty of river scenery," Joseph and Elizabeth Pennell write that "the Thames from Streatley to Tilehurst is one uninterrupted stretch of loveliness passing before you like a pageant" (157). The word *pageant* implies a show put on for the benefit of a spectator, and in particular, a show that constitutes a kind of cultural or nationalistic display. Andrew Wynter, writing in 1847, itemizes the variety of scenes that pass before him, from the "delicious scene . . . beneath one of the cool, grey arches" to the "scene" created by the dripping of the water, "like molten gold upon the glassy surface." He marvels that "a short, quick pull brought [him] to a different scene," and then notes that this "picture for a summer evening" might have been sketched by Cuyp (63). River travel becomes less a physical experience than a mechanism for display of a series of scenes to be admired. Inverting the dynamic of the moving panorama that unrolls before the spectator, the river journey passes the spectator before the scenes, in an early example of the kind of "mobilized gaze" that Anne Friedberg describes as integral to the development of cinema.[4]

The ability of the river to provide a continuous, natural gallery of pictures is a large part of its charm, and aligns its aesthetic qualities with the linearity that makes it an apt vehicle for virtual travel. James Thorne notes that "one of the many advantages of following the course of a river is, that we are thereby . . . brought to see a continous variety of objects" (126), while Thomas Cornish describes the way in which the continuousness of river scenery allows one to see subtle variations in the landscape more clearly: "[Nature] can give a constant succession of pastoral scenes, charming in its detail . . . nice gradations, so intimately blended with one another, where a peculiar tint of the foliage, or a sudden curve to the bank, serve to destroy the uniformity" (1842, vii). The aesthetic experience of viewing river scenery is qualitatively different from the mental "framing" of picturesque scenes that characterizes eighteenth- and early nineteenth-century topographical poetry and landscape description. There, the goal was to identify and admire singular, striking scenes, which were prized for the degree to which they stood out from the surrounding scenery and presented themselves as pictures. Here, individual scenes are admired, but always within the linear context of a stream of pictures that allows the traveller to see subtleties of color and arrangement that might be invisible were these views encountered in isolation. Moreover, the fact that these visual effects are presented in an unbroken sequence gives an immersive quality to the experience that enhances its power over the imagination. Even today, we recognize that a river trip can effectively immerse the viewer in a series of tableaux by providing a naturalistic motive for one's movement through them: among the most popular imaginative environments created at Disneyland and Disney World are the boat rides "Pirates of the Caribbean," "Jungle Cruise," and "20,000 Leagues Under the Sea."

The quality of continuousness noted by writers contributed to the Thames's appeal for painters, too, particularly painters seeking to represent effects of light or atmospheric moods rather than well-defined "sights." Donald Holden says of James McNeil Whistler, that "like Turner . . . [he] had chosen the water's edge for his most innovative pictures. Here space becomes a subject in itself, continuous, ambiguous, dissolving objects in a diffused light that abolishes edges, defies interruption, and insists on becoming a field of modulated color" (19). Pictures such as "Nocturne in Blue and Silver: Battersea Reach" (ca. 1870) and "Nocturne in Black and Gold: Entrance to Southampton Water" (1872 or 1874) show the Thames as a blurred strip of color that balances the line of the horizon at the top of the painting, creating an analogy between the flowing river and the endless sky above.[5]

The nineteenth century saw an explosion of interest in forms of visual depiction that attempted to recreate the sense of continuity associated with travelling an entire stretch of river, suggesting that the river's linear unrolling of scenes was more significant than the value of individual sights along the way. Sets of engravings depicting the river's major sights in order of appearance were very popular. Many maps of the Thames, often partly illustrated or topographic, appeared in the nineteenth century, generally as long, foldout, panoramic strips. One circa 1830s representation, *Panorama of the Thames, from London to Richmond*, consists of a total of 56 engraved panels, connected, folded, and pasted between covers. It depicts both sides of the river (facing each other, so that one is upside down) in a continuous illustration of buildings, landscape, and bridges between the two points (fig. 6). The popular *Boyle's Thames Guide* (1840) was a detailed depiction of the riverside consisting of 47 strips of approximately 11 inches, arranged horizontally, three to a page. All buildings are numbered to correspond with labels and brief descriptions underneath. Even a straightforward map like the *Thames Angler's Guide* (1887) folds out into a continuous strip, rather than being arranged onto pages in a booklet. Representations such as these attempted to combine maplike comprehensiveness of information with a format that replicated the sequential nature of the rivergoing experience. They

Fig. 6. *Panorama of the Thames, from London to Richmond*. ca. 1840. Reprinted courtesy of the Bodleian Libraries, University of Oxford.

anticipate, in many ways, the description of the spatial dimensions of "virtual worlds" offered by geographer Jonathan Taylor: they have "internal extents and boundaries," and "users orient their way through them using direction" (J. Taylor, 179).

The unbroken stream of the river lent itself to easy organization of verbal depictions as well as visual ones. John Murray admits that the river provides an organic structure for his account, as he pursues a policy of "considering the subjects of our work in their natural juxta-position" (197), and certainly the popularity of Thames narratives can be attributed in part to the effortless organization of such accounts. Any travel narrative is shaped by the journey, of course, but a river journey requires few decisions about where to go next. All of the accounts cited above owe much of their internal coherence to the sense of connection that the river provides between otherwise disparate scenes. The clearly established structure of the river narrative made it a useful genre to play off of for the authors of two more ambitious accounts: Jerome K. Jerome and William Morris. They resisted the temptation of the prepackaged format, choosing instead to mix elements of the traditional Thames narrative with more elaborate thematic structures. Nevertheless, in very different ways, both works create an abstract vision of the Thames in which the river occupies no particular time and no particular place. Instead, it offers the traveller an escape, a virtual journey that allows England to function simultaneously as home, and away from home.

4. BLOGGING THE TRIP:
THREE MEN IN A BOAT

The power of the Thames fantasy made it tempting to deflate. While Jerome K. Jerome's *Three Men in a Boat* (1889) seems at first to present itself as a familiar example of the river journey, the book's style quickly undermines any sense of specificity or sequence of location, creating instead a narrative that does not attempt to accurately represent or replicate the Thames-going experience. Instead, it contrasts the classic picturesque idealization of river travel with a more realistic depiction. The guidebook format was so well established by the end of the century that it could be brilliantly parodied by Jerome's book, the success of which both confirmed and reinforced the popularity of pleasure boating on the upper Thames in the final decades of the century. Jerome's consciously au courant narrative reveals how well entrenched this form of leisure had become, and how familiar the literary tropes associated with it. Jerome's satire of the Thames river experience as described in the earlier narratives and guidebooks offers a humorous inversion of the generic conventions of the "journey back to nature" enjoyed by his predecessors. *Three Men in a Boat* touches on virtually all of the themes seen in other river accounts but adopts these rhetorical tropes only to undermine them through an ironic stance that feels surprisingly modern. Jerome's narrative in many ways resembles a twenty-first-century blog in its casual, intimate tone; moment-to-moment level of detail; frequent linkage to anecdotes about other people, places, and events; and ironic, almost snarky, attitude. For Jerome, a trip up the Thames is no trip at all. Every thing he sees is utterly familiar, and everything one can say about the Thames has been said before. The only new thing he brings to the table is himself. The point of the book is his random commentary on other things.

Jerome later claimed that he had not originally intended to write a funny book; it was to have been "'The Story of the Thames,' its scenery and history." But "somehow it would not come." The episodes of "humorous relief" with which he expected to sprinkle the work began to dominate it, and the "slabs of history" he labored hard to add were mostly removed by his discerning editor (1926, 82). Jerome, who already had established a reputation as a humorist in his periodical essays and book *Idle Thoughts of an Idle Fellow* (1886), may have exaggerated his own pretensions to seriousness in this account in order to suggest that the book's comedy was entirely spontaneous. In fact, few readers will recall any of the scenic or historical description. The book's best-known passages involve a nearly fatal attempt to open a tin of pineapple without an opener; the narrator J's comments on the "excitement" of being towed by girls; and the dramatic reversals of fortune experienced when George angers J. by laughing at his having dropped his shirt in the water—until they discover that the wet shirt is not J.'s at all, but George's, a situation that strikes George as less, and J. as more, amusing.

Unlike other Thames narratives, *Three Men and a Boat* is not a knowledgeable exploration of national landscape and history, or even an introspective account of the author's escape from urban stresses. It is a series of vignettes depicting the efforts of three friends to spend several days on the river without coming to blows. *Three Men in a Boat* exposes the episodic nature of typical Thames travel accounts by rejecting the automatic coherence and continuity associated with narratives organized around river journeys. Instead of relying on the smoothly flowing chronological sequence of scenes through which they pass to order his narrative, Jerome follows a comic pattern of haphazard association that has an effect not unlike links in a blog: he jumps without warning from a given scene to something that occurred previously, or to something that happened last time he went boating, or to something that once happened to Harris's father. The resulting narrative is not shaped by the Thames's path but instead forms a labyrinthine counterpoint to the winding river landscape through which they pass.

The journey seems at first to be motivated by the same impulses that drew other travellers to the Thames. The three friends decide that they are overstrained and need "rest and a complete change," so Jerome suggests that they should "seek out some retired and old-world spot, far from the madding crowd, and dream away a sunny week among its drowsy lanes—some half-forgotten nook . . . —some quaint-perched eyrie on the cliffs of Time, from whence the surging waves of the nineteenth century would sound far-off and faint" (9). As in so many of these accounts, escape from the city is conflated with escape from the present. Like Wynter and Murray, the friends are suddenly struck by a perfect notion.

> George said: "Let's go up the river."
>
> He said we should have fresh air, exercise, and quiet; the constant change of scene would occupy our minds (including what there was of Harris's); and the hard work would give us a good appetite, and make us sleep well.
>
> Harris said he didn't think George ought to do anything that would have a tendency to make him sleepier than he already was, as it might be dangerous. He said he didn't very well understand how George was going to sleep any more than he did now, seeing that there were only twenty-four hours in each day, summer and winter alike; but he thought that if he *did* sleep any more, he might just as well be dead, and so save his board and lodging. (12–13)

In other accounts we have seen, the suggestion of "a trip up the Thames!" is a call to action that propels the author out of his sluggish urban stupor, causing him to leap to his feet and run to the lovely, cool river as quickly as if his life depended on it. Here, the narrative drifts slowly along as the idea is mulled over by the three friends in an idly contentious manner that will become the book's characteristic tone.

Throughout the book, Jerome frequently satirizes the picturesque impulses that lead people to undertake river journeys. Many passages begin in the gently admiring tone that is familiar from other descriptions of the Thames, then quickly lapse into a more concrete and realistic mode. Of his first night on the river, Jerome writes:

> We had originally intended to go on to Magna Charta island, a sweetly pretty part of the river, where it winds through a soft, green valley, and to camp in one of the many picturesque inlets to be found round that tiny shore. But somehow, we did not feel that we yearned for the picturesque nearly so much now as we had earlier in the day. A bit of water between a coal-barge and a gas-works would have quite satisfied us for that night. We did not want scenery. We wanted to have our supper and go to bed. (76)

While many other writers make a point of lamenting the presence of signs of industrialization along the river, Jerome admits that physical comforts are a higher priority than pristine riparian beauty and tacitly accepts the inevitability of coal-barges and gas-works in a world that aims to be comfortable.

Jerome and his friends are familiar enough with the traditions of topographic description to attempt to emulate the state of mind portrayed in works like *Rambles by Rivers*. But maintaining this perspective can be difficult when circumstances are less than ideal.

> We rowed on all that day through the rain. . . . We pretended, at first, that we enjoyed it. We said it was a change, and that we liked to see the river under all its different aspects. We said we could not expect to have it all sunshine, nor should we wish it. We told each other that Nature was beautiful, even in her tears.
>
> Indeed, Harris and I were quite enthusiastic about the business, for the first few hours. And we sang a song about a gipsy's life. . . . free to storm and sunshine, and to every wind that blew! . . .
>
> George took the fun more soberly, and stuck to the umbrella. (155)

Here and throughout the book, Jerome's humor is based not simply on a contrast between a standard, idealized perspective and the more realistic one he takes himself, but on a contrast between his own attempts to maintain the proper frame of mind and the doubts that inevitably surface. The popular idea of the Thames experience as a leisurely escape from worldly cares is undermined by Jerome's relentless emphasis on the more prosaic aspects of this form of travel.

Jerome attempts at times to provide the kind of general descriptive commentary and historical background that typify other Thames guides and narratives. But he exposes the tedium of repeating well-known facts by allowing his own narrative to wander immediately to less elevated topics. Oxford, for example, usually the subject of one or two full chapters in Thames guidebooks, is disposed of quickly and unceremoniously: "We spent two very pleasant days in Oxford. There are plenty of dogs in the town of Oxford. Montmorency had eleven fights on the first day, and fourteen on the second, and evidently thought he had got to heaven" (152). The arbitrariness of any designation of what is "historic" is pointed up by Jerome's comments on Kingston. At first, his description follows the pattern of typical Thames guides, as he is led to "muse" on the passing scene, a device that allows him to retrieve a few historic tidbits.

> I mused on Kingston, or "Kyngestun," as it was once called in the days when Saxon "kinges" were crowned there. Great Caesar crossed the river there, and

the Roman legions camped on its sloping uplands. Caesar, like, in later years, Elizabeth, seems to have stopped everywhere: only he was more respectable than good Queen Bess; he didn't put up at public-houses.

She was nuts on public-houses, was England's Virgin Queen. There's scarcely a pub. of any attractions within ten miles of London that she does not seem to have looked in at, stopped at, or slept at, some time or other. I wonder now, supposing Harris, say, turned over a new leaf, and became a great and good man, and got to be Prime Minister, and died, if they would put up signs over the public-houses that he had patronised: "Harris had a glass of bitter in this house"; "Harris had two of Scotch cold here in the summer of '88"; "Harris was chucked from here in December, 1886."

No, there would be too many of them! It would only be the houses that he had never entered that would become famous. "Only house in South London that Harris never had a drink in!" The people would flock to it to see what could have been the matter with it. (42)

The absurdity of a place distinguishing itself on the arbitrary basis of a single royal visit is highlighted by Jerome's imagining a similar fetishism of the presence of a random individual like Harris. In a neatly deconstructive turn, Jerome points out that Harris's presence would in fact be less significant than his absence. Had Jerome really been writing "The Story of the Thames," he would have felt obliged to linger longer on the historical significance of Kingston, instead of moving quickly to an irreverent suggestion that Elizabeth I was "nuts on public-houses." This kind of colloquial language drew unfavorable notice from reviewers, but, as the 1911 publication of a book entitled *Slang and Cant in Jerome K. Jerome's Works* (Bosson) suggests, early readers don't seem to have minded learning more about contemporary slang than about ancient history from Jerome's book.

Even the few historical set-pieces that do appear in the book are framed and, one must admit, eclipsed by the humorous episodes that surround them. Chapter XI, for example, includes an extended historical fantasy that begins in a serious tone that is sustained for several pages.

> The sun had got more powerful by the time we had finished breakfast . . . it was as lovely a morning as one could desire. Little was in sight to remind us of the nineteenth century; and, as we looked out upon the river . . . we could almost fancy that the centuries between us and that ever-to-be-famous June morning of 1215 had been drawn aside, and that we, English yeoman's sons in homespun cloth . . . were waiting there to witness the writing of that stupendous page of history. . . .

> It is a fine summer morning—sunny, soft, and still. But through the air there
> runs a thrill of coming stir. King John has slept at Ducroft Hall, and all the day
> before the little town of Staines has echoed to the clang of armoured men. (90)

The serene scene instigates a kind of imaginative time-travel that would be
echoed by William Morris two years later, when his trip on the Thames became
a pathway, not into the past, but into the future. Here, Jerome indulges in a
few pages of present-tense historical fantasy, ending with the stirring announcement: "And King John has stepped upon the shore, and we wait in breathless
silence till a great shout cleaves the air, and the great cornerstone in England's
temple of liberty has, now we know, been firmly laid" (93). The next chapter,
however, brings him firmly back to reality: "I was sitting on the bank, conjuring
up this scene to myself, when George remarked that when I was quite rested,
perhaps I would not mind helping to wash up" (93). The scene Jerome creates,
which he describes in the chapter headnote as "Historical retrospect, specially
inserted for the use of schools" (84), is in any case wholly outshone by the de-
bacle that immediately precedes it, Harris's attempt to scramble eggs.

Jerome inverted the usual priorities of the river-journey genre, allowing incidental anecdotes to take precedence over the "main" narrative—the expected
"potted history and scenic description." As we have seen, in all of these Thames
accounts, the destination of the journey is irrelevant. The traveller's goal is not
a single end point but multiple stopping points on the way to nowhere. Jerome
takes this diffusion of destination one step further, treating the specific locations through which they pass as mere scenic backdrop to the social drama being played out on the boat. Even the events on the boat are subsidiary to Jerome's own narrative, which often incorporates anecdotes and information that
are entirely external to the journey at hand. It has been suggested that Jerome's
"narrative meanderings" not only resemble the river but also "recall George's
own anecdote about his experience of the maze at Hampton Court, where after
forays down various paths . . . he kept finding himself at the point at which
he started" (Harvey, xvi). The structure of Jerome's story replicates the agenda
behind his journey: the goal is not to get anywhere in particular, but to pass the
time in a pleasant manner by pausing at whatever points happen to catch one's
interest. Jerome's casual surfing from site to site creates an experience that is less
about place than about movement.

The real point of *Three Men in a Boat*, and the reason for its strangely contemporary feel, is the sense of mobility it embodies. This may help explain the
mystery of its enduring popularity. It was not only a bestseller in its own time,
it has been continuously in print ever since, in many languages, and has seen

numerous stage and television adaptations (including a BBC television version by Tom Stoppard). It is a primary source for Connie Willis's 1997 Hugo Award–winning science fiction novel, *To Say Nothing of the Dog*. But perhaps its most emblematic contemporary incarnation takes the form of a Google Earth tour, available on the web, that allows you to recreate Jerome's precise journey through satellite photography: just click onto the path, sit back, and watch the river landscape unroll beneath you.

5. BACK TO THE FUTURE:
NEWS FROM NOWHERE

The Internet is full of websites that function as virtual museums, preserving the experience of sites and places that have long since vanished. Virtual tours of the Acropolis (http://www.acropolis360.com/) or the now-inaccessible Cave of Lascaux (http://www.culture.gouv.fr/culture/arcnat/lascaux/en/) allow visitors not only to see specific aspects of these sites but to have the sensation of moving through them, giving a more vivid sense of reality to the experience. While these virtual tours sometimes involve video clips and at other times are merely comprehensive maps with pictures, the visitor's ability to click on different portions of the site and linger at the places that interest him or her most creates a sense of individual interaction with the environment.

Similarly, the leisurely, contemplative pace and sense of continuousness that characterized traditional river travel, combined with an awareness of the historical significance of the Thames itself and of the many important sites through which it passes, fostered a sense that travel on the Thames was a kind of virtual travel into the past. Herendeen notes that "in topographical literature—from the writing of Genesis, to the classical and medieval descriptions of the world, through the Renaissance—the river offers simultaneously a return in time and to nature: to the *fons et origo* where mind and matter, *logos* and *numen* were unseparated" (125). Schama also describes the classical association between rivers and a sense of return to a primeval past, in which "the ultimate origin was represented as a fountainhead" (267).

The Thames is often portrayed in these guidebooks and narratives as a generically pastoral and traditional setting that is best experienced through old-fashioned modes of transport. In fact, the necessarily slow-paced and somewhat archaic means of travel required by the river journey is a large part of its charm.

It has been noted that contemporary ecotourists follow a long tradition of travellers who deliberately "eschew the technologies heralded by industrialization," and that "since the European nature tours of the Romantic period, the history of modern Western travel has been marked by a nostalgic investment in objects and activities that might be used to recreate experiences from a bygone era" (Gilbert, "Belated Journeys," 260). In the Victorian period we see that as the railroads stretched further into the countryside and superseded river and canal travel as a convenient means of public transportation between major towns, the earlier mode of transportation continued to be valued not just in spite of, but because of, its obsolescence.

Yet many Thames narratives begin on the railway before moving to the river, evincing a structure that is also apparent in twentieth-century ecotourism, according to Gilbert: the preference for progressively more primitive forms of travel on a single trip. In this layering of multiple travel experiences, the "movement through specific spaces is transformed into a journey back in time through a mutually constitutive process: decreasing mechanical complexity in the modes of transport signals an increasing temporal distance from contemporary urban life in the Western world, a process which, in turn, casts specific destinations as belonging to the past" (Gilbert, 258). In the nineteenth-century texts, the framing of the river excursion by an introductory railway journey has the effect of highlighting the contrast between pastoral simplicity and the cutting-edge technology represented by the railway, which in turn reinforces a sense that the sights seen along the Thames are not just spatially removed but also temporally distant from modern London.

In many of these narratives, progression up the river is linked with regression in historical time, as the traveller becomes gradually more immersed in the past. The river is seen as providing a form of access to specific moments in history through its display of the scenes at which significant events took place. Many of the guidebooks and narratives pause to expound on the historic events connected to such sites as Magna Charta Island, Godstow Abbey, or Hampton Court, so that the passing landscape becomes a historical pageant for our edification. Godfrey Turner's comments encapsulate this view of the Thames as a river into the past.

> We drift on the tide of the Thames, as on the tide of Time, away from the Norman to the Plantagenet to the Tudor, and it is the life of England that we can scan as the waters flow past scenes which, through all the mutations of the ages, through all the seasons' difference, year after year, are ever freshly, strongly, characteristically, English. (*Royal River*, 161)

This capacity of the Thames to provide a sense of time travel would be exploited and inverted by William Morris in his utopian fantasy *News from Nowhere*. In Morris's book, a trip up the Thames becomes literally a voyage to Nowhere, as the narrator enters a world of the future that in many ways resembles the past. The "Guest" is only a temporary sojourner, however, and his trip leaves him exactly where he began.

News from Nowhere begins with a man pondering the prospect of a "new society" and saying to himself, "'if I could but see a day of it . . . if I could but see it'" (44), an incantation that seems to magically call the desired picture into being. The river acts as a kind of time machine, the moment of transition registered only in the traveller's slightly altered perception of the scene.

> He came right down to the river-side, and lingered a little, looking over the low wall to note the moonlit river, near upon high water, go swirling and glittering up to Chiswick Eyot; as for the ugly bridge below, he did not notice it or think of it, except when for a moment . . . it struck him that he missed the row of lights downstream. (44)

He goes to bed and awakens to find the season has changed, but is reassured to see that "there was still the Thames sparkling under the sun" (45). Nevertheless, the speech of the boatman who greets him, so unlike what he would expect from "a Hammersmith waterman," as much as the unexpected sight of salmon-nets in a place where salmon had long since disappeared, confuse him: "I was going to say, 'But is this the Thames?' but held my peace in my wonder" (47). The identification of the Thames with England, and, more abstractly, with the condition of England, is reflected in Morris's use of the Thames throughout *News from Nowhere* as a touchstone of the extent and value of the changes he describes.

James Buzard notes that in spite of the word *Nowhere* in its title, Morris's book emphasizes the specificity of the places described. The "particularized utopian terrain" of the novel runs along the Thames between Morris's two houses in Hammersmith and Oxfordshire (1997, 452). The world of the novel is a timeless one, "beyond the succession of 'epochs'"—a world whose inhabitants "are of course the products of history" but "do not live historically" (452). The space of the novel offers a "temporary refuge" for the narrator, allowing him to escape the tensions and conflicts of his own period (Buzard, 452).

Morris's decision to cast the major portion of his utopian fable in the mold of a Thames travel narrative reflects the degree to which the river, as charted by earlier narratives, was seen as uniquely reflective of England as a whole. The major structural element in this actionless and expository narrative is provided by the Guest's trip up the Thames with his helpful and informative companion, Dick. Like the voice of the river guide in a Thames handbook, Dick helps the traveller to navigate both literal and metaphoric twists and turns. But of course Morris's traveller knows the territory well—in his own time. Thus, his sightseeing tour enacts a continuous dialectic between the future he sees and the past he knows.

The upriver Thames, as we have seen, was experienced as a distant, idyllic, archaic world by most nineteenth-century river travellers, and Morris's treatment is an elaboration of that fantasy. For Morris's narrator, the journey upstream is a process of bringing into alignment the different worlds under comparison: the future, his present, and his own past. He notes that as they "went higher up the river, there was less difference between the Thames of the day and the Thames as I remembered it." The Thames as he remembers it is both the river as it was when his adventure began, as well as the river he recalls from his own past.

> For setting aside the hideous vulgarity of the cockney villas of the well-to-do, stockbrokers and other such, which in older time marred the beauty of the bough-hung banks, even in this beginning of the country the Thames was always beautiful; and as we slipped between the lovely summer greenery, I almost felt my youth come back to me, and as if I were on one of those water excursions which I used to enjoy so much in days when I was too happy to think that there could be much amiss anywhere. (Morris, 169)

The farther upriver he goes, the less jarring the disjunction between what he sees now and the Thames of his day. When his knowledgeable reference to a particular stretch of the river is challenged by an old man who asks, "Oho! . . . so you know the Thames, do you?" he is led into a discussion of the relative merits of the two Thames. The old man functions as a kind of devil's advocate in the text, asking the narrator if he does not find the river "much changed for the worse," and noting that in "old times" one could see many "big and fine houses" that showed that "England was an important place in those days" (180), a simplified version of the interpretation of the landscape found in most of the Thames guidebooks discussed here. The old man's statement enables the narrator to argue against this comfortable view of the picturesque Thames and to summarize his own feeling that the changes demonstrate that now "everybody can live comfortably and happily, and not a few damned thieves only, who were centres of vulgarity and corruption wherever they were, and who, as to this lovely river, destroyed its beauty morally, and had almost destroyed it physically, when they were thrown out of it" (180).

The improved vistas along the Thames confirm Morris's vision of what Marcus Waithe has called "a reconciliation of society and space" (460). Waithe describes the novel as being torn between the idea of cyclicity, of return, and the "growth of linearity," the need for new narrative (469). The river itself is an important aspect of the novel's drive toward linearity, and the associations Morris's readers would bring to the idea of a journey upriver make the idea of a permanent river idyll, a world from which one never returns to London, very appealing.

Although it is true that *News from Nowhere* is full of specific, minutely described locations, these places no longer seem to have a distinctive identity. Even the narrator's favorite spots along the river seem part of a hazy, pleasant tableau in which one scene melds imperceptibly into the next. When the narrator is given the opportunity to ask Dick's great-grandfather, Hammond, some questions, he seeks information on many familiar areas around London and on the Thames, asking what now lies east of Bloomsbury, or what it is now like south of the river. In each case, it seems that the formerly specific place has not simply changed but virtually ceased to exist as a discrete entity. Hammond tells him that the Docks are there, "but are not so thronged as they once were, since we discourage centralization all we can, and we have long ago dropped the pretension to be the market of the world." The area contains "a few good houses," though it is "not inhabited by many people" (101). Hammond's report on other industrial towns reflects the experience of London: "As to the big murky places which were once, as we know, the centres of manufacture, they have, like the brick and mortar desert of London, disappeared" (102). The suburbs "have melted away into the general country" (102). A general dispersal of people across the land has virtually eliminated familiar geographic categories, making all of England a nowhere land in which specific and distinctive sites have been replaced by a pleasant but undifferentiated landscape. Like the continuous panorama of Thames scenery prized by river writers, it is a landscape that offers no specific destinations, but a nowhere/everywhere that is the essence of England.

The Guest's trip up the river dramatizes the physical changes that accompanied this social upheaval that intervened between his time and the present. Yet while he admires the improved state of things, the narrator is undeniably relieved to see that some aspects of the world appear unchanged, as if this continuity between past and present might affirm the reality of the future he sees. Patrick Brantlinger claims that Morris considered this vision of a society based on the writings of Marx and Engels to be at least "a possible future in most of its details" (1975, 39). It is not a future dreamt up out of whole cloth but a projection based on a specific ideology, and the Thames serves as a touchstone of the imagined transformation, the success of which is gauged according to its effect on the passing panorama of the river.

Jacques Rancière has described utopia as "the power of mapping together a discursive space and a territorial space, the capacity to make each concept correspond to a point in reality and each argument coincide with an itinerary on a map" (31).[6] Thus, providing a specific map for the utopian landscape helps to reinforce Morris's reading of British culture. Morris's choice of what Buzard calls "the most familiar territory possible" (453) for his vision suggests that "the British utopia is already *there* to be uncovered, could we but excavate beneath the layer of Industrial detritus that hides it" (Buzard, 454). In this sense Morris's utopia is simply a literalized and intensified version of the utopia already found along the Thames in other river narratives. Where other writers present the Thames river trip as a journey into the past, Morris presents it as a journey into the future, into a timeless space where the most idyllic elements of an earlier age are combined with wisdom achieved through experiences yet to come.

The book's subtitle, "An Epoch of Rest," suggests the tensions inherent in its use of the travelogue form to portray a society characterized by restfulness, by freedom from the restless search for novelty often associated with travel. By appropriating the genre of the Thames narrative, however, Morris was able to map a utopian landscape that was specific enough to seem plausible. At the same time, it allowed him take his readers on a journey to a landscape that already enjoyed the status of a kind of mythic no-man's-land. The Victorians were accustomed to viewing a trip up the Thames as a trip to nowhere.

6. RIVER OF OBLIVION:
THE LONDON THAMES

The guidebooks and travel accounts examined earlier, as well as the literary texts that appropriated many of their themes and structures, create a timeless, pastoral, and largely affirmative vision of England through their emphasis on the restorative power of the Thames and its capacity to remove the viewer/traveller from specific, quotidian, reality. The novel, however, presents a different story. Novelists who turned to the Thames as a setting present a realist's view, one that acknowledges the degree to which the Thames, as symbol of the nation, reflected its disgraces as well as its glories. The vision of the Thames that we see in Dickens and George Eliot is not only influenced by specific controversies

involving the polluted state of the river itself; it also channels a more generalized sense of anxiety about modernity and metropolitan life into representations of the London river as a "nowhere" site of lost ideals and homeless souls.
Rather than transcending space and time, the London Thames of these novels
erases the local and the particular, sweeping them away in a muddy backwash
of oblivion that suggests the primary danger of modern life: the loss of identity
and rootedness in the swiftly flowing waters of change. The appealingly timeless and spaceless Thames that we saw in nonfiction accounts and guidebooks
becomes, in the realist novel, an unsettling aporia.

The expansion of industrialization and growth of population in and around
London over the course of the century had its inevitable effect on the city's infrastructure, an infrastructure of which the Thames was a central artery. In earlier times, as we have seen, the great London river combined beauty and commerce to form a powerful symbol of the British Empire, and over the course of
the nineteenth century, writers continued to acknowledge its centrality to an
understanding of Britain's economic dominance and imperial expansion. However, commentators also began to stress the darker side of the river landscape,
the degree to which it reflected the perceived physical, moral, and psychic ill-
health of the city as a whole. These less picturesque aspects of the river were not
seen as anomalous or contradictory. They were the inevitable by-products, the
logical consequence, of the economic and industrial success that the river itself
had fostered. These dark undercurrents to the imperial tide began to flow closer
to the surface as the century progressed, as it became harder to ignore the social
cost of Britain's power. The idea of the river as both timeless and placeless was
reinforced in a darker key by an emerging image of the Thames as a sewer that
was everywhere and nowhere, a constant presence below the surface of Victorian life that was always threatening to emerge.

The contrast between the pastoral Thames north of London and the appearance of the river as it approached the city itself highlighted the commercial
and industrial character of the London Thames. Travel on this Thames was an
exercise in realism rather than nostalgia. Henry James acknowledged that the
upriver Thames was "in its recreative character . . . absolutely unique," admitting,
"I know of no other classic stream that is so splashed about for the mere fun of
it"; the river above London seems at times so crowded that "it is the busiest suburb of London" (*English Hours*, 26). The commercial end of the river, however,
is altogether different. It is also, he claims, "pictorial," though in a different way.
James paints a picture that seems like a photographic negative of the continuous
picturesque banks that lined the upriver Thames: "For miles and miles you see
nothing but the sooty backs of warehouses, or perhaps they are the sooty faces:

in buildings so utterly expressionless it is impossible to distinguish. They stand massed together on the banks of the wide turbid stream, which is fortunately of too opaque a quality to reflect the dismal image" (103).

The continuous, repetitive scenery that had unrolled itself to such soothing effect during upstream travel here produces monotony rather than charm. Instead of the distinctive landmarks that punctuated views of the upriver Thames, we see interchangeable, expressionless buildings in a monochromatic landscape. "A damp-looking, dirty blackness is the universal tone. The river is almost black, and is covered with black barges; above the black housetops, from among the far-stretching docks and basins, rises a dusky wilderness of masts." Though gloomy, the view is in its way striking, as "the whole picture, glazed over with the glutinous London mist, becomes a masterly composition" (James, 103).

Though he canvasses the scene's aesthetic dimension, James is more interested in the river's symbolic significance than in its appearance. He finds it "very impressive in spite of its want of lightness and brightness," and suggests that "though it is ugly it is anything but trivial." In fact, when viewed in an "intellectual light,"

> the polluted river, the sprawling barges, the dead-faced warehouses, the frowsy people, the atmospheric impurities become richly suggestive. . . . all this smudgy detail may remind you of nothing less than the wealth and power of the British Empire at large; so that a kind of metaphysical magnificence hovers over the scene . . . I know that when I look off to the left at the East India Docks, or pass under the dark hugely piled bridges, where the railway trains and the human processions are for ever moving, I feel a kind of imaginative thrill. The tremendous piers of the bridges, in especial, seem the very pillars of the Empire aforesaid. (103)

James's awareness that the river is to a large degree responsible for the wealth and power of the nation blends with his aesthetic apprehension of the scene to produce a kind of "thrill." This thrill is indefinite, "suggestive," being partly a response to the scene and partly the effect of his own imagination. The scene is fascinating precisely because its unattractiveness obscures the tremendous potential that lies hidden beneath it. The paradox of "smudgy detail" evoking "the wealth and power of the British Empire" is a statement about the connection between commerce and expansion, between messy industrialization and the shining glory of Empire.

James's response is stronger, I would argue, because of the fact that he is moving through a succession of scenes rather than contemplating a single bridge or building. As he passes the East India Docks, then moves under the bridges, past the railways and the crowds, the immensity of the panorama invests each of its details with significance. Finally, the very piers of the bridges seem symbolic, the "pillars of Empire." These bridges join the old world with the new; they span the river that has been the historic sign of Britain's greatness but carry the railways that represent the core of Britain's power in the modern age.

Though the Thames is the essence of England, it is not a specific and unitary place: it is a conduit that connects many disparate sites, linking the old with the new, London with the British countryside, and England to the world. The nineteenth century saw a considerable expansion of the industrial and commercial landscape along the river that changed the character of the Thames just as industrialization changed the character of the English countryside as a whole. The inadequacy of the number of Legal Quays and licensed "sufferance wharves" that existed in the eighteenth century led to the building of the East India Docks at Blackwall in 1803–6, and of the West India Docks at the Isle of Dogs, followed by additional docks at Wapping and Rotherhithe. The need to accommodate larger ships led to a second phase of building, which included the Royal Victoria Dock, in the 1850s. Though there was little need for additional space beyond what these provided, the growth of the railway system made alternative locations necessary, and at the end of the century further docks were added (Williamson and Pevsner, 22).

The river also provided an ideal site for industries generating waste that could be discharged into the water. The author of *Up the River from Westminster to Windsor* (1876) admits that on the south bank, "the majesty and refinement of the past give place to the might of modern England; and we lose, in sentiment at least, by the exchange. From monumental chimneys gin, vitriol, and soap works obscure the sunlight, and insult the nose" (6). While admitting the value of all this industry, the author is anxious to "leave behind these homes of progress, and get into the unprogressive country" (6). Paradoxically, the purpose of his progress up the river is to avoid progress—to go to a place where time appears to stand still.

In addition to symbolizing commercial power, however, the city river was also seen as emblematic of the criminal or poverty-stricken dimensions of London life that were connected in part to industrial expansion and the population pressures it engendered. Charles Mackay commented in 1839 that the "manufactories and gasworks, belching out volumes of smoke ... darken the atmosphere" (379), but even so, he preferred the public buildings and industrial warehouses on the London side of the river to the Southwerk and Lambeth side, which he describes as "low and flat, and meanly built," containing a "population with a

squalid, dejected, and debauched look." While blaming their "unhealthy appearance" on the low, swampy land on which they dwell, he seems to see a moral
equivalence between the squalor of the setting and the "dissolute" appearance
of its inhabitants. The riverside areas of Southwerk and Lambeth, he claims,
are "the great sinks and common receptacles of all the vice and immorality of
London" (376). This image of the riverside as a kind of moral drainage basin
into which all the city's filth is poured would be echoed and intensified over the
course of the following three decades, as the river itself became notorious as the
city's literal sewer.

Throughout the late 1840s and 1850s, the river's foul appearance and odour
were frequently noted and satirized in the popular press, and the possible relationship between the condition of the river and the state of public health became a subject of increasing controversy. Public outrage peaked in 1858, known
as the year of "The Great Stink," when a particularly hot, dry summer made
the condition of the river so noxious that Parliament itself was unable to hold
committee meetings on some days, as the stench wafting through the windows
was unbearable.

A famous July 1858 *Punch* illustration of Death rowing a boat on the Thames
ironically inverts a popular image of carefree recreation to suggest that the river
was no longer a conduit for escape but a pathway to oblivion. Eventually, sufficient funding was provided to the Metropolitan Board of Works to enable it to
adopt Sir Joseph Bazalgette's complex plan for a system of intercepting sewers,
embankments, and pumping stations that would deposit the city's sewage at a
safe distance downstream, a project completed in 1875. In addition to improving
public health, the Main Drainage and Thames Embankment had a dramatic
effect on the character of the river, transforming its "polluted, smelly, and un-
sightly commercial waterfront" into "an architectural monument" that "restored
the Thames to London" (Porter, 4).

But the "restored" Thames had changed. Once a shining image of the glories
of British commerce and culture, it now presented a darker picture. Depictions
of the Thames began to mirror generalized concerns about pollution, disease,
and crime associated with the river. A number of genre paintings, like G. F.
Watts's "Found Drowned" and Luke Fildes's "Found Dead on the Embankment"
depicted the river as the scene of human tragedy and the final repository of
London's outcasts. In particular, the Thames frequently figures as the last refuge
of despairing women. As Martin Meisel has noted, paintings, literature, and
theater of the period share a recurrent iconographic image involving "the concat-
enation of the stone arch, the river, the night, and the fallen woman contemplating or committing suicide" (138). Charles Mackay's "Rambles Among the Rivers"

praises the view from Waterloo Bridge while acknowledging that it was famous for "love assignations" and suicides. In fact, Mackay speculates, "to many a poor girl the assignation over one arch of Waterloo Bridge is but the prelude to the fatal leap from another" (378).

The sense of the Thames as a conduit rather than a place, a means of transit rather than a fixed location, begins to take on a more sinister implication as the Thames becomes an image of the rootlessness and transience of modern life. When George Eliot's Daniel Deronda sees Mirah Lapidoth sitting alone in a boat on the Thames, dipping her cloak in the water, he instantly deduces that she is fashioning a shroud for herself. Mirah turns out to be a homeless, rather than fallen, woman. Like Deronda's own feeling that the river provided a seclusion obtainable "nowhere else" (225), her plaintive explanation—"I have nowhere to go—nobody belonging to me in all this land" (231) —reinforces the idea of the river as a non-place and the "forsaken girl" as a wayfarer whose only home is, indeed, "nowhere." Mirah expects the river to be a conduit to oblivion, but instead it delivers her to Deronda, who magically provides a home for her. The river seems to represent an indeterminate, liminal space that is always in danger of becoming a void.

This sense of the river as both deeply familiar and deeply estranging makes it an apt image for the complexities of modern life. As a place that is not really any place, it prefigures the kinds of non-places described by Marc Augé and Fredric Jameson, as touched upon in the Introduction. By associating the river with death, nineteenth-century writers emphasized the dangers inherent in this absence of locatedness. Once a proud image of British history, by the end of the century the Thames represented the loss of historical memory and straining of social connections within the swirling waters of cultural change. Seen in this context, it offers a threat to the most vulnerable members of modern society. Even *Three Men in a Boat* includes a jarring episode in which the friends encounter the corpse of a woman floating in the water as they approach Streatley. Jerome claims to have discovered her story later—"the old, old vulgar tragedy"—and takes a page to tell it. The river had "taken [the girl] into its gentle arms, and had laid her weary head upon its bosom, and had hushed away the pain" (138). Death in the river represents a kind of oblivion, a return to the comforting breast of Mother Nature.

The inclusion of this tragic story in Jerome's otherwise jaunty narrative suggests that the image of the river as the final resting place of the fallen woman was such a standard part of Thames iconography that no tour would be complete without it. A number of Dickens's novels and essays also reinforce the common association of the river with "lost" women. Dickens's *Uncommercial*

Traveller describes the area around Waterloo Bridge as a nightmarish scene in which the reflected lights of the river seem like beacons held "by the spectres of suicides" (129). When Dickens spends a night with the Thames Police, the man attending Waterloo Bridge treats him to a disquisition on the best spots to jump from, the reasons behind many suicides, and the outcomes of some particularly memorable attempts (529).

In *David Copperfield*, an extended description of the filth and debris in the Thames ends with the prostitute Martha standing by "the polluted stream," looking "as if she were a part of the refuse it had cast out, and left to corruption and decay" (chap. xlvii). In *Oliver Twist*, Nancy meets Rose and Mr. Brown on London Bridge, a secret rendezvous that will lead to her murder by Bill Sikes. She tells Rose, "Look before you, lady. Look at that dark water. How many times do you read of such as I who spring into the tide, and leave no living thing, to care for, or bewail them" (316). When searching for the disgraced Lady Dedlock, *Bleak House*'s Inspector Bucket takes Esther to the river, where a posted bill reading "FOUND DROWNED" warns Esther of his suspicions. To Esther, the river has "a fearful look, so overcast and secret, creeping away so fast between the low flat lines of shore" (771). Though Lady Dedlock's body is eventually found in the cemetery, not the river, the riverside search confirms Lady Dedlock's status as a fallen woman and the Thames's status as the expected end point of her tragic story. The earlier image of the Thames as a carefree pathway to nowhere in particular is ironically reversed in this negative image of it as a place for those who have nowhere else to go.

The Thames and the neighborhoods around it are linked with crime in general in many nineteenth-century commentaries, including Mayhew's *London Labour and the London Poor*, as well as in visual art. Gustav Doré's illustrations for Jerrold's *London: A Pilgrimage* (1872) include a number of pictures of life along the river that convey its liveliness but also its squalor. "The Docks-Night," for example, shows a violent mob of workers struggling to get into the door of a building, presumably the public house where they would collect, and drink away, their wages. The image of Bill Sikes running through "Folly's Ditch," a Thames inlet, to escape his pursuers, before finally hanging himself there, is typical of popular perceptions of riverside neighborhoods. The fact that the city had a specific police force devoted to the river, the Thames Police, is perhaps indicative of the level of crime expected on and around the river, a scene of significant economic activity inhabited by a highly transient population. Among the sixteen etchings of the river that form part of Whistler's well-known "Thames set" is a drawing of the Thames Police, showing the police boats docked outside their headquarters. Dickens's essay "Down with the Tide" reveals the novelist's interest in the Thames police, and his son Charles Dickens Jr.'s *Dictionary of the Thames* describes their work in some detail.

> An important portion of the duties of the Thames division consists in search-
> ing for and dealing with the bodies of suicides, murdered persons, and persons
> accidentally drowned. The dragging process is only carried on for one tide, after
> which it is considered that the missing body will pretty certainly have been car-
> ried out of reach, and it occasionally happens that a corpse will drift into a hole
> and become covered over before it becomes sufficiently bouyant to rise. Should
> it be eventually recovered, it is first photographed and then preserved as long as
> possible for identification, not at the station, but at the parish dead-house. (206)

Bracebridge Hemyng, the prolific author of many books and stories on trendy topics (e.g., *Secrets of the Turf* [1868], *On the Road: Tales of a Commercial Travel-ler* [1868], *The Girl of the Period* [1876]), exploited popular interest in the Thames Police in his "edited" collection of anecdotes and stories, *Secrets of the River. By a Thames Policeman* (1870). Many of these stories, such as "Found Drowned" and "The Secret of the Dead Body Which No One Would Own," use the discovery of a body, generally "part of an ordinary night's work" for a Thames policeman (Hemyng, 72), as an excuse to tell the sad tale behind a suicide or murder. A number of these stories resemble *Our Mutual Friend* in their emphasis on the contradictory role of the river, which seems at first to erase a person's life and identity, yet persists in bringing its remnants to the surface again. Suicides and criminals may dream of the Thames as a path to oblivion that will allow them to slip away unnoticed; instead, it makes its victims and their tragedies more prominent than ever, as each becomes the subject of a poster announcing "Dead Body Found" and promising a reward for information.

The association of the Thames with crime in many of Dickens's novels sug-gests that crime is inevitable, an expected waste product of contemporary so-ciety. In *Great Expectations*, Pip, protecting the convict who has been his bene-factor, uses the river in an attempt to help the criminal escape. Pip notes that while his friend Herbert took comfort from the knowledge that the river "was flowing, with everything it bore, toward Clara," his beloved, he himself "thought with dread that it was flowing towards Magwitch, and that any black mark on its surface might be his pursuers, going swiftly, silently, and surely, to take him" (381). The inescapable movement of the river seems emblematic of the workings of an inevitable fate. The pursuit of Magwitch along the river culminates in his capture, and Pip returns back up the Thames to London with the convict. But in spite of the novel's association of the river with criminality and guilt, it is important to recall that the Battery marshes were the scene of many of Pip's pleasantest early experiences, and that the river becomes the source of Pip's regeneration after he has nearly drowned. Just as the river looks different to Herbert and to Pip because of his differing situations, so the effect of it on each character is determined by their own attitude and conscience.[7]

In *Our Mutual Friend*, the Thames provides a horrifying livelihood for Lizzie Hexam's father, a "dredger" who retrieves drowned corpses for rewards or for what he can scavenge from their bodies. The sense of defilement that Lizzie feels as a result of her participation in this grim work amazes her father, who, noting her reluctance to sit near a corpse in the boat, reproaches her, "As if it wasn't your living! As if it wasn't meat and drink to you!" (1).[8] He represents the furthest extreme of capitalist enterprise, an entrepreneur who feeds on the waste discarded by the system. Dickens conveys the horror of urban poverty by emphasizing the inescapability of its products: what the culture attempts to dispose of will always float to the surface again.

This is a world beyond individual control. The charming passivity of upriver journeys is here presented as powerless vulnerability to larger forces. The novel's opening image of Hexam and Lizzie presents them as a kind of flotsam directed by the water.

> In these times of ours, though concerning the exact year there is no need to be precise, a boat of dirty and disreputable appearance, with two figures in it, floated on the Thames, between Southwark Bridge which is of iron, and London Bridge which is of stone, as an autumn evening was closing in. (43)

In a ghastly parody of the intent gaze that tourists directed at the lovely scenery of the upper Thames, Dickens emphasizes the "dread or horror" (43) with which Lizzie surveys the scene, and her reluctance to look at anything other than her father's face. While upriver leisure travellers admired the continuously changing views, Lizzie is dragged through a far less picturesque scene.

> The girl pulled the hood of a cloak she wore, over her head and over her face, and looking backward so that the front folds of this hood were turned down the river, kept the boat in that direction going before the tide. Until now, the boat had barely held her own, and had hovered about one spot; but now, the banks changed swiftly, and the deepening shadows and the kindling lights of London Bridge were passed, and the tiers of shipping lay on either hand. (45)

Dickens describes the river and riverside as containing more than its share of the city's filth; it is not just a sample but a repository of the city's waste. When Eugene and Mortimer ride down to Hexam's house with Charlie, the view from their window charts a descent into the depths of London, to a place where only the dregs remain.

> The wheels rolled on, and rolled down by the Monument and by the Tower, and by the Docks; down by Ratcliffe, and by Rotherhithe; down by where accumulated scum of humanity seemed to be washed from higher grounds, like so much moral sewage, and to be pausing until its own weight forced it over the bank and sunk it in the river. In and out among vessels that seem to have got ashore, and houses that seem to have got afloat . . . the wheels rolled on . . . (63)

Here, the river's boundaries seem permeable, with ships pulled onto the ground and houses perched out over the water on stilts. As a kind of "moral sewage" that flows freely through the city, finding its own level, the riverside community is a barometer of the city's poverty and degradation.

This riverside neighborhood seems tenuous and unstable. The pub frequented by the riverfolk, the Six Jolly Fellowship Porters, is described as "a narrow lopsided wooden jumble" that leans so far out over the water that it seemed "to have got into the condition of a faint-hearted diver who has paused so long on the brink that he will never go in at all" (104–5). But it has a resilient energy all its own. The narrator's confident claim that "it had outlasted, and clearly would yet outlast, many a better-trimmed building" (104) turns out to be well-founded: the favorite pub that Dickens had in mind, then called "The Bunch of Grapes," still stands in Limehouse. A 1937 photographic panorama of the river between London Bridge and Greenwich shows the public house in its row of eighteenth-century buildings much as they appeared in Dickens's time; in a duplicate panorama executed in 1997–2000, "The Grapes" is still clearly visible.[9]

The permeability of the riverside reinforces the river's status as a non-place and is emblematic of the many boundary inversions of a novel in which a "living-dead man" (430) returns from an apparent grave, a living woman struggles with spells of "deadness," and nobody is really what they seem. When Mortimer tells the story of John Harmon at the Veneerings' dinner party, Harmon is called both the "Man from Somewhere" and the "Man from Nowhere," as if these categories were interchangeable (55)—which, in the peculiar geography of this novel, they are. Dickens describes Podsnap's pervasive worldview as a belief that other countries were in general "a mistake," that "whatever he put behind him he put out of existence," and that beyond the habits and customs of his own "not . . . very large world," nothing else was "To Be—anywhere!" (174–75). Anywhere or somewhere becomes nowhere if it does not fit into the well-defined social topography of this society. The "Nowhere" from whence Harmon emerges is, in fact, the river, which erases his earlier identity and allows him to reinvent himself.

George Eliot's late-century depiction of rowing on the Thames, in *Daniel Deronda*, adds a darker shade of modern complexity, of almost fin de siècle angst, to the picturesque musings of earlier "upriver" writers and affirms the status of the Thames as a fluid image of a changing England. As we have noted, Eliot chose to situate a key scene in the novel—Daniel's first encounter with Mirah Lapidoth—on the river.[10] Book Two of the novel is titled "Meeting Streams," and Eliot uses the river as a central motif throughout this section to convey a sense of merging destinies.

Eliot characterizes Deronda's predilection for rowing as a common genteel pastime that offers him a unique opportunity for solitude and introspection. Chapter 7 begins:

> On a fine evening near the end of July, Deronda was rowing himself on the Thames . . . His old love of boating had revived with the more force now that he was in town with the Mallingers, because he could nowhere else get the same still seclusion which the river gave him. He had a boat of his own at Putney, and whenever Sir Hugo did not want him, it was his chief holiday to row till past sunset and come in again with the stars. Not that he was in a sentimental stage; but he was in another sort of contemplative mood perhaps more common in the young men of our day—that of questioning whether it were worth while to take part in the battle of the world. (225)

Eliot presents Daniel as representative of a particular form of modern anxiety and thus portrays him indulging in what had by this time become a typical, even trendy, activity for a young gentleman of the period.[11] (The novel was published in 1878; its time frame has been identified as 1864, though critics agree it is generally reflective of the 1870s.) Eliot emphasizes the ordinary nature of this occurrence; after describing the impression Deronda might make on an observer, she adds, "It is precisely such impressions that happen just now to be of importance in relation to Deronda, rowing on the Thames in very ordinary equipment for a young Englishman at leisure, and passing under Kew Bridge with no thought of an adventure in which his appearance was likely to play any part" (226).

The river is not only a conduit but a conductor, sparking a palpable, almost electric sense of affinity between Deronda and Mirah, and moving their lives into convergence with each other. Deronda's first glimpse of Mirah arrests his attention, as he is struck by a mysterious sense of congruity between his own dissatisfaction, expressed in the Rossini music he is singing, and the young woman he sees by the river. Deronda thinks about Mirah as he continues on his course, a course determined entirely by the river itself. In this journey, as in his life at this moment in time, he is aiming for no particular destination.

> He used his oars little, satisfied to go with the tide and be taken back by it. It was his habit to indulge himself in that solemn passivity which easily comes with the lengthening shadows and mellowing light, when thinking and desiring melt together imperceptibly. . . . By the time he had come back again with the tide past Richmond Bridge the sun was near setting. . . . He looked out for a perfectly solitary spot where he could lodge his boat against the bank, and throwing himself back with his head propped on the cushions, could watch out the light of sunset. (229)

He chooses a bend in the river just opposite Kew Gardens, "where he had a great breadth of water before him reflecting the glory of the sky, while he himself was in shadow." Deronda is an observer, not a participant, in the scene, and lies peering over the edge of his boat so that he "could not be seen by any one at a few yards' distance; and for a long while he never turned his eyes from the view right in front of him" (229). Like other Thames travellers, Deronda gives himself up to the visual pleasure of the scene before him. But his reverie goes deeper, as he uses the scene to focus his own efforts to define a sense of himself.

> He was forgetting everything else in a half-speculative, half-involuntary identi-fication of himself with the objects he was looking at, thinking how far it might be possible habitually to shift his centre till his own personality would be no less outside him than the landscape. (229–30)

Deronda's self-willed disorientation, his effort to stand outside himself, is reminiscent of the kind of virtual travel that we saw in the panorama accounts of Part One. Like the panorama viewer who enjoys standing on the edge of a sense of being someplace else, Deronda cultivates a sense of suspended subjectivity that positions him in a mediated space that is neither here nor there. The modernity of his attitude is encapsulated in this dual perspective, this sense of alternating interiority and exteriority.[12] Eliot uses the Thames as the locus of a journey to nowhere that is really an exploration of the self.

As we have seen, even the darker side of the Thames offered a powerful medium for cultural self-examination. The contrast between the pastoral England of the upriver Thames and the grittier reality of the London riverside exemplified the contradictions of a changing nation. This self-examination or auto-ethnography was rendered more compelling by the way in which writers and novelists were able to use the Thames to evoke a sense of mingled spectatorship and immersion in the world they depicted. The London Thames represented the threat as well as the opportunity of modernity. The river was a conduit to oblivion that erased the past, leaving you either with a chance at a fresh start— or no place at all.

7. CHANGE OF PACE:
THE RUSH TOWARD LEISURE

The idea of the Thames as a generalized and generalizable non-place was reinforced by the way in which river travel effaced the difference between public and private space, focusing attention on the speed and quality of travel itself and on the subjective experience of the traveller. While the chance contiguity of other people is a feature of many other forms of travel (and, as we will see in Part Three, figures importantly in descriptions of railway travel), river travel was unique in its blending of individual and shared experience. Travelling in a private boat was not as solitary as walking but also not as collective as travelling in a railway carriage, omnibus, or steam launch. One travelled at one's own pace, but along the same path and direction as others following the river's course. Some accounts note the dreamy meditativeness fostered by the solitary experience of drifting or rowing along the river. Many others, however, stress the social dimensions of river travel, which might involve friends travelling together or interactions with the different boats and parties encountered along the way.

The river's liminal status as a public space, bordered by primarily private property, made it the focus of debates not just about where one could travel on the river but also about *how* one could or should travel. The London Thames had always been crowded with a variety of vessels, more so in the eighteenth and early nineteenth centuries than by the mid- to late 1800s. But increasing public demand for greater clarity in rules of navigation was heightened in 1878 following the *Princess Alice* disaster, a collision between an excursion paddle steamer and another ship, the *Bywell Castle*, that claimed 640 lives. During the series of inquests and investigations that followed, "much was made of the igno-rance of the rules of navigation displayed by the various watermen" (Thurston, 168), and this calamitous event reinforced a general perception that river traffic had become chaotic and dangerous.[13] The upper waterways, too, became more difficult to negotiate later in the century, as amateurs in small boats began to clog the river, and steam launches entered the scene, much to the dismay of the small boaters. Accounts of boating on the Thames often contain impassioned complaints about property owners who post signs forbidding mooring along their property, and the question of who "owned" the water itself was brought to the fore by increasing hostility toward the large steam launches that came to dominate river traffic toward the end of the century.

Many of the river narratives we have been examining include hostile com-mentary on the growing nuisance presented by steam launches, which not only disrupted smaller craft with their large wakes but also annoyed seekers of pas-toral peace by transporting large and rowdy parties. G. Turner describes them as "the most unpopular and best-hated craft on the Thames," a "one-sided con-venience, esteemed by the selfish, the lazy, and the fast" (*Royal River*, 169), and the moral equivalence he implies between selfishness and the desire for speed is typical. Charles Dickens Jr.'s *Dictionary of the Thames* refers slightingly to the "people who pay their L5 5s. a day for the hire of a launch, and whose idea of a holiday is the truly British notion of getting over as much ground as possible in a given time." However, he notes that the "offences against courtesy and good behavior" of these "steam-launch 'Arries," in the popular phrase, are influenced by the "selfish example" set by "people who ought to know very much better" (237).

Dickens was not alone in seeing the steam-launches as a somewhat déclassé form of travel; given the limited holiday time available to the working classes and the effort made to tempt them into steam and rail excursions with cheaper fares, one- or two-day boat excursions certainly had great appeal for workers and their families, as well as for aspirants to middle-class gentility who could afford a few days on the Thames more easily than a month on the Rhine. The terms of the steam-launch debate will seem familiar to twenty-first-century readers: the conflicting attitudes toward particular modes of river travel we see developing toward the end of the nineteenth century are a precursor of the kinds of debates played out today between cross-country skiers and snowmobilers, or canoers and jet-skiers. Genteel travellers rowing traditional Thames boats maintained their right to a quiet, peaceful river environment, while proponents of the steam launches argued for easier, more rapid access to the river for larger groups of people. We will see in Part Three that similar questions of access formed an important undercurrent of debate about the railway. By removing the exclusivity of a particular mode of travel, new forms of transport had the potential to devalue the travel experience for upper-class travellers.

While the steam-launch opponents did not have the specific environmental objections that motivate contemporary opposition to highly motorized, "gas-guzzling" forms of travel, in all of these cases the preference for speed is perceived as a threat to the entire ethos of recreational travel. The speed of the steam launch, or snowmobile, is not the utilitarian speed of efficient commuter transportation to a specific and necessary destination, but the optional speed of accelerated travel to no place in particular. It is speed primarily for its own sake, for the pleasure of dramatic movement and the sensation of mastering the terrain that passes so quickly. From the point of view of those with time to spare, the primary virtues of paddling or canoeing upriver are the enforced slowness of the pace, the peaceful ambience, the relative isolation, and the opportunity, even necessity, of looking thoughtfully at the slowly changing scene. The exciting pace, rapidly shifting landscape, and highly social atmosphere of the steam launch seemed a rejection of the very values that drew boaters to the Thames to begin with.

Though printed commentary and satiric cartoons in this period universally condemn steam launches and the inconsiderate louts riding them, this mode of river travel increased dramatically in popularity during the 1870s and 1880s, so many people evidently ignored their scruples and enjoyed the ride. Perhaps the most realistic perspective is provided by Jerome, who while rowing his own boat complains endlessly about the launches and humorously describes his own deliberate efforts to get in the way of steamers; but who also appreciates the convenience of getting a tow from a friend's steam launch, and then complains, with self-conscious irony, about the "wretched small boats" that keep blocking their way (137).

Some river enthusiasts objected to launches on principle, not just because of their effect on other boats but because it was felt that they provided an inferior experience to the passengers themselves. As Buzard notes of nineteenth-century travel in general, "Critics tended to hold the tangible evidence of modernization in travel (improved roads, carriages, steamboats, railways) responsible for destroying the true character of travel . . . they allegedly laid waste the self-improving potential of valid travel" (1993, 32). As an artist, G. D. Leslie paid close attention to the visual experience of travelling on the river, and he claimed that it was not possible to fully appreciate the view from on board a launch: "The motion of the boat causes the perspective, both in front and behind, to alter so rapidly in a converging and diverging manner, as to have on the eye quite a painful effect"—not to mention that "in this part of the vessel the passengers generally sit . . . with their backs to the view" (256). Leslie's argument here resembles the similar complaint often made about rail travel, that the high speed at which one passed through landscape rendered it impossible to see.

As we saw earlier, most river travellers enjoyed the sense of ceding control of their journey to the river itself, which determined their path and, to some degree, their speed. As the pace quickened, travellers on steamboats had conflicting feelings about the rate at which they were moved through the scenery. A traveller on the Rhine says at first that he "regretted the rapidity" with which the "paddle-wheel hurried us away" from the magnificent scenery (Quin, 118) but then adds:

> Nevertheless, perhaps the very circumstance of our velocity of motion gave a fresh charm to each scene; for knowing that we could scarcely behold it before it vanished from our view, our attention was in a state of perpetual excitement. The presentation to the eye of a majestic pile of rocks and ruins, and the immediate substitution for it of declivities teeming with vines, or of fertile valleys . . . seemed to be the work of some enchanter, who had the power to change the objects before us at a stroke of his wand. (119)

This description of enforced refocusing on rapidly changing visual stimuli seems to prefigure the commentary that would arise in relation to railway travel, and later, in relation to movies and television and their control over the viewer's attention span. Here, the viewer appreciates the novelty of having the pictures changed rapidly in front of him, without any effort or design on his part. Like the balloon travellers who saw the scenery unroll magically beneath them, Quin finds a kind of enchantment in the movement of the landscape.

Here as in other descriptions, the aesthetic quality of the scene is enhanced by distance, and rapid movement through the landscape improves the viewer's capacity to see these objects as a picture rather than as an immediate environment. Quin notes that he prefers the "retrospective scenery" to the scenery around him for precisely this reason.

> The panorama always seemed to me more perfect in its outline and accessories when contemplated in that way than in the reverse. All the objects are then seen assembled, but arranged in their proper places . . . whereas when we are going through them in detail, we are not able to appreciate their individual value in the general prospect. (121–22)

The scene becomes a "panorama" when seen as a whole, behind him, and he prefers this sensation to the immersion in detail that accompanies his actual passage along the banks.

The high level of hostile commentary attracted by steam launches suggests that the popular association of river travel with a leisurely, pastoral, premodern form of existence was too powerful to be easily abandoned. Clearly, many travellers felt that the presence of large, mechanized boats on the Thames was an affront to their archaic image of the river, and a threat to their image of themselves as travellers to Britain's agrarian past.

The contrast between the pastoral pleasures of river travel and the pressures of modern technology that we see in the small boat–versus–launch debate was even more strongly marked in the frequent comparison of river travel to train travel in these accounts. As we have already seen, many of these accounts are shaped by a contrast between the journey itself and the framing experience of taking a train to and from the point of embarkation. These accounts dramatize the extent to which recreational river travel and train travel were deeply interconnected. It is not an exaggeration to state that the Thames riverboat boom could not have occurred without the expansion of excursion trains to key points along the river that took place in the middle of the century. The Great Western Railway added routes to Maidenhead, Reading, Pangbourne, Goring, and Moulsford in 1840, to Oxford in 1844, and to Windsor in 1849. The Twyford to Henley branch appeared in 1857. The addition of these stations certainly reflected the potential market for travel to riverside towns, and as the train system expanded, so did interest in exploring the upper reaches of the Thames.

As noted earlier, many travellers along the river did not take boats from London but instead took trains to popular departure points such as Oxford, and rented boats from there. The tourist industry that sprang up around boat travel clearly depended on the convenience of trains not only for bringing travellers out of the city but also for shipping luggage and boats to wherever they were needed. Charles Dickens Jr.'s *Dictionary of the Thames* includes, among the facts of "practical information to oarsmen, anglers, yachtsmen, and others directly interested in the river" (3), detailed train timetables and clear instructions about where trains disembark and what services or amenities they offer, while an advertisement for Salter's at the front of the book notes the availability of combined rail and steamer tickets. In all of the guidebooks, advertisements for boat-hire shops and hotels in riverside towns stress their proximity to the rail station.

The confluence of river and rail travel in this pattern of popular excursions highlights the irony of the emerging Victorian attitude toward leisure travel. Only the availability of rapid transit to popular spots along the river enabled travellers to indulge in the luxury of a leisurely, timeless voyage up or down the Thames. Whether one took the popular route of taking a quick train up to Oxford and then rowing down, or followed Jerome and his friends, who row up to Pangbourne and then jump on a train that gets them back to town in time to enjoy a snug dinner at their favorite chophouse, the mass transit provided by the rail system was an essential part of the trip. This new "hurry up and wait" pattern of using rapid transit to free up time for deliberately leisured travel reveals the strong investment of Victorian travellers in the travel experience itself. The goal of these trips was not to get to Oxford or Lechlade—you could do that in two hours. The goal was to enjoy the process of returning from there, or the process of getting to a place that was no longer a destination, but merely a train station from which to depart for home.

Many of these river narratives display the contradictions inherent in a form of excursion that privileges one form of travel while continuing to exploit another. James Thorne, for example, waxes indignant on the "rapid whirl of modern travelling" in which "men visit many places, and learn to despise them all," and contrasts it to his own "companionship" with the Thames. At the same time, he advises readers to take the railway to Maidenhead or other picturesque spots in order to then stroll along the river (202). As we have seen already, there is a strong sense of moral superiority in the slow traveller. G. Turner paradoxically claims that "the lazy are often restless in their inert desire to be conveyed swiftly from place to place; for they have no energy for idling" (170), suggesting that effortless transportation from one place to another allows one to escape the mental labor of observation required by a more leisurely pace. Like a flâneur strolling through a Parisian arcade—or like Jerome in the essays published in the journal he named *The Idler*— Turner valorizes "idling" over more efficient forms of travel, a stance that is clearly dependent on a degree of leisure that many of the new Victorian travellers could not enjoy.

While Andrew Wynter describes the Great Western train he takes to Maidenhead as a "monster that eats up a hundred miles in an hour with ease," he nevertheless seems to appreciate the fact that "the pace was accordingly first-rate" (62). The contrast between the continuous, slowly shifting view along the river and his view from the train is clear.

As [the train] got into the open country the trees seemed engaged in a perpetual waltz, those in the middle distance and those afar off continually changing places; then the furrows of the fields appeared to revolve like the spokes of an enormous wheel; bridges were passed with a rush like the sound of a pump-ball; then the express-train met us, and disappeared. (62–63)

Wynter sees the structural elements of the scene, but they pass by too quickly to cohere into any kind of picture. The natural elements of the scene become themselves mechanized in this process, as trees seem to automatically shift back and forth, while furrows turn into spokes in a wheel. Wynter's account ends with the passage, cited earlier, that describes him shooting "like a rocket" out of the train at Paddington. Like so many other Victorian travellers, he enjoys the opportunity to have it both ways: to experience the sensation of undertaking a leisurely journey while at the same time enjoying the convenience that modern technology provides.

These late-century debates about the nature and value of river travel echoed some of the same concerns that had been aroused by the expansion of the railways decades earlier. As we will see in Part Three, the Victorians understood that the dramatic, almost magical, expansion of their horizons offered by railway travel came at a cost. The popularity of recreational river travel in the second half of the century clearly reflects a nostalgia for a kind of travel experience that few people had the leisure or inclination to pursue in an increasingly fast-paced world. Trips on the Thames captured, in a concentrated and marketable form, many of the characteristics that made other forms of travel appealing: the sense of exploration associated with more exotic river journeys; the sense of cultural sophistication associated with viewing and appreciating a wide array of historic and picturesque scenes; the feeling of timelessness that comes from being wholly removed from one's everyday world. Moreover, Thames travel provided all these sensations within the context of a cultivated sense of pride in British landscape and, by extension, British culture. But while earlier nonfiction prose accounts stress this affirmative vision, Victorian novels reflect the darker side of that culture, mirroring the polluted waters of the London river.

All of these representations of the river share an emphasis on its capacity to transcend time and place, to become a virtual space that functions as a conduit rather than a location. This is the key to the unique role of the Thames in the geography of nineteenth-century British culture. By being everywhere and nowhere at the same time, it offered Victorians the opportunity to experience the sensation of travel, its displacement and restoration of self, without threatening their increasingly fragile sense of imperial mastery. A trip on the Thames did not require any engagement with foreign culture, or present any threat to British authority. On the contrary, it served as an affirmation of the traveller's own identity. It offered total immersion in the experience of being English.

Like the panorama exhibitions examined in Part One, Thames trips provided a form of virtual travel: they were mere imitations of more elaborate and authentic kinds of journeys. By the end of the century, river trips were so packaged and scripted, and accounts of them so ubiquitous, that the difference between actually travelling up the Thames, and merely reading about it, seemed beside the point. As with panorama viewing, the appeal of this form of travel lay precisely in its careful positioning in the space between representation and reality. In the depictions of railway travel we will examine in Part Three, we will see an even more self-conscious awareness of the disorientation created by this kind of separation of physical and imaginative experience. The emotional dislocation experienced by characters like Deronda and Mirah will be figured as literal dislocation in many late nineteenth-century novels—but with travel itself offering, at the same time, the opportunity to forge new networks of communication and connection.

Part Three

HIGH-SPEED CONNECTION
The Railway Network

> Going by railroad I do not consider as travelling at all; it is merely "being sent" to a place, and very little different from becoming a parcel.
>
> —John Ruskin, *Modern Painters* III, 1846

> He stepped out and caught sight of a white holographic cigar suspended against the wall of the station, FREESIDE pulsing beneath it in contorted capitals.... WHY WAIT? pulsed the sign. A blunt white spindle, flanged and studded with grids and radiators, docks, domes. He'd seen the ad, or others like it, thousands of times. It had never appealed to him. With his deck, he could reach the Freeside banks as easily as he could reach Atlanta. Travel was a meat thing.
>
> —William Gibson, *Neuromancer*, chap. 5, 1984

It was a new technology that seemed to herald a new age. A network that was initially designed for use by a limited number of professionals quickly grew into an indispensable infrastructure that changed a whole society's sense of distance, scale, and community. Though its eventual impact was impossible to predict, its capacity to bring together people and ideas from widely dispersed locations promised the dawn of a new era. At the same time, it seemed to speed up all aspects of life, creating new pressures in an increasingly harried modern world. Many feared that the patterns of social interaction it created would erode local communities and strain intimate relationships. The railway was in many ways the Internet of its era.[1]

The rapid development of the railway in the nineteenth century has long been seen as a critical harbinger of modernity. Not only did rail travel have an enormous economic and social impact, it also created a radical reconfiguration of our perceptual experience. Wolfgang Schivelbusch's seminal work, *The Rail-way Journey: The Industrialization of Time and Space in the Nineteenth Century* (1977), explored the ramifications of this new, mechanized form of travel for nineteenth-century European and American culture, showing how it altered "the traditional space-time consciousness" (37) in a way that would define the modern sensibility. Schivelbusch suggested that "the diminution of transport distances seemed to create a new, reduced geography" (35), creating a kind of "temporal shrinkage" (34). Schivelbusch's analysis emphasizes the industrial as-pect of railway transportation, in contrast to earlier forms, famously describing the "machine ensemble" created by the engine's dependence on the external ap-paratus of railway tracks and tunnels. This created, according to Schivelbusch, an artificial mode of perception in which "the traveler perceived the landscape as it was filtered through the machine ensemble" (24).[2]

In the final section of this study, I suggest that railways created the same disorienting feeling of suspension between two places that we saw in the ex-perience of panoramas, and in the leisurely Thames journeys of Part Two. In comparing a third form of virtual travel to the two already discussed, I will show that this new technology achieved perceptual effects that were not in fact completely new. Where panorama viewers stood still and succumbed to an il-lusion of movement, and river travellers drifted through a timeless, generalized landscape, railway travellers arrived at distant destinations without feeling the sensation of having gone there. All three modes of experience involve a continu-ous slippage between the subject and the surrounding environment. As we will see, virtual travel is valued for precisely this destabilization and disorientation of the self.

Through close examination of the representation of railways and railway travel, Part Three explores Victorian conceptions of the relationship of the self to the modern world. I begin with some historical and cultural background on the development of the railway, not with the goal of providing a comprehensive overview but in order to identify some key themes and aspects of rail travel that would become important to its textual manifestations. Among the texts I then offer in illustration of these themes are a range of little-known railway guides, periodical accounts of rail journeys, and pieces of popular short fiction. These accounts, many studied here for the first time, share an emphasis on the ambi-guity of railway space, and the complexity of the social relations that developed in this new, less class-stratified, domain. As in previous sections, I examine some specific rhetorical moves in these short pieces that will reappear in fictional rep-resentations of the railway in novels by Stoker, Dickens, Braddon, and Eliot. Finally, I will draw on film and media theory in order to illuminate the relationship between the linear visual perception associated with the railway, and the cinematic culture that emerged at the end of the century. This will pave the way for some concluding reflections on the general relationship between Victorian realism, modernity, and postmodernity.

From the very beginning, contemporary writers saw the potential for this new form of travel to reshape their economy, their recreational habits, their social relations, their very understanding of the world around them. The coming of the railway was seen as having profound symbolic significance, representing the triumph of mankind over fundamental physical constraints, in much the same way that the Internet would later be credited with the potential to bring about radical cultural change. As one commentator wrote in 1884, "There is an ozone in the nineteenth century air, much of which can be traced to railways. Men are for ever waging war against obstacles, and when a great victory is won over any one of these, the morale of the whole army is strengthened" (Foxwell, 17). The railway had considerable social and political significance, offering as it did unprecedented mobility to classes of people who were able to travel freely around the country for the first time. The expansion of railway networks would change popular conceptions about the size and accessibility of the country and world, much as the Internet would later shape the idea of the "global village." Modern critics disagree about the importance of the railway within the larger context of the industrial revolution, and indeed about the extent to which that "revolution" was revolutionary or evolutionary. But no one disputes the centrality of railways to the social and economic changes that took place in Britain over the course of the nineteenth century.

I suggested earlier that over the course of the nineteenth century, the idea of travel was gradually sifted into two distinct and opposing categories: first, the kind of leisure travel that was self-consciously valorized in Thames river narratives; and second, the efficient transportation epitomized by rail travel. These two very different forms of travel created a similar effect: they produced a model of disembodied travel that separated physical presence from a "sense of place." This separation, I would argue, is a first step toward understanding the disembodiment of information represented by modern developments in electronic media and communication. We will see, in fact, that railway travel is often represented in Victorian texts as a kind of communication, an activity that engenders a transmittal of information more than a transmittal of goods or people.

We saw in Part Two that the popularity of river travel was contingent on the development of the railways, and in a sense, the reverse is true as well. Rail travel was recognized as an entirely different mode of experience from earlier types of travel, and the nostalgic displacement of the more leisured sense of travel onto specific forms like river journeys or walking tours made it possible for the Victorians to revel in the brute efficiency of the railway journey. Railway travel had the effect of separating the desire to *be* someplace else from the desire to experience the process of getting there. It represents a complete inversion of river travel as described in Part Two. River journeys, as we saw, were a fundamentally nonpurposive form of travel, in which the continuous experience was more important than the destination. In rail travel, by contrast, we see that destination is everything. The traveller has a sense of having been magically transported from one place to another, without fully experiencing the transition.

While river journeys allowed the traveller to savor the passing scene, rail journeys generally proceeded at a pace that prevented assimilation or appreciation of the countryside between the point of departure and the destination. The effect, as we will see, was a kind of experiential erasure of the intervening space. The journey itself becomes a gap. This gap, the imperceptible distance between two points, resembles "the perceived gap between experience and 'the actual'" that defines virtuality (Boellstorf, 19). This gap can run in either direction. Panoramic travel, as we saw, was a simulated, fictive experience that felt real. Train travel offered the opposite experience: travel that was real but felt fictive.

This examination of railway narratives will show that both journalistic and fictional accounts of railway journeys tend to focus on the mechanics of travel— processes and procedures, arrival and departure—rather than the experience of passing through a particular landscape, reflecting a sense that the trip itself was essentially unassimilable. At the same time, however, a burgeoning genre of timetables and guidebooks offered a kind of user's manual that focused the traveller's perceptions on the practical aspects—the nuts and bolts, or bits and bytes—of the experience.

In fact, though other critics have emphasized the role of railway travel in fostering a critical reorientation of visual perspective with regard to external landscapes, I will suggest that in the majority of railway narratives, external space is largely ignored in favor of the social space defined by the interior of the railway carriage. The texts I examine here suggest that the railways did indeed reconfigure the spatial context of travel, but by focusing the attention of the traveller inward, either on the new social world created by the mix of passengers in a carriage, or on the private, interiorized space of a newspaper or novel to be read. The railway experience can thus be seen as the first step of a gradual dissociation of self from the travel experience that is manifested today in the iPods, laptops, and cell phones that allow contemporary travellers to ignore their immediate surroundings while on the move.

For Victorian writers who sought to reinforce the realism of their narrative worlds, the railway network provided an infrastructure that helped the reader to orient him- or herself within the fictional environment. Allusions to rail travel in Dickens and Eliot serve as symbols of progress that allowed those novelists to comment on the ambiguities of the changes taking place in the modern world. More frequent and detailed representations of train travel in works by Doyle, Braddon, and Stoker form an overlay of spatiotemporal markers that seek to align these fictional worlds in a more literal manner with the urban and sub-urban landscapes of modern British life. These representations share, however, a sense of rail travel as a virtual experience in which the physical body, what Gibson's cyber-cowboy Case calls "meat," is separated from the mental universe of the traveller.

Kevin Robins has said that in "the new world order" created by cyberspace, "old and trusted boundaries—between human and machine, self and other, body and mind, hallucination and reality—are dissolved and deconstructed. With the erosion of clear distinctions, the emphasis is on interfaces, combina-tions, and altered states" (140). Much the same can be said of the new world order represented by the railway, which the Victorians described in terms that emphasize its power to challenge the boundary not only between man and machine, but between corporeal and mental experience. Victorian railway nar-ratives acknowledge the unique sensory and physical demands of the railway, with its unprecedented speed, power, and potential for disaster. At the same time, they reflect the difficulty of describing or even apprehending the railway journey itself, which is often elided, superseded, or invested with the hallucina-tory qualities of a dream. The Victorians also recognized the importance of the railway system as an interface that would enable individuals to connect with new people, new places, and new sources of information more rapidly than ever before.

A single phrase epitomizes, for nineteenth-century commentators and for contemporary critics, the radical change in perception brought about by railway travel: "the annihilation of space and time." A cliché among the Victorians, it is still used to convey the sense in which this form of travel profoundly altered people's sense of their relationship to, and control over, the world around them. David Harvey, in a discussion of Balzac's penchant for the metaphor, notes its "latent" use in Marx, where it signifies "the revolutionary qualities of capitalism's penchant for geographical expansion and acceleration (speed up) in the circula-tion of capital." In Balzac, Harvey suggests, the annihilation of space and time is part of a quest for the "sublime moment" of insight in which "all the forces of the world become internalized within the mind and being of a monadic individual" (2001, 72). Harvey quotes Balzac as praising man's power of "isolating himself from the milieu in which he resides," and declaring to the universe, "I am here and I have the power to be elsewhere! I am dependent upon neither time, nor space, nor distance. The world is my servant" (quoted in Harvey, 74). Harvey sees this as a "distinctively capitalistic and bourgeois version of the sublime" (74) that is linked to a "totalizing vision" (67) of the city—specifically, Paris—that may remind us of the panorama.

Schivelbusch, like Dolf Sternberger, describes the railway experience as "panoramic," and many critics have followed them in using the term to characterize the visual apprehension of landscape from a railway train. Sternberger claims that the view from the window of a train enforced an indiscriminate view of landscape, in which all scenes meld into "the same panoramic world that stretches all around and is, at each and every point, merely a painted surface" (57). We saw in Part One that the development of panoramic perception over the course of the century had taught Victorians to appreciate grand, sweeping overviews, and the sense of mastery associated with taking a broad perspective. In the case of railway travel, that power is reinforced by the sense of technological mastery of the landscape created by what were seen as the extraordinary, even magical, capacities of the steam engine.

We have already seen that the continuousness of a representation contributes to the degree of immersiveness it offers. As was the case with river journeys, the linear quality of the railway experience made it well suited to panoramic representation in a variety of formats. As early as 1834, the Baker Street Bazaar exhibited a "Padorama" that displayed model railway trains in front of a 10,000-square-foot dioramic strip wound on drums, showing "'the most interesting parts of the country traversed by the Liverpool and Manchester Railway'" (Altick, 203). An 1894 panorama would take a nostalgic look back at the same famous line, using four 24-inch strips to depict "Travelling on the Liverpool and Manchester Railway."[3] This panoramic strip allows the train itself to be represented in its entirety, showing the different classes of carriages. Many railway companies commissioned promotional lithographs of trains passing through scenic landscapes, and these often attempted to convey a sense of both the impressive length of the train and the panoramic quality of the landscape around it. While these small representations cannot be said to reproduce the effect of a full-scale panorama, they allude to that effect, suggesting to the viewer that a railway journey might be expected to offer some of the same pleasures as a panorama.

But while there are many similarities between the kind of panoramic perception described in Part One, and the perception of landscape described by Schivelbusch and others, it is important to note the difference between an individual's perception, from a stationary point, of a world spread out beneath him, and the collective experience of a group of people who see a landscape moving past them but are powerless to control the pace or duration of their apprehension of it. While many of the texts discussed here demonstrate the sense of pride and domination associated with the coming of the railways, that pride is felt on behalf of mankind or England, not on behalf of individual efforts of their own. As representatives of the English nation, travellers felt awed by the power of steam locomotives and proud of the logistical and organizational effort needed to make trains run on time. As individuals, however, train travellers frequently felt disempowered, threatened, and diminished by the experience. Their attitude contrasts strongly both with the sense of adventure associated with foreign travel and with the sense of leisured privilege associated with river travel. The sense of disempowerment registered in many railway narratives may also reflect the less privileged class status of many railway travellers.

The need to rapidly grasp a greatly increased number of visual impressions when travelling by train requires a form of perception that many critics have characterized as distinctly modern. Today, this kind of rapid overview might be described as surfing, browsing, or scanning, and occurs most often in front of a computer screen. Schivelbusch sees it as an example of what Georg Simmel calls "urban perception" (Schivelbusch, 60) and links it further with the kind of "mobility of vision" created by consumerism (66). This idea is in turn echoed in Anne Friedberg's notion of the "mobilized virtual gaze" evoked by the visual demands of commodity culture. And, as we will see, it had important consequences for the development of cinema as an alternative method of absorbing a continuous flow of visual images.

But while Sternberger suggests that train travel "turned the traveler's eyes outward and offered them the opulent nourishment of ever changing images that were the only possible thing that could be experienced during the journey" (57), many travel accounts suggest that travellers took only occasional note of this passing panorama, and that the primary experience of rail travel had less to do with the view and more to do with what was happening on this side of the window. We saw in Part One that an important aspect of panoramic travel was the degree to which the surrounding apparatus, general context, and viewer's expectations contributed to the overall experience. The panoramic perspective was valued precisely because its scale and context allowed it to transcend the merely visual and become a more comprehensive sensory experience.

In fact, rail travel most closely resembled the panoramic perspective not in its specific visual characteristics but in its separation of the sensations or experience of travel from the physical fact of being somewhere else. The Victorians were fascinated by the capacity of the railway to whisk them to a new location so quickly that it *felt* as if they could not possibly be there yet. Accounts of rail travel typically note that "the passenger can scarcely credit he is really passing over the ground at such a rapid pace" ("Manchester," 168). As we will see, there was certainly a sense of danger and disorientation associated with this form of travel. But the perceptual incongruity of the experience seemed in general to contribute to a sense of its value. The time lag between one's intuitive sense of one's location and one's actual arrival gave an aura of magic to train travel, a sense that technology had outstripped physical obstacles and allowed the impossible to happen. To the Victorians, this seemed at first as amazing as the science-fiction transporter beams that allow starship crewmembers to materialize on distant planets.

In this way, the railway journey seems to anticipate Fredric Jameson's "postmodern hyperspace," alluded to in the discussion of panoramas in Part One, a space that "has finally succeeded in transcending the capacities of the individual human body to locate itself, to organize its surroundings perceptually, and cognitively to map its position in a mappable external world" (43). Victorian travellers found it difficult to locate themselves on the rapidly moving panorama of the world outside their windows, focusing instead on the interior world of the railway car, a comprehensible space that offered temporary shelter from the whirlwind around them. Jameson suggests that the "alarming disjunction between the body and its built environment" that he sees in contemporary society is a "symbol" for the cognitive disjunction that makes it difficult for us to position ourselves as subjects within "the great global multinational and decentered communication network" (44). In the Victorian period, the undeniable physical dislocations of the railway (both in its effect on individual bodies and in its effect on disrupted communities) were thought to be the unavoidable price paid for the possibility of a national and global communications network that would reduce the fragmentation of modern life.

Some new technologies are so radical as to seem uncanny. The belief in their capacity to transcend material constraints found expression in the nineteenth century in a level of rhetoric that James Carey and John Quirk labeled "the electrical sublime" (Carey, 121), and David Nye has called "the technological sublime."[4] Even as the railways were lauded as a supreme achievement of science and technology, they were described in language that associated them with magic. John Hollingshead claimed in 1867 that the train carried him to his destination "swifter than the genii bore Aladdin from city to city" (727), an image that is literalized in an illustration to an 1839 railway guidebook that shows a cherub astride a magic lamp (*Home and Country*, 7). The same guide notes that the railways would have seemed to our ancestors to be "proofs of our necromantic powers and triumph in all the black arts" (*Home and Country*, 34). Robert Bell, writing in *Bentley's Miscellany*, carries this theme a step further, suggesting that railway speed "is nothing short of witchcraft," and that "if Mr. Stephenson, or Mr. Gooch, or any other philosopher of their cloth, lived in the days of the Stuarts . . . he would have been burned at the stake" (454). Bell also wrote a novel, *The Ladder of Gold* (1850), about the rise and fall of a railway magnate, and there, too, he characterized the railroad as "a new element of power" akin to magic: "Science was the magician that had called it into existence, and money was the spell by which it was to be worked" (Bell, *Ladder* I, 273).[5] If the railway was magic, it was magic created through the alchemy of science and money.

Although there were a number of Christian tracts based on railway themes and metaphors, as we will see, the emphasis remained on the railroad as a product of human ingenuity. At times, this undertaking was seen as the reverse of Christian, as if only the devil could wield this kind of untrammeled power. There was understood to be a kind of hubris in the undertaking that led more than one writer to label the railway magic "Faustian." Thomas Carlyle, for example, in a frequently quoted 1839 letter to John Carlyle, described an early train journey as "likest thing to a Faust's flight on the Devil's mantle" (Jennings, 212), an image that suggests not simply demonic power but the very capacity that the railways promised and Goethe's hero achieved: the power to annihilate space and time. The fire and steam of the engine itself led many writers to describe railway scenes as hellish, a cliché that was used to comic effect by Charles Lever in his *Tales of the Trains; by Tilbury Tramp* (1845). One of his tales includes a dream interlude in which "the convulsive beating and heaving of the black monster itself" leads to a nightmare of wild goblins dancing and brandishing "bars of seething iron." They sing a devilish "Song of the Stoker": "Rake, rake, rake, / Ashes, cinders, and coal; / The fire we make, / Must never slake, / Like the fire that roasts a soul" (37). Similar imagery pervades the anonymous 1838 work *The Ghost of John Bull; or, the Devil's Railroad*, a facetious political allegory that satirizes the Poor Laws and various other subjects as well as the new railroads. "John Bull" is driven out of one town after another and forced to travel by train on a road made by the devil; only when the train crashes is his spirit able to debate the devil and expose the truth.

These demonic images of the railway convey menace as well as power, of course, and became even more common in the wake of the second round of "railway mania" in 1844–47. In 1845, the same year that Lever's book was published, George Cruikshank's *Table-Book* included a cartoon of "The Railway Dragon," a railway engine with an open, flaming mouth chanting: "I come to dine. I come to sup / I come—I come—to eat you up!" as it bears down upon a family's holiday meal. "Oh, the Monster! . . . Oh, my beef! and oh, my babbies!" the parents cry, the implication being that their family finances have been ruined by unlucky railway speculation. A century and a half before the promise of Internet riches fueled the dot-com bubble, the "railway bubble" devastated the Victorian financial world, demonstrating that the promise of this new technology had yet to be fully understood.

I. FRANKENSTEIN'S MONSTER: THE CYBORG ENGINE

The Victorians were not entirely confident that the power of the railway could be predicted and controlled. E. Foxwell's image of "Distance . . . led captive across the land in triumphal possession at forty miles an hour" (17), and his claim that "men who were once the serfs of distance, are now free" (18), suggests that in overcoming physical constraints, man had freed himself from a kind of enslavement. But the railway "monster" was often compared to Mary Shelley's monster, who is powerful enough to escape the shackles of the scientist who created him.

The analogy to Frankenstein's monster may seem surprising, given that it occurs in contexts presenting a largely enthusiastic vision of the railway. Alexander Anderson, in his "Song of the Engine," refers to the engine as "this monster of ours, that for ages lay/ In the depths of the dreaming earth," till he is brought out by man (46); then, "like the monster of Frankenstein's, / This great wild being was nigh; / Till at length he rose up in his sinews and strength," causing both pride and fear (46). The fact that Anderson is announced on the title page of his collection as a "Railway Surfaceman," and pictured with a pick and shovel, suggests that his working-class perspective may take into account the employment opportunities created by this new industry. In another poem, "On the Engine by Night," Anderson has the engine himself speak, saying, "Let the Frankensteins who made me / Keep the guiding of my feet" (79). This image of barely restrained power in need of careful guidance emphasizes the hybridity of this partly artificial, partly human creation.

The specter of Frankenstein's monster seems to lurk beneath the surface, too, in images that attribute an electrifying, galvanizing power to the railway. Foxwell, for example, uses a complex organic metaphor to describe the ability of railway speed to further the progress of thought: "Such swift speed makes

one organic whole of the practical ideas scattered here and there, so that the
local vigour of the country pervades the whole mass in through currents, which
return to revivify the centres of their birth; industrial life becomes intensified as
bodily functions are by the establishment of cerebro-spinal nerve tracks among
the 'sympathetic ganglia'" (5). Here, the railway seems to function as the electric
current that gives life to a previously lifeless "mass." Iwan Morus has described
the transformation of electricity from an unstable, dangerous form of experimentation and entertainment in the 1820s and 1830s into an integral part of
public and commercial life from the 1840s onward, and the frequent use of electrical images in relation to steam-powered locomotives seems intended to place
them on the same trajectory of acceptance.

The animating, life-giving power of the railway is stressed in the London
and Birmingham railway guide. The guide muses, as the route passes through
a cemetery:

> Here is the dead creature—there the living, moving, all but speaking monster,
> which had its origins from intelligences like those which once inhabited the
> mortal remains around us. The powers of Frankenstein's monster are here ex-
> ceeded, and these were created by man. (Freeling, 39–40)

This striking juxtaposition of the transience of human life emblematized by the
rotting corpses, and the immortality of human intelligence embodied in the railway engine, suggests that the engine is an independent creature that will outlast
its creators. To see the power of this new technology as exceeding the capacity
to animate dead flesh is to credit man with almost godlike powers that stand in
ironic contrast to his inescapable mortality.

The anxieties about the dehumanizing effects of technology that led Victorian writers to personify the railway as a kind of monster are echoed today
in the cyborg figures that populate science fiction novels, films, and television
shows. Contemporary theorists have rehabilitated the figure of the cyborg, seeing in these "hybrids of machine and organism" a progressive image of "trans-
gressed boundaries, potent fusions, and dangerous possibilities" that led Donna
Haraway to declare, famously, "we are cyborgs" (516). But representations of
cyborgs in popular culture clearly reflect a fear that evolving technology might
push us too far past the human/artificial divide. The Victorians' portrayal of
the railway as Frankenstein's monster is an early example of the same kind of
projection. This fear is also evident in an obsession with the body—in all its
dimensions, as corporeal presence and as social actor—that is prominent in a
number of railway narratives. As we will see, these texts emphasize a central

paradox of railway travel: the way in which one's body was able to outrun one's mental perception of place. This disjunction made railway travel an apt image for a general and persistent fear that the power of technology will exceed our ability to understand and control it.

2. NEITHER HERE NOR THERE:
THE BODY IN TRANSIT

An obsession with the speeds achieved by railway trains is evident in virtually all accounts of railway travel. The earliest "Bradshaw," the standard railway guide, was like a pocket calculator, providing, as one author notes, "a pleasant little chart, by which we can make amusing calculations on the rate of travelling per hour, per minute, or any fractional portion—pocket Babbage, which might beguile a weary hour" ("Old Guide," 546). Many accounts make reference to such calculations and are often quite specific in their description of time elapsed on particular legs of a journey. One traveller recounts a chance meeting with a man whom he desires to question further about a mutual acquaintance, and notes ruefully: "But only fifteen miles remained, and I recollect calling to mind . . . that the gradients were against me . . . and that the journey would be over in twenty-four minutes" ("What Are We Coming To?" 284). The idea that the railroad quickly altered travellers' expectations about travel time is borne out by the opening of a story in which a journalist orders a "special engine" for his trip to London. He writes, "I was the bearer of despatches of great importance for a London morning newspaper, and somewhat more than three hours was the utmost space of time I could afford to shoot over the 200 miles of rail which separated me from the office in the Strand" ("Nightmare on the Rails," 522).

Long after the novelty of train speed might be expected to have worn off, Sherlock Holmes is very attentive to the speed of travel: "'We are going well,' said he, looking out of the window, and glancing at his watch. 'Our rate at present is fifty-three and a half miles an hour.'" When Watson protests that he has seen no quarter-mile posts, Holmes replies, "'Nor have I. But the telegraph poles on this line are sixty yards apart, and the calculation is a simple one'" ("Adventure of Silver Blaze," 291). As we will see, Holmes makes good use of travel time to converse with Watson or with clients; one such conversation begins when he notes with satisfaction, "'We have a clear run here of seventy minutes. . . . I want you, Mr. Hall Pycroft, to tell my friend your very interesting experience'" ("Adventure of the Stockbroker's Clerk," 332). As we will see, an important by-product of train travel was the pressure it created to use the travel time productively.

Many writers compare train speed to carriage or horse speed, as they struggle to come to terms with the capacity of steam to exceed the fastest speeds achievable in nature. An 1833 description of the new Manchester to Liverpool Rail-Road helpfully explains to readers that the train runs "at a speed equal to the gallop of a race-horse" ("Manchester," 168), while by 1849, an account describes the "fearful momentum" of a train as it "rush[es] forward faster than any race-horse can gallop" (quoted in Simmons, 211). Trains are frequently described as "steam-horses," and the celebrated railway poet Alexander Anderson characterized the train as both a "black beast of burden" and a "thunder-horse" (78, 48).

Other writers sought mechanical analogies in attempting to convey the physical power behind this new form of transportation. We saw in Part Two that Andrew Wynter described himself as being shot "like a rocket" out of a train at the end of his journey, and trains were often compared to rifles or cannons. Dickens describes the passage of an express train, which "was like all other expresses, as every express is and must be," this way.

> Here, were station after station, swallowed up by the express without stopping; here, stations where it fired itself in like a volley of cannon-balls, swooped away four country-people. . . . and fired itself off again, bang, bang, bang! (Dickens and Collins, "Idle Apprentices")

In a nostalgic description in *Felix Holt* of the stage-coach culture of "five and thirty years ago," George Eliot contrasts pleasant memories of long coach journeys with contemporary travel experience.

> Posterity may be shot, like a bullet through a tube, by atmospheric pressure from Winchester to Newcastle: that is a fine result to have among our hopes; but the slow old-fashioned way of getting from one end of our country to the other is the better thing to have in the memory. The tube-journey can never lend much to picture or narrative. (5)

Eliot's image of the future embeds a wistful complaint about contemporary travel within a facetious reference to what was then experimental technology. Pneumatic trains had at one time seemed a logical next development for the railways, and an 1864 illustration from the *Illustrated London News* shows a "working model" of a "pneumatic railway for passengers" exhibited on the grounds of the Crystal Palace at Sydenham. It did indeed shoot passengers through a tube over a distance of 600 yards in 50 seconds (*ILN*, Sept. 10, 1864: 275–76). An artist's rendering of the Victoria Embankment in 1867 shows, in addition to the sewer, underground railway line, and utility pipes that were eventually built into the embankment, a proposed pneumatic railway crossing the Thames (Halliday, 159). Eliot would comment again on the pace of modern life in *Daniel Deronda*, a novel that includes many train journeys, noting the relativity of time and the absurdity of equating time with inherent value (771).

The speed of railway trains was seen as typical of the age, as both contributing to and reflecting a sense in which life had simply sped up. An anonymous 1877 writer in *Blackwood's* mourns the transformation of more difficult forms of travel into mere "touring," but acknowledges, "the course of time has swept us along with it; as knowledge has been increased, facilities of communication have been multiplied; the indulgence of a privileged class has become the recreation or necessity of the many; and the pace of our busier life has been accelerated" ("Rambles," 605). As early as 1849, a writer notes the "locomotive propensities of the age" and uses the railway as a metaphor for contemporary existence, "the headlong bustle and the toil of life, with its steam always up, and its engine, when not going at full speed, generally preparing for a start" ("Railway Literature," 280). A staunch train enthusiast, E. Foxwell, is less regretful about the change of pace, suggesting that "the hottest advocate of past times would be the first to desert his colours if confronted with the travelling realities of fifty years ago." He praises the "modern gift of speed" that has "opened out new worlds in life" (Foxwell, 4).

There were critics who argued that railway speed closed as many doors as it opened. John Ruskin, who objected strenuously to railways both because of their effect on the landscape and because he felt that they degraded the scenic experience of travel, insisted many times that it was impossible to visually apprehend and appreciate landscape when it passed by so rapidly.[6] The vastly increased speed of train travel certainly had an effect on travellers' perceptions of distance, or, more abstractly, of space in general. Places did not seem as far apart when they could be reached so easily. Stephen Kern, among others, has explored this phenomenon in the period from 1880 to 1918, pointing out that first trains and then "technical innovations including the telephone, wireless telegraph, x-ray, cinema, bicycle, [and] automobiles" led to a "reorientation" of thinking about space and time, while such "independent cultural developments . . . as the stream-of-consciousness novel, psychoanalysis, Cubism, and the theory of relativity shaped consciousness directly" (Kern, 1). Michael Freeman describes "railway space" as an abstract kind of "relational space" that is epitomized by the railway timetable, which raises well-connected areas into prominence while erasing others from notice completely (78).

But while the effect undoubtedly grew more pronounced as more people experienced railway travel and fewer people remembered coach travel, this sense of a collapsing of space between two points is evident in the earliest accounts of travelling by train. The 1833 Manchester to Liverpool account cited earlier states that "remote places are, by this means, virtually brought near to each other; and thus, while intelligence is diffused, an impulse is given to commerce, each of which advantages most powerfully affects the condition of the people" (161). As we will see, this emphasis on the railway as a form of communication, rather than mere transport, would become central to an understanding of its value. More important, however, the use of the term *virtual* demonstrates the immediate recognition that by changing one's experience of time, the train in effect changed one's perception of space, so that places themselves seem to move closer together in their own virtual travel. There was less of a distinction between places that were near and places that were far, so a traveller's choice of destination need not be based primarily on proximity and convenience. We recognize today that "distance means less and less in the digital world" (Negroponte, 78), because the speed and format of our communication is the same regardless of whether a loved one or work colleague is two floors away or two continents away. In the nineteenth century we see the beginning of this gradual dissociation of space from time.

The author of *Bradshaw's Monthly Descriptive Guide* notes that railways send people wherever they are not, through an equalizing exchange in which "the denizen of the town seeks health upon the sea-shore, or regales his eye with the verdure of meadows.... the rural population seeks the life and bustle of the town, its antiquities, and its museums. The operative of the manufacturing district visits the enchanting scenery of the Lakes.... The dweller in villages visiting the distant city is brought to some great cathedral ... and lives anew in the fervour of medieval piety" (vi). This is perhaps an optimistic characterization of each traveller's appetite for the cultural opportunities he or she has missed—advertisements for special excursion trains to London suggest, for example, that major attractions for many visitors were not museums but sporting matches, temperance events, panorama exhibitions, and Madame Tussaud's. But it is significant in its assumption that railway traffic flows in all directions. Preference for one location over another is less evident than a preferred *difference* in location that leads people everywhere to trade places.

These comments emphasize a sense of the railway as offering a kind of universal access, so that, once plugged into this network, the traveller could go anywhere. One effect of this new mobility was to diminish the dependence of individual holidaymakers on the destinations closest to home. Hollingshead describes this as a kind of emotional abandonment of "old pleasures and old friends": "Our withered tea-gardens on the borders of the city beckoned to us in vain, and looked at us reproachfully as we hurried past. . . . Our old taverns pined for our presence; our fishing-punts, on the London rivers, rotted with neglect . . . the slopes of Hampstead became a desert" (729). But while this may be an accurate evocation of Hollingshead's own attitude toward formerly fa-miliar places, it is not an accurate description of the popularity of such sites of recreation. They may have become less appealing to the most local inhabitants, but other travellers from farther away were happy to take the place of London-ers who no longer frequented suburban tea-gardens. And while the popularity of going on the Thames may have diminished in the 1860s, when Hollingshead was writing, the resurgence of interest in river travel a decade or two later was a direct result, as we have seen, of the "opening-up" of space by the railways.

The collapsing of space associated with the railway led many to anticipate a new era of peace and brotherhood. Alexander Somerville, author of *Autobi-ography of a Working Man*, writes that when he "first saw the railway uniting Liverpool and Manchester," he imagined "nation exchanging with nation their products freely; thoughts exchanging themselves for thoughts, and never taking note of the geographical space they have to pass over," and finally, "man hold-ing free fellowship with man" (Jennings, 235–36). This language of universal brotherhood would be echoed more than a century later by the rhetoric of what Fred Turner and others have called "digital utopianism." In the early days of the Internet, "the cybernetic notion of the globe as a single, interlinked pattern of information was deeply comforting"; in these linkages between cultures and the sharing of information that would result, "many thought they could see the pos-sibility of global harmony" (Turner, 5). The high level of rhetoric associated with these claims (which has been referred to as "cyperbole" [Imken, 102]) follows a long-standing tradition of overestimating the social benefits of new technology.

Railway developers and supporters exploited the popular association of the railway with progress, making it seem unpatriotic to stand in the way of some-thing that was often described as if it were a disinterested effort to foster greater human understanding, rather than the moneymaking proposition it was. In his novel *Ladder of Gold*, Robert Bell notes that "the people had believed in the South Sea, in the Mississippi. . . . why should they not believe in the conquest of time and space by practical science . . . ?" (274). The association of science with belief in the unseen found many expressions in the period, but here Bell empha-

sizes the ability of people to believe in the existence of faraway places they know
only by report. The railway made distant places seem so near, conventional geography was almost meaningless; the Mississippi might as well be the Thames.
But Bell also satirizes the assumption of ease associated with railway expansion.

> Mountains were to be cut through, as you would cut a cheese; valleys were to be
> lifted; the skies were to be scaled; the earth was to be tunnelled. . . . the shriek-
> ing engine was to carry the riot of the town into the sylvan retreats of pastoral
> life. . . . hissing locomotives were to rush over the tops of houses; and it was not
> quite decided whether an attempt would not be made to run a railway to the
> moon. (I, 274)

Bell claims that the "foundations" of this belief were strong enough, but "the
superstructure was a fantastic dream" (I, 274), and the bursting of the "railway
bubble" exposed the overoptimism, or outright greed, that led to overinvestment
in the railroads.

Trollope's vivid depiction in *The Way We Live Now* (1874–75) of the financial world defined by the railroads reinforces this image of the enthusiasm engendered by the railways taking on a life of its own, as what had once been a
bold belief in emerging technology soon developed into a speculative fever that
ignored common sense. Trollope's description of an American railway company
spokesman's speech to the prospective board of the prospective railway makes a
clear distinction between the familiar rhetoric of the enterprise and the underlying reality.

> Without giving it word for word, which would be tedious, I could not ade-
> quately set before the reader's eye the speaker's pleasing picture of world-wide
> commercial love and harmony which was to be produced by a railway from Salt
> Lake City to Vera Cruz, nor explain the extent of gratitude from the world at
> large which might be claimed by, and would finally be accorded to, the great
> firms of Melmotte & Co. of London, and Fisker, Montague, and Montague of
> San Francisco. (78)

But for all that, "there was not one of them then present who had not after
some fashion been given to understand that his fortune was to be made, not by
the construction of the railway, but by the floating of the railway shares" (78).
In fact, it becomes increasingly clear that the railway will never be built—and
perhaps was never intended to be built. It exists only as an object of investment.
When we are told that the novel's most decent character, Roger Carbury, "did

not believe in the railway" (108), his lack of belief in that project symbolizes a lack of belief in the entire social world that has been constructed on that shaky foundation. The railway represents an early instance of what might be called the increased virtuality of value, the gradual dissociation of economic worth from material production. Economic historians have compared the railway boom of the mid-1800s with the introduction of the Internet, noting that "then, as now, stock markets found that pricing shares associated with an exciting new technology is extremely difficult, reflecting considerable uncertainty about the value of the technology" (Baines et al.). As a new technology with an unpredictable future, the railway had a virtual existence in the public imagination and the financial marketplace that was distinct from its material development.

In addition to the dislocations of space and bodily experience we have noted, another fundamental dimension of perception affected by railway travel was the sense of time. The much-lauded ability of the railway to "save time" was not always seen as an unmitigated benefit. Enthusiastic travellers argued that the time required by walking tours or even coach travel was time well spent, and that the traveller who sped up his journey to save time was merely reducing the value of the experience. Purists seemed to posit a direct ratio in which the value of a trip was measured not by miles covered but by depth of experience multiplied by hours spent. John Ruskin wrote that "a man who really loves travelling would as soon consent to pack a day of such happiness into an hour of railroad, as one who loved eating would agree . . . to concentrate his dinner into a pill" (III, 370–71).

One might expect that the capacity of the railway to save time by increasing the speed of travel would create a sense of increased time at one's disposal. But in a paradoxical manner that is nonetheless strangely familiar to our modern sensibilities, the promise of "saving" time seems to have instead increased the pressure on notions of time in general. The need for coordination among railway timetables created the push for standard time that resulted in the adoption of Greenwich mean time by most of the nation when the Royal Observatory, in conjunction with the South Eastern Railway, began telegraphing time-signals in 1852.[7] But not only did the railways engender a greater emphasis on punctuality that spilled over into other areas of life, the idea of saving time by accomplishing a journey more quickly than ever before seems to have reinforced a quintessentially Victorian notion that one should expend wisely the time thus saved.

The railway generated not only a new expectation of punctuality but a new attitude toward the time spent on a journey. For the first time, the trip was not an event in itself but a space to be filled. Previously, the impracticality of attempting to read, let alone write, while travelling by coach or boat had meant that there was no expectation that a traveller would be doing anything other than travelling: looking at the scenery, talking to companions, perhaps sleeping or eating. The relative smoothness of railway travel, however, created the possibility of doing other things, and travel time was no longer given over entirely to the experience of travel. People began to consider other ways to "pass the time." While railway travel saved time, it also created the perceived burden of "wasted" time spent sitting at railway stations, and an imperative that the time spent on the train itself should be usefully employed. The rail journey was not, like a coach or river journey, a world unto itself; it was a non-space, a vacuum to be filled.

The dislocated sense of time created by rail travel is a primary plot element in Margaret Oliphant's 1873 story "A Railway Junction." Oliphant locates her story in "one of those purgatories of modern existence, those limbos of the weary and restless spirit" (419), a railway junction. The story centers on the relationship between a man and woman who encounter each other at the station, and much of the plot is determined by the unique constraints of waiting for a train. Oliphant emphasizes the tedium of the wait, the way in which "time and patience wear out the solemn hours" (420), while various problems arise from the dislocated sense of time created by the wait itself. The young man, Captain Cuttle, misses his own party on a departing train when he pauses to address a young lady of his acquaintance; they find themselves strolling about the station area "to 'pass the time'" (431), but "time passes very quickly under such circumstances" (433), and she then misses her train, obliging him to help her send a telegram to her waiting father. She then becomes upset by the realization that Cuttle himself has now missed a train to his own destination. In the end, of course, they fall in love and eventually marry, so the enforced wait has had a fortuitous outcome.

But Oliphant's story focuses less on the romance than on the stretching and compression of time under these circumstances, the way in which a period of intolerable boredom is transformed into insufficient time when a welcome distraction is offered. Although this story takes place at a station, rather than in a railroad car, many commentaries share this emphasis on the way in which railways trap passengers and take control of their most precious commodity, time, which they must then struggle to recapture through some meaningful "pastime."

The anonymous poet of the 1846 *Railroad Eclogues* satirizes the speeding-up of modern time and questions the value of the time thus "saved."

> No, no, our world's a world of hurly burly;
> We're late to bed, and we arise right early.
> Time's precious—up!—would you a fortune make,

Your maniac journey by express take.
Sounds the loud whistle—but, with all this pother,
Time saved one way is wasted in another. (Eclogue IV, ll. 88–93)

The poet goes on to note that when you send your lawyer to London by train, he "finds something there / Which must detain him," and "dips into your purse," while the doctor who travels down from London to attend you "travels cheap, saves time," but does not charge you a penny the less (IV, 94–103 passim).

The emergence of this new block of time created options for the traveller that had never existed before. As we will see, the railway generated new forms of social interactions with fellow travellers. But railway travel also fostered a new interiority, a focus on private activities such as reading and writing, that seems to represent a first step in the direction of what one contemporary critic has called the "capsularization" of travel: the increasing tendency of travellers to use devices such as iPods and cell phones to insulate themselves from the travel experience. Lieven de Cauter suggests that the more mobile we become, the greater our reliance on "virtual capsules" that protect us from the sensory overload of modern experience (95). Sherry Turkle has noted that in modern railway stations and airports, technology allows travellers to be not simply anonymous but "absent," as they focus their attention on electronic devices that connect them to people elsewhere (2011, 155). For the Victorians, the preferred medium for isolating oneself was the text.

Reading was quickly established as a favored activity of rail travel. The connections that were initially established between railway lines and newspaper distribution made it natural that newspapers should be readily available and, in fact, aggressively touted at railway stations. (Nineteenth-century cartoons frequently show newsboys thrusting papers and periodicals in the windows of departing trains.)[8] With the establishment of the first railway bookstall concession in 1841, a market was established for the sale of suitable reading materials. Many critics have credited the railways with a general expansion in recreational reading during this period, as people found themselves buying books during idle moments at the railway station and then—theoretically—perusing them on the train.[9] Guidebooks and popular novels initially dominated railway bookstalls, but a number of publishers soon established special cheap editions of more reputable works. The establishment of "Routledge's Railway Library," "Bentley's Railroad Library," "Murray's Railway Reading," and "Longman's Travellers' Library" made a mark on the publishing patterns of the day, creating a competitive market for good but inexpensive literature. Schivelbusch notes that an examination of typical offerings suggests that "the reading public is almost exclusively bourgeois." In fact, he suggests, "reading while traveling is an exclusively bourgeois occupation," one that does not appeal to the "less privileged strata" in the large, uncompartmentalized third- and fourth-class carriages (69).

Railway reading was a highly interiorized and even self-referential experience. Although reading was an activity undertaken in order to distract one from a tedious journey, the journey itself was an organizing principle behind many works of railway literature. Among the most popular formats for books designed with railway readers in mind was the collection of railway-related tales, jokes, anecdotes, and inspirational stories. Even the authors of religious tracts attempted to capitalize on the popularity of railway reading with collections like *Reading for the Railroad: Being Interesting and Instructive Selections from various Christian Authors* (1848) and *Railway Incidents* (1859), a collection of evangelical tracts describing spiritually significant experiences on rail journeys. In many of these essays and short stories, railway terms are applied to religious issues, and metaphors like "the railway of life" are extended to improbable lengths. Many aspects of rail travel—the inevitability of one's destination, the random assortment of fellow passengers who share one's journey, the suddenness with which disaster can strike—seemed to lend themselves to religious allegory. The railway journey could be a narrative unto itself.

Richard Pike's 1884 collection of miscellaneous pieces, *Railway Adventures and Anecdotes: Extending Over More than Fifty Years*, includes praise for the development of railway bookstalls dating back several decades. One writer connected the longer works of literature that became available at stations with the increased length of the journeys themselves: "As the iron lengthened, and as cities remote from each other were brought closer, the time spent in the railway carriage extended, travellers multiplied, and the newspaper ceased to be sufficient for the journey" (Pike, 131). An 1851 newspaper clipping cited by Pike also praises railway bookstalls, lamenting, "How many hours are wasted at railway stations by people well to do in the world, with a taste for books but no time to read advertisements or to drop in at a bookseller's to see what is new?" (Pike, 132). The key dimension in this modern dilemma, it seems, is time: paradoxically, the person who is so busy he cannot even read the advertisements for books is also the person who has time to kill at the railway station. The job of railway literature, it seems, is to adapt itself to the specific slot of time available.

The growing fear that this new technology was having an effect on people's reading habits is reflected in an anonymous 1849 article entitled "Railway Literature" in which the author complains that "the headlong bustle and the toil of life . . . leave men small leisure save to skim the surface of books." The pandering of writers to this limited attention span has led to "a quantity of literature, if literature it can be called, fit for little else, save to be read in a railway carriage or steamboat" ("Railway Literature," 280). The traveller is unable to avoid buying one or two of the miscellaneous works that are thrust upon him, "which, having stuffed into his pocket, he will probably think of no more, until, arrived at his journey's end, the advent of some rainy day or idle evening may tempt him to explore their mysteries" (280), at which point he is likely to be disappointed. This description presents what seems a recurrent image of the harassed traveller who feels obligated to buy something to read, but somehow ends up not reading it. The railway creates a pressure for productivity that travellers are unable to avoid.

We may see an anticipation of contemporary claims about how technology contributes to diminished attention spans in the frequent suggestion that the Victorian public was losing its capacity to digest meaningful literature. One writer suggests that it is absurd to imagine that anyone could read anything of substance while engaged in railway travel. He marvels at the expectation: "Never did I suppose it possible for I don't know how many intelligent publishers to commence I can't say how many libraries, for persons to read while travelling by railway!" (483). The title of his article, "Railway Reading," is exposed as an oxymoron: "I defy—and this, I beg to say, forms the principal argument of my paper—I defy the most constant of all 'constant readers' to make either head or tail of even a child's primer while in a travelling railway carriage" (483). To prove his point, he presents an anecdote about a traveller who more or less involuntarily finds himself trying to read *Tristram Shandy* on a train. This traveller, Allen assures us, was not much of a reader, in fact "had been known to say that he had never read a book throughout since he left school." But "seeing the book-stall, and being reminded of the many, many times he had seen the words 'Railway Reading' among advertisements that had recently come his way," he thinks to himself, "'I shall find my journey long . . . I have a good mind to buy a book to wear away the time'" (484). Allen amusingly alternates impressions of the journey with lines from *Tristram Shandy* in order to simulate the effect on the reader's mind of attempting to assimilate Sterne's elliptical prose while also listening to loud engine noises and the conversations of other passengers. The above passage emphasizes the traveller's susceptibility to advertising, the way in which his train of thought replays what he has been told until he hypnotically performs the recommended action. This association of even the benign presence of unquestionably "good" literature with mindless consumerism suggests the extent to which the railway was seen as implicated in the emergence of a new and potentially threatening commercial culture. If railway travel could force an indifferent reader to attempt *Tristram Shandy*, anything was possible.

The sense that modern media might prove dangerously absorbing is reflected in the satiric association of railway reading with a "modern" taste in literature in Elizabeth Gaskell's *Cranford* (1853). The book's opening chapter dwells at length on a dispute between Miss Jenkyns and Captain Brown that arises when he praises the writing of "Boz," whom she considers a vulgar upstart not to be compared with her favorite, Dr. Johnson. Duelling passages are read aloud without either reader abandoning their preference, and their friendship is severely strained by this difference of opinion. Soon after, Captain Brown is killed in a railway accident. He is sitting by the tracks, absorbed in a book, when his attention is belatedly caught by a child who has wandered into a train's path, and he dies in the act of saving her. When Miss Jenkyns reads in the newspaper account that "'the gallant gentleman was deeply engaged in a number of 'Pickwick,' which he had just received,'" she sighs sadly, "'poor, dear, infatuated man!'" (chap. 2: 21). He has paid a high price for his plebeian tastes.

Once reading on a train had been mastered, it was a small step to a further enhancement of productivity: writing. Railway travellers were amazed to find that the motion was smooth enough to permit writing, if one were properly equipped. Of course, the indefatigable traveller Anthony Trollope wrote many of his novels, beginning with *Barchester Towers*, while riding on the train. It is difficult to see any effect on his prose; given his famous self-discipline about writing, one imagines that the strictly delimited time frame of a journey exactly suited his usual writing habits, and that he may have produced his novels according to a formula of words-per-milepost. In any case, *Barchester Towers* was written at approximately five times the speed of its predecessor, *The Warden* (Hall, 145). A number of Victorian diaries and letters casually mention that they have been written in the course of a railway journey. Some accounts make little mention of the journey itself and sound much like any other letter or entry; others, particularly those written when railways were still a novelty, attempt to capture the experience of the writer. A journal entry written by Elizabeth King (sister of William Thompson, Lord Kelvin) in May 1839, records a trip from Liverpool to London.

> Long stop at Warrington, with steam puffing loudly; afterwards undulating country. Now we pass through a deep cutting—now a tunnel! Now trees flying past! A pretty country—a canal—across a valley; rushing at the rate of thirty-three miles an hour on an embankment high above the surrounding country— Father holding his watch in hand marking speed by the mile-posts. Now run-

Fig 7. "The Queen's Return from the Highlands: Her Majesty Crossing Tay Bridge, Dundee." *Illustrated London News*, 1879. Reprinted courtesy of the Mary Evans Picture Library.

ning over a tedious, tame district—level and bleak . . . Now a lovely little blue
hill far away in Derbyshire! . . . Going at a tremendous rate—no less than thirty-
six miles an hour! (Jennings 209)

The constant repetition of "now" emphasizes the rapidity with which the scene
changes, and the writer's desperate attempt at a real-time record of her experience is apparent in the breathless quality of her prose. Robert Louis Stevenson
not only wrote about trains in a number of his poems and stories, he wrote on
trains as well. One letter is dated "Train between Edinburgh and Chester, 8
August 1874," and begins, "My father and mother reading. I think I shall talk
to you for a moment or two." The letter combines more general musings with
comments on the scenery and on the journey itself. At one point, Stevenson describes the "combination of lowland and highland beauties" in terms that show
his appreciation of the distant, structured view a train window can provide:
"The outline of the blue hills is broken by the outline of many tumultuous tree-
clumps; and the broad spaces of moorland are balanced by a network of deep
hedgerows that might rival Suffolk, in the foreground." However, he immediately goes on to complain, "How a railway journey shakes and discomposes one,
mind and body! I grow blacker and blacker in humour as the day goes on" (I,
207–9). But however discomposed he may feel, he cannot resist the impulse to
capture his experience on paper.

These efforts to write bespeak not only the desire to use the time productively but a struggle to create some sort of alignment between one's mental universe, and the world rushing by outside the window. This challenge is visible in
a picture from the *Illustrated London News* from 1879, showing Queen Victoria
crossing the ill-fated Tay Bridge (fig. 7).[10] The picture is startlingly modern-
looking both in its foreshortened perspective, which brings the viewer directly
into the picture space, and in the casual way in which the Queen hangs outside
the window of the railway car, looking at the river below. Like many textual representations of railway travel, the picture has an immersive quality that invites
us to go along for the ride.

3. USER'S MANUALS:
THE RAILWAY GUIDE

This effort at mental alignment is made explicit in reading material designed

specifically for the railway traveller: railway guides and handbooks. The railways generated a unique body of texts that sought to fill the perceptual gap created by this disorienting form of travel. Like an "iPad for Dummies" book, these
railway guides were indispensable companions to the potentially intimidating
experience of new technology. Combining scenic description with timetables
and practical advice, railway guides played an important role in making this
new, complicated form of travel accessible. Travellers rapidly came to rely on the
iconic "Bradshaws" to lead them through the maze of connecting and competing
train schedules. The novelty of the railway itself, as a mechanism, also made ex-
planatory information about speeds, inclines, embankment levels, and viaduct
construction a useful addition to many guides. But perhaps the primary role of
the guidebook was to mediate between the insular experience of train travel and
the external world through which the traveller was passing. The idea of reading
about scenery, perhaps at the precise moment one was passing through it, seems
intended to counter the sense of dislocation and alienation from the landscape
that was so prominent a feature of the rail travel experience.

The overall format of railway guides generally resembles that of the river
guidebooks examined in Part Two—they present scenic description and historical background to the places encountered on a specific route. But the tone
and pace of the narrative is quite different. Guides to the Thames generally position themselves in relation to a reader who may consult them in advance of
a journey, or indeed, instead of a journey. As we saw, their rhetoric encourages
the reader to feel a sense of vicarious participation in an experience that may
in fact substitute for their own journey. The relatively slow pace of river travel
ensured that if the reader was literally following along during the actual trip,
there would be plenty of time to absorb both scenery and description. Many of
the Thames books were oversized volumes with elaborate, foldout illustrations,
clearly not meant to be handled on a boat. Railway guides, however, were con-
veniently sized books that seem to assume that they are being read during the
course of the journey. Yet the rapid pace of travel meant that the "objects worthy
of notice" to which our attention is being drawn generally pass by so quickly that
it is difficult to imagine both reading the text and viewing the real sights that
are being described.

One of the very earliest railway guides, a pocket-sized *Freeling's Railway
Companion* for the London to Liverpool, Manchester, and Birmingham line
(1838), explains its purpose to the reader as a hope that "the book will not only
profitably pass away the few hours during which the passenger is passing along
the line, but will be the means of recalling many an interesting historical in-
cident to him, when re-seated in his domestic circle" (Freeling, vi). The triple

recurrence of forms of the word *pass* in this single sentence is an insistent reminder not only of the railway's status as a transitional space, a corridor through which one passes, but of the inescapable passing of time during the journey, time that must be profitably harnessed in some way.

Like the Thames guidebooks examined in Part Two, and the panorama exhibition guides discussed in Part One, railway guides establish a rhetorical fiction that the author and reader are taking a "real time" journey together. They far outrun these other formats, however, in the level of control they appear to exert on the reader's experience. Train guidebooks offer themselves as on-the-spot guides to places and experiences as they present themselves. They project a clear expectation that they will be read not before, not after, not instead of, but *during* the specific journey described, and that the perspective they offer will be adopted by the reader.

The *Railway Companion,* as the title suggests, expects to accompany the passenger every step of the way and promises that information is arranged "so that every object worthy of notice may be easily referred to as the trains pass along, reference being made to each from the mile-post nearest to it." The author has paced his own narrative to suit the journey, evidently, for "notwithstanding the amazing rapidity of transit, the traveller may, by looking to the work a little before he arrives at a particular post, easily obtain the desired view" (v). Desirable views, objects "worthy of notice," have not only been identified in advance, they have been mapped out with great precision. The guide maintains this highly directive stance, offering detailed instructions about what to notice: "Here we will pass under another handsome bridge of three arches. The traveller will observe the mode of laying the rails has been changed" (38); "The traveller will here observe the picturesque appearance of this cutting, arising from the rocks having been left, without trimming, in the form in which they were rent when blasted" (179). The reader is told what to look at, and even what to notice about it. It is perhaps not coincidental that many of these directives refer to aspects of the railway project itself, encouraging the reader to find the arches and cuttings "handsome" and "picturesque."

Similarly, a guide to the South Eastern Railway, written by George Measom (1853), sees itself as having a very specific mission. At one point, Measom admits the temptation to describe a lovely spot in detail, adding apologetically, "but as this is a railway guide—that is, a companion for railway travellers to indicate their whereabouts from one place to another, and tell them of the principal objects of interest," he will have to resist (38). The pace of the journey evidently demands a less leisurely description. Measom's definition of the main function of a railway guide is indicative of the spatial dislocation engendered by rail travel.

The guidebook becomes a kind of GPS system that helps the traveller to track his precise location.

Measom attempts to orient his reader by sketching a detailed scenario and placing the reader within it.

> Behold us now quietly and cozily seated in our carriage; for we have taken good care—and do you, gentle reader and fellow-traveller, always take a similar precaution—*to be in time* . . . .
>
> But now—the carriages begin to move—throb—throb—throb, clack—clack, &c., from presto to prestissimo; and we are convinced we are leaving the station and in earnest commencing our journey . . .
>
> The view . . . from the carriage window, after leaving the station, is very peculiar, looking over chimney-tops and house-roofs, and into streets . . . (11)

From his insistence on punctuality to his present-tense rendering of the motion of "their" train, Measom keeps a tight rein on his "fellow-traveller." An even higher level of control is exhibited in an 1884 guide to the Midland railway, which makes no claims about the joys of railway travel but rather "seeks to beguile the tedium of a long railway journey" with useful information (*Official Guide*, 5). This author give his or her primary objective as "definiteness," promising that "the traveller is never left in doubt as to whether an object to which his attention is directed is on his right or on his left; and where it is not close to the line, but has to be looked for, its distance is approximately indicated." The guide notes helpfully that you will need to reverse "right" and "left" if you are sitting backward; and if you are travelling in the opposite direction, you "will, of course, have to read back to the beginning." In that case, the reader "will do well to sit with his back to the engine, for there will then be no need to reverse the expressions 'right' and 'left'" (6–7). One can imagine the obedient reader shifting seats and riffling backward through the volume in an effort to follow along.

A single guide quickly dominated the market, becoming a brand-name that was synonymous with railway guides. Short stories, essays, and novels affirm its status in their numerous references to the need to buy "a Bradshaw" before embarking on a journey. In *Lady Audley's Secret* (1862), for example, we see that the book forms an important link in the chain of transportation that enables Robert Audley to pursue his investigation. We feel the author's sense of pleasure in the efficiency of her character's movements when Braddon notes, "Robert had consulted a volume of *Bradshaw*, and had discovered that Villebrumeuse lay out of the track of all railway traffic, and was only approachable by diligence from Brussels. The mail for Dover left London Bridge at nine o'clock, and could be

easily caught by Robert and his charge, as the seven o'clock up-train from Audley reached Shoreditch at a quarter past eight" (382–83). And of course Phileas
Fogg consults a Bradshaw in order to begin planning his journey around the
world in eighty days. Bradshaw's dominance was sufficiently well established
to make it a frequent source of satire in *Punch*, which proposed that learning
to read a railway timetable should be offered as part of the regular school cur-
riculum (Freeman, 69).

The format of Bradshaw's volumes changed considerably over the course of
the century, growing larger and adding more information. A number of guidebooks, of varying sizes and formats, some printed monthly and some annu-
ally, appeared under the Bradshaw's imprimatur. In the year 1865, for example, a
"Bradshaw" could be *Bradshaw's Monthly Railway and Steam Navigation Guide
of Great Britain and Ireland; Bradshaw's Threepenny Guide for all the Railways;
Bradshaw's Illustrated Guide and General Hand-Book for Great Britain and Ireland; Bradshaw's Illustrated Sections of Great Britain and Ireland; Bradshaw's Railway Itinerary and General Conveyance Guide to every Town, Village, and Parish
in Great Britain, for 1865; Bradshaw's Railway Manual, Shareholder's Guide, and
Official Directory for 1865* ("Bradshaws," 367–68). There were individual guides
to particular lines that included timetables, descriptions of local sights, and, as
a *Bradshaw's Pocket Handbook to the London, Brighton, and South Coast Railway* promises, "useful particulars in regard to the Company, and to the manage-
ment of its concerns for the public benefit" ("Preface," n.p.). A visitor to London
might purchase *Bradshaw's London Railway Guide, Commercial Companion and
Advertiser*, which contained omnibus routes, steamship departures, lists of popular sights, and, of course, advertisements. The inclusion of a list of "Residences
of Foreign Ambassadors and Consuls" (32) suggests that visitors from abroad
formed an important part of its audience.

The more detailed descriptions of *Bradshaw's Monthly Descriptive Railway
Guide and Illustrated Hand-Book of England, Wales, Scotland, and Ireland* (1857),
however, are addressed specifically to a domestic audience. Though it bills itself as "a travelling companion, not only to Englishmen, but to Foreigners" (v),
its preface focuses on the way that the railways have changed the Englishman's
relationship to his own land, claiming, "The British Traveller of the present
day is, generally speaking, a *much better* informed person." It notes, somewhat
defensively, that "an observant man of business is not necessarily indifferent or
insensible to the picturesque beauties of nature, or to the exquisite scenery with
which a country abounds" (v). While English scenery cannot provide the complete "change of air and locality that refreshes the jaded mind and weary brain of
the overwrought man of business," nevertheless, "the people of England . . . are

now beginning to discover that there are numerous spots on the sea-coast, and the interior of the United Kingdom, deserving of their admiration" (v). It would seem that it is not simply the traveller, or even the "people of England," but the "Englishman," and, more specifically still, the "man of business," perhaps a commuter from the suburbs, who constitutes the imagined audience of this text.

Over time, guidebooks seemed to become more elaborate and regulatory, presenting themselves as necessary interpreters of an increasingly complex system. One commentator, writing in 1866, noted the evolution of the small, six-page "Railway Companion" sold for a shilling into the current volume of 300 pages covering some 8,000 train runs, seeing this as evidence of the "greatness of this peaceful revolution" in transportation ("Bradshaws," 369). But another writer mourns this change, claiming that the newer Bradshaw, with its maps, tables, figures, "keys to his keys, indexes to his indexes," grows "more unwieldy by the hour." He likens it to "a huge panorama, that you spread out on your knees over your railway-rug, and look into wearily and laboriously" ("An Old Guide," 545). The author sees the "good-natured, confiding way in which little instructions are given to travellers" (546) in the old Bradshaw as charmingly quaint, bespeaking a "kindly disposition" toward the reader, whereas the new guides leave him "to follow out columns, or discover that two are to be swallowed up in one, or to trust to the lame guidance of the red figures, which will cast him loose in a thicket of black ones" (547). In fact, the new Bradshaw is symptomatic of the information overload of the age: it offers "a strange symbolical lesson as to the marvellous growth of things earthly in these days of ours, and headlong, tempestuous, five hundred horse-power growth, with which has kept pace the growth of our book, the traveller's bible" (547).

As we have seen, the railway guide offered itself as a very specific text for a very specific purpose. It was intended to be a helpful "companion" to the traveller through a particular stretch of country, generally on a particular railway line, over a well-defined period of time. To call a Bradshaw a "bible" reveals the extent of the railway's world-making powers. The railway spawned an entire industry of related services and products, a mutually reinforcing web of commodities that helped to solidify the central place of the railway in the public consciousness. Dickens describes, in a well-known passage in *Dombey and Son*, the incursion of the railway into a particular neighborhood, and the immediate ubiquity of its presence: "There were railway patterns in its drapers' shops, and railway journals in the windows of its newsmen. There were railway hotels, office-houses, lodging-houses . . . railway plans, maps, views, wrappers, bottles, sandwich-boxes, and time-tables; railway hackney-coaches and cabstands . . . There was even railway time observed in clocks, as if the sun itself had given in" (290). Journals and timetables are equivalent to hotels and sandwich-boxes: they are all part of a vast apparatus that attempted to link the railway to every facet of Victorian life. The railway guide sought to control the traveller's time and consciousness in the same way the railway itself controlled his movements. Like the railway stories that offered coherent narratives structured around the self-enclosed railway journey, railway guides presented a textual, virtual version of the trip that attempted to fill in the invisible space between embarkation and destination.

4. CHAT ROOMS:
THE SOCIAL SPACE OF TRAINS

The sense of control over the reader that is increasingly evident in railway guides mirrors the overall experience of railway travel for most passengers. Travelling by rail was often figured as a complete surrendering of individual agency and control. The precise time of departure and arrival were dictated by the railway company; the precise location of one's seat was dictated by the ticket purchased; the nature of one's travelling companions was dictated by chance. The safety of the journey itself was in question, and the early practice of locking passengers into cars contributed to fears about railway accidents. In addition to reading, the other way in which railway travellers sought to pass the time during their journey was, of course, through conversation with fellow passengers. But this, too, seemed to offer danger to the unwary. Like visitors to Internet chat rooms, railway travellers found themselves in a fluid environment that lacked many of the usual markers of social class and identity.

River travel, as we saw in Part Two, was prized for its partial control over the movements of the traveller, who felt pleasurably relieved from responsibility as he or she drifted slowly up or down the Thames. Rail travel, however, combined a predetermined route with additional aspects of control over the traveller's movements, rendering the overall effect far less relaxing. Many short stories and accounts of railway journeys reveal a strong current of anxiety about entering a space that was so clearly marked "no exit." For many travellers, the experience of rail travel was not defined by the external space covered as much as by the interior space occupied during the journey. Railway cars became the focus of anxieties about personal space, physical danger, and the erosion of class and gender boundaries. While railway guidebooks meticulously covered every inch of the journey, railway narratives, in stark contrast, seldom refer to the actual journey at all. Railway travel was defined as the experience of being shut up in a room with other people. Where the room happened to be going was irrelevant.

In spite of the rhetoric of freedom associated with the railway's opening-up of travel, the accounts of individual travellers often focused on a physically and psychologically intimidating experience of confinement. A controversial early policy of most railways, the locking of all doors while the train was in motion, provoked numerous letters and articles of protest. An 1842 letter to the *Morning Chronicle* criticizing the Great Western Railway not only outlines the physical dangers involved in preventing passengers from exiting in the event of an accident, but also comments on "the effects which [locking the doors] has upon the imagination." The author claims that "a journey comes to be contemplated with horror" when taken with "the knowledge that escape is impossible," and suggests that "the females of the family" in particular are oppressed by their association of rail travel with "abominable tyranny and perilous imprisonment" (Simmons 1951, 201). In an 1840 story by "Miles Ryder," the sensation of entrapment is apparent in the growing unease felt by a group of passengers whose fellow traveller insists on recounting lurid tales of train disasters; their anxiety culminates in one man's horrified realization, "And, by Heaven . . . we are locked in here!" ("Railway Trip," 238–39). While many cartoons and commentaries attest to the unpopularity of this policy, which was eventually discontinued, the strength of this writer's objections are indicative of a more generalized fear of restricted movement that had as much to do with one's fellow passengers as it did with the prospect of a railway disaster.

For most passengers, the most radical change brought about by the railway was not its amazing speed but the necessity for travelling in close contiguity with random strangers from a range of social classes. Unlike American railroad cars, which were filled with rows of front-facing seats, British railway cars were more closely modelled on coaches and were divided into separate carriages holding four, six, eight, or even twelve passengers. A traveller with the appropriate-sized party could reserve an entire "saloon" or "family" carriage, but anyone travelling alone or in a pair would have to take their chances in a shared car. The pleasure of having a carriage to oneself is apparent in a description of one of Robert Audley's train journeys, when, having caught an express leaving Brentwood at three, he "settled himself comfortably in a corner of an empty first-class carriage, coiled up in a couple of huge railway rugs . . . smoking a cigar in mild defiance of the authorities" (Braddon, 143). But such luxury was unusual. Most travellers could expect to share a space small enough to seem to require some mutual acknowledgment or polite attempt at conversation. As Wolfgang Schivelbusch notes, upper-class passengers were likely to be embarrassed by this proximity, and to avoid conversation, while the second- and third-class cars were generally filled with conversation (76).

While railway trains and even some railway stations carefully differentiated the accommodations offered to different classes of passengers (Freeman, 110–11), railway travellers could still expect to encounter a diverse group of people in a railway carriage. A dominant theme in a wide variety of journalistic accounts, short stories, and representations of railway travel in the nineteenth century was the unique opportunity—or threat—of meeting people from all walks of life. This "levelling" tendency of railway travel was often lauded as an indicator of social progress, but stories and anecdotes of railway travel reveal underlying discomfort about this unrestrained mixing. If the Internet is, in Sherry Turkle's words, "a significant social laboratory for experimenting with the constructions and reconstructions of self that characterize postmodern life" (1996, 180), the railway was a similarly experimental space, offering the opportunity for travellers to fashion new identities for themselves in their anonymous interactions with fellow passengers.

The *British Quarterly Review* essay on "Bradshaws" notes that "there is one demand for the safety and comfort of passengers that we hope will be inexorably extorted from all railway companies," which is "some means of enabling passengers to communicate, in cases of emergency, with those in charge of the trains" (408). What, exactly, would constitute such an emergency? According to a supposed "Lord Advocate" quoted in the essay, a traveller "might be shut up with a murderer, a madman, with a drunkard or a villain; he might die of apoplexy, he might have his throat cut" (408). The essay goes on to recount several supposedly well-known examples of assaults on trains. Numerous periodical essays throughout the period make similar points, expressing a particular fear that female passengers will find themselves insulted by male passengers.

Many short stories and humorous accounts of railway travel reflect and exploit this popular suspicion of the unknown fellow passenger. Although the kind of rhetoric seen above focused on the fear of actual physical assault, it also seems to reflect deeper anxieties about the ambiguous social space of a railway carriage, where all passengers are a blank page to each other. Many railway stories and anecdotes are essentially descriptions of elaborate con games in which a credulous passenger is duped by a fellow traveller. In much the same way that late twentieth-century articles about the Internet worried about the dangers of unbridled communication with people of whom you know nothing, nineteenth-century accounts of train travel focus almost obsessively on the dangerous, fascinating, or merely embarrassing consequences of being forced into temporary intimacy with complete strangers. As Eliot notes wryly in *Daniel Deronda*, even strangers, when travelling together by train, "are liable to become excessively confidential" (832).

A surprising number of railway stories and anecdotes seem to boil down to nineteenth-century precursors of the famous Peter Steiner cartoon from the *New Yorker*, "On the internet, nobody knows you're a dog" (July 5, 1993). In an environment that offers no external verification of an individual's social status, the potential for exaggeration, as well as outright deception, is great. The absence of substantiating contexts that might help to identify other passengers is compounded by the concentrated nature of the experience. In the tales told by Charles Lever as "Tilbury Tramp," as well as in other accounts and stories, the special circumstances of the railway journey create a false sense of intimacy that an unwary traveller can mistake for genuine knowledge of his or her companion.

Lever's tales all revolve around mistaken identities or deliberate deceptions by fellow passengers, often involving misrepresentation of social class. "The Coupe of the North Midland" is the story of a man who strikes up a conversation with a gentlemanly looking fellow on the train, who carries luggage labelled "Duke of Devonshire" and freely admits to this identity. This "gentleman" seems educated and well-versed in political questions of the day, and a stimulating conversation ends with the narrator being promised a dinner at the duke's home. Lured by dreams of aristocratic patronage, the narrator presents himself to the baffled and indignant Duke of Devonshire, who throws him out of the house. His gentlemanly fellow traveller was, of course, the Duke's manservant.

Many versions of this story, in which a servant is mistaken for his or her master or mistress, can be found in other rail travel accounts, suggesting that travellers feared the absence of a stable context that would help one to socially place one's fellow passengers. While there certainly are travel stories set on steamships or coaches that also involve questions of status or identity, the more typical problem faced by travellers in these stories is that of knowing the social milieu of one's companions all too well, and finding it difficult to escape either their condescension or their encroachments. As we have seen, in a world in which "everyone goes on the Rhine," there are few surprises on the ship manifest. But the more democratic world of railway travel brought a wider variety of people together, and the difference in fares in the different classes of carriages was not great enough to guarantee that first-class carriages carried only upper-class travellers.

Excursion trains, which were developed primarily to serve working-class and lower-middle-class passengers, exerted a particular fascination by bringing together and making visible an assortment of travellers from widely different backgrounds.[11] The "ethnographic" impulse that James Buzard has documented in nineteenth-century travel writing is evident in many analyses of the excursion train experience. Middle- and upper-class commentators often present themselves as sociologists studying the habits of a different species. Charles Lever notes "the strange and curious views of life presented by railroad travelling," claiming that "a peep into the several carriages of a train is like obtaining a section of society" (110). John Hollingshead writes, "We are all fond of excursion trains, more or less," claiming that, once established, they infected everyone with such a sense of "restless activity" that soon "the whole town was on the move. Barbers, potboys, and milkmen disappeared for a few hours, and came back with strange stories of mountains, lakes, and caverns" (729). The power of the "magic Bronze Horse" acts as a leveller, and now "clerk, shopman, servant, costermonger, or sweep, can cling to the long tail of the fiery steed, and ride roughshod over the laws of time and space" (727).

Hollingshead's itemization of the different workers represented on an excursion train establishes a sense of distance between regular railway travellers like himself and the kind of person now served by the railway. His essay takes the familiar form of a survey of passengers on a supposed train journey: "Let us peep inside one of these excursion trains, going to Dover and back for half-a-crown, and take a few portraits of the travellers as they sit in a row" (730). A similar documentary impulse informs many other accounts that simply describe a cross-section of "typical" passengers, as well as pictorial representations such as the well-known *Illustrated London News* print "Waiting for the Excursion Train."[12]

Not only did the railway bring one into contact with a wider variety of people, the shorter length of most railway trips meant that time spent with one's companions was brief, so that social interactions were inevitably compressed and intensified. The many Victorian stories that focus on the romantic possibilities of this kind of accelerated relationship might almost be contemporary descriptions of Internet dating. They acknowledge that it is exciting to come into contact with new people, but reveal that all too often, people are not what they seem. In Margaret Majendie's "A Railway Journey," a young girl travelling alone for the first time is relieved to be joined at the last minute by an unknown relative, whom she takes for a youthful uncle, but who is in fact her cousin. He maintains his avuncular identity in order to forestall any sense of impropriety in their sharing a carriage alone, and they are able to spend the day chatting and sharing food in a very intimate manner. The supposed "uncle" finally reveals himself, and proposes, at the end of their journey, saying, "Do you know, Edith, I seem to have known you for years! You have shown today every good quality a woman can possibly possess. . . . I should like to go on travelling with you, like this, for ever and ever . . ." (503). By creating a false identity that makes an unknown young man a perfectly acceptable companion for a young girl, the author is able to exploit the romantic potential of the situation without compromising the delicacy of her heroine.

Other stories present a more sinister take on the anonymity of train acquaintanceship. Railway travel made it easier for unescorted females to travel by reducing the need to stay alone at hotels along the way, and several of the "Tilbury Tramp" stories focus on the machinations of scheming females who dupe unwary male travellers. In "The White Lace Bonnet," a traveller describes for his companions an earlier journey in which he encountered an eloping couple, and, moved by their plight, helped them surmount various difficulties and tie the knot. One of his present listeners turns out to be the enraged father of the groom, who reveals that the supposedly genteel young lady had turned out to be a twice-married adventuress without a penny to her name. Far from enjoying a happy life with his blushing bride, the groom ended up paying her 500 pounds to disappear. Another of Lever's stories, "Fast Asleep and Wide Awake," features a bitter narrator who warns a fellow traveller about the wiles of women who travel alone. He had himself been deceived on a long trip by a young lady who exploited his protection and won his heart, but turned out to have a fiancé waiting at the other end of the line. All of these stories evince a contradictory fear of both excessive intimacy and excessive anonymity.

Clearly, the possibility of finding oneself isolated in close proximity with a member of the opposite sex was fraught with tension for both women and men. Many contemporary accounts evince concern on behalf of female travellers who might face male insults in an isolated railway carriage, and by 1845 some railways had established separate "Ladies Only" compartments, though they resisted proposals that provision of such compartments become compulsory. In 1892, *Sala's Journal* was still warning that "something must be done . . . to stamp out the rapidly increasing practice of ladies being insulted and assaulted in railway carriages," noting further that "outrages in first class carriages have not been by any means infrequent" (97). The author makes some elliptical references to Col. Valentine Baker, who was involved in a famous assault case in 1875. In spite of this concern for women, many commentators seemed equally worried about the plight of male travellers who could be victimized by false claims made by female companions. *Punch* argued that if separate compartments were to be provided, women should be required to use them, lest male passengers fall prey to attempts at extortion.[13]

The generalized anxiety about the body that is reflected in these debates about the physical proximity of other passengers found even stronger expression in public concern about railway accidents. Peter Sinnema has shown that while the *Illustrated London News* offered many articles and pictures on railway accidents, the actual interplay between word and image created a "dilution of potential trauma" (116) that prevented reports of such catastrophes from undercutting the journal's positive view of a "pioneering technology" that "further[ed] human dominance over natural obstacles while apparently remaining in harmony with the environment" (131). Victorian fears may seem disproportionate to the actual risks faced, but are certainly explicable when seen in the context of the general loss of individual agency associated with rail travel.

A number of accounts of rail journeys include the author's fears about the possibility of an accident, and many railway anecdotes and short stories focus on acts of heroism or personal tragedies connected with railway accidents. One humorous story features an obnoxious passenger who antagonizes his fellow travellers by recounting gory tales of train accidents in which he has been involved. No one is sorry when a slight accident does occur and he is the only one seriously injured. While the traveller's superior attitude is satirized by the narrator, his prediction that "something will happen to us today" turns out to be true ("Railway Trip," 242). Many of the poems in Alexander Anderson's collection describe the gruesome deaths of railway workers struck down by trains, often in the attempt to save passengers' lives.

Several Victorian novels contain passing references to train disasters that are presented offstage, as past events in the lives of characters, suggesting that they had come to be considered part of the routine fabric of life, like other kinds of misfortune. In Gissing's *New Grub Street*, for example, a down-on-his-luck doctor explains that the source of his decline was the mental breakdown he suffered as a result of losing his wife and child in a rail accident: "One minute I was talking with them . . . my wife was laughing at something I had said; the next, there were two crushed, bleeding bodies at my feet" (443). There, the sudden arbitrariness of the disaster reinforces the novel's relentless emphasis on the difficulty of controlling one's own career and destiny in the face of the larger social forces at work in the increasingly commercialized London of the novel.

The general sense of disembodiment associated with railway travel made the possibility of accidents, and physical injury, even more striking and incongruous. The suddenness of a train crash, the contrast between the pleasant experience of a journey and the unexpected intervention of disaster, seems a key component to the fascination it exerted. A letter writer who complained in 1842 about the locking of railway carriages noted the uniquely shocking nature of a recent accident on the Paris railway: it was "a massacre so sudden, so full of torment—death at the moment of pleasure—death aggravated by all the amazement, fear, and pain which can be condensed into the last moments of existence" (quoted in Simmons 1951, 200).

The railway was seen as having a profound effect on human experience that was symptomatic of many "shocks of the new." Nicholas Daly has traced a connection between the advent of the railways and the development of both sensation drama and sensation fiction, suggesting that the nervousness brought about by the "heightened time-consciousness" of train travellers has its analogue in the frenzied pace of plot developments in sensation fiction, which often depend on a "rapid succession of diverse locations" (473). Daly's argument is consistent with the general trend toward what Ben Singer has called "a *neurological* conception of modernity," a conception that follows the work of Georg Simmel, Siegfried Kracauer, and Walter Benjamin in understanding modernity "in terms of a fundamentally different register of subjective experience, characterized by the physical and perceptual shocks of the modern urban environment" (Singer, 72). The railway stands as a perfect exemplar of this new mode of experience.

Dickens portrayed the railway's disturbing effect upon both individuals and communities as a kind of trauma. Among many references to the railway throughout *Dombey and Son,* three set pieces stand out: the long passage in chapter 20 in which Dombey thinks about his lost son and sees the railway engine as an image of the "remorseless monster, Death" (354); the elaborate description in chapter 15 of "Staggs's Gardens," a neighborhood experiencing "the first shock of a great earthquake" (218), the coming of the railway; and the description of Carker's death on a railway track, in chapter 55. These scenes have received a great deal of attention from critics, individually and collectively. Some see the novel's connection of the railway with death as an indictment of the industrial world, while others argue that this "linkage is subjective and takes place in Dombey's stunted imagination" (Baumgarten, 71). Harland Nelson claims that Dickens's description of Stagg's Gardens emphasizes a "dehumanization of the neighborhood" (50), showing the power of "a great force that turns everything upside down in its passing" (52), while F. S. Schwarzbach sees *Dombey and Son* as demonstrating "Dickens's recognition of the revolutionary social importance of the railway and the developing industrial technology it symbolized," but suggests that the description of Staggs's Gardens displays a very equivocal optimism: "The railway universe that replaces Staggs's Gardens may be for the best after all—perhaps" (113).

In his famous postscript to *Our Mutual Friend,* Dickens refers to his own experience in the Staplehurst accident on the South Eastern Railway in 1865.

He does not describe the accident but instead uses it to humorously substantiate the reality of his characters, who he claims to have rescued from the wreck. Dickens did in fact reenter his precariously dangling railway carriage to retrieve his manuscript of *Our Mutual Friend,* but his more personal account of the accident in a letter to a friend also describes his efforts to free actual fellow passengers from the carriage. By identifying himself as Charles Dickens, he was able to claim the attention of a railway guard and persuade him to give up the key that was needed to unlock the doors of the carriage. He also assisted several dying passengers. He wrote to his friend, "I don't want to be examined at the inquest and I don't want to write about it" (quoted in Simmons 1951, 211).

Jill Matus has analyzed this episode in detail in her essay on "railway trauma," noting that railway accidents were seen as producing a specific and identifiable psychological trauma in survivors, a form of trauma linked to the kind of "overwhelming and unassimilable" events made possible by the material technologies of modernity (414–15).[14] Matus sees reverberations from Dickens's train accident in "The Signalman," one of the *Mugby Junction* stories, which features a signalman whose occasional nightmares about impending train crashes seem to be actual premonitions. The story ends in a sensational manner, with the signalman envisioning the disaster that in fact claims his own life. An 1852 story by Charles B. Henry that also features a prescient railway worker offers a different twist: an escaped embezzler's recurring nightmare of his pursuer arriving on a night train finally turns into reality—and the embezzler uses his position as railway guard to send a false signal that causes the train to crash. These stories fit into a larger pattern in railway stories and anecdotes, what might almost be labelled an entire subgenre of "railway dreams" that are often railway nightmares.

5. GAME OVER: THE RAILWAY JOURNEY AS DREAM AND NIGHTMARE

The discrete experience of a railway journey seemed to lend itself to a narrative structure whereby the journey defines a specific imaginative episode that might be a dream, a nightmare, or, in a frequent pun, a specific "train of thought." The journey becomes a world of its own, with its own rules and logic; nothing is certain except the fact that it will eventually end. Like the fictive world of a video game, the dream world of the journey unfolds on a predetermined path that is not always apparent.

A. K. H. Boyd's "How I Mused in the Railway Train," for example, begins with the sleepy narrator, on an early-morning train, commenting on the dreaminess of the scene before him: "I can hard believe it substantially exists. . . . very often the evidence of sense comes no nearer to producing the solid conviction of reality than does that widely different evidence on which we believe the existence of all that is not material" (146). He extends this analogy further, noting that when you are admiring a landscape at a distance, you cannot "*feel* that the landscape before you was solid reality," and that your belief in the landscape can be verified "no more substantially" than can a belief in "a country beyond the grave" (146). The narrator feels a sense of disassociation between the reality he knows is out there and the reality of his senses, which are not able to fully register the fast-moving landscape.

The frequent use of the railway as a metaphor for life is fully played out in a kind of dream-fantasy by J. A. Froude, "A Siding at a Railway Station" (1879). The story begins with an air of almost sociological concreteness, as Froude describes the various passengers on the train, "numerous and of all ranks and sorts," including commercial travellers, judges, businessmen, idle young gentlemen, a duke and duchess, tourists, and laborers in search of employment. Froude notes their contrasting accommodations, from the Pullman cars and saloon carriages occupied by those at the upper end of the spectrum, to the crowded third-class cars, where "no more consideration was shown [the passengers] than if they had been cattle." Froude comments, however, that the languid and fretful "fine people in the large compartments" seemed to enjoy the journey less than the poorer folk, who seemed good-humored and merry, perhaps because they "had found life go hard with them wherever they had been, and could be as happy in one place as in another." The train itself seems like no place in particular, and the precise geographical space of this journey is indeterminate: Froude says merely that he was travelling by railway, "no matter whence or whither" (622).

When the train is unexpectedly pulled into a siding and everyone forced to alight, matters become no clearer. To repeated enquiries about where they will go and what they will do, the stationmaster replies enigmatically, "'You will see'" (624). Each person is called forward by an examiner to claim his or her personal belongings, but their boxes, when opened, prove to contain not clothes or money but "simply samples of the work which he had done in his life," which are also carefully itemized in an account book, along with the number of days worked (625). In addition, the account book lists each passenger's actions—"his affection for his parents, or his wife and children, his self-denials, his chari-ties . . . or, it might be, ugly catalogues of sins and oaths and drunkenness and brutality" (625).

Froude describes in detail the evaluation of what each person has contrib-uted and how "unprofitable" most of the passengers turned out to have been: "speculators who had done nothing but handle money which had clung to their fingers in passing through them, divines who had preached a morality which they did not practise. . . . distinguished pleaders who had defeated justice while they established points of law, writers of books upon subjects of which they knew enough to mislead their readers . . ." (627). Unlike the workers whose products are a testament to their lives' value, these passengers are defined by absences and negative accomplishments—things they have failed to do.

In the end, the most dishonest and unproductive passengers are sent back to continue their journeys, amid many promises that they will do better in the future. Those who remain are examined closely and encouraged to see the po-tential for improvement in their own lives. Froude himself is found "unworthy" but "not wholly unworthy," and so is not assigned a different existence to live out but is permitted to resume his journey. As we have seen, the railway serves as neutral territory, a transitional space in which individuals appear stripped of their usual contexts and identities. Here, that space becomes a blank page upon which Froude can write an allegory that naturalizes what in another context would seem an artificial circumstance: the chance gathering of a wide array of people from all walks of life.

A theological framework also shapes an anonymous story, "By the Under-ground Railway," from 1886. The narrator, "Jones," finds himself in a railway car-riage with a friend who reveals he has just attended a Positivist service; a curate of Jones's acquaintance (whom he despises); a young lady who has just returned from a service at St. Paul's; a "dissenting minister"; and a "suspicious-looking individual with dirty collar and cuffs," whom Jones determines to keep an eye on (497). This somewhat implausible cast of characters sets the stage for an animated religious dispute. Things get to the point that Jones's friend is accused of "'rank blasphemy, schism, and worse,'" and finally, the narrator describes the entire group being "off on a future life now, at our end of the carriage, going at it hammer and tongs, the curate and all" (499). The narrator maintains an ironic distance, marvelling at the vehemence with which his companions address this "endless question, which will be settled beyond all discussion if people would only have the manners to wait until their turn comes."

But when an "appalling crash" is followed by screams and sounds of misery, the narrator suddenly finds himself "lying in a brilliant light, somewhere, I don't know where" (500). The scene includes not only a flowered plain and choirs of angels, but the dissenting parson, beaming away. Jones and his friend find that they don't like the look of heaven, with its bland, undifferentiated pleasures. An angel takes pity on them and sends back these "poor souls," "unhappy in Heaven, still bound to earth, mortals amidst immortality" (507).

The tale initially hints at a concrete political explanation for the crash. The narrator of this 1886 story mentions early on that it was "a season of explosions," referring presumably to the dramatic increase in anarchist activity, particularly involving dynamite, in London in the 1880s. Following close upon a series of explosions in 1884, including one at Victoria Station that coincided with the discovery of "infernal machines" at Charing-Cross and Paddington Stations (Melchiori, 13–14), the year 1885 saw what Barbara Melchiori has called "the great day of the dynamitards": on January 24, Fenian activists caused explosions at Westminster Hall, in the Houses of Parliament, and at the Tower of London. Many people were injured, and these coordinated attacks "spread panic throughout London" (21). It is perhaps not surprising, then, that the narrator of "On the Underground Railway" is initially suspicious of a shabby-looking man on the train and is determined to keep an eye on him. When he wakes up after the crash, the narrator assumes that the man he spotted had tried to blow up the train, but he is told it was "only a collision," in which two people were killed (508). Thus what had been presented as a possible terrorist attack turns out to be a routine railway disaster.

Here, as in Froude's piece, the railway journey is primarily a hook upon which the author hangs his or her depiction of contemporary attitudes toward religious doctrine, but the choice of venue seems to exploit the common metaphoric association of a railway journey with "the journey of life." The transitional space of the railway trip is used as an image of the ultimate waiting station. This allegorical use of railways is consistent both with the "infernal" verbal imagery that was, as we have seen, applied to trains from the very beginning, and with a pictorial trope that associated the vast spaces of railway architecture, and the power of the trains themselves, with visions of heaven and hell. Michael Freeman has noted the use of train images in apocalyptic paintings by John Martin, such as *The Last Judgment*. The long-standing tradition of allegorizing life's journey as an actual trip takes on an additional resonance when the route is no longer a path or road but a railway track. The train journey represents a predetermined path, but one shaped by man as well as by God.

An early, anonymous story entitled "Nightmare on the Rails" (1846) also turns the neutral space of a train journey into the unreal space of a nightmare. In this tale, a single passenger on a specially commissioned train finds that his engine driver is a madman, deranged by the suicide of the woman he loved. The train itself bounds along the rails "like a mad thing" (524), and the narrator gives a vivid description of the blurring of the scenery as the train's speed increases to dangerous levels.

> The hedges of the wayside flew by in a long, dusky line, which might have been shrubs, or a stone wall, or wooden palings.... The white poles which supported the wires of the electric telegraph flew by as though defiling in rapid procession; bridges loomed a moment before us like dark stripes culling the sky, and then, with a steam shriek and a bound, were left behind. (523–24)

The train has become a "steam monster" that "seemed instinct with life" (524), and the engine driver seems like a demon as he mutters to himself and stokes the fires faster and faster. The passenger describes the "thrill of horror" that goes through him as he realizes that they are "going at a pace to which all others that [he] had ever travelled were child's play." The most frightening aspect of the experience is the recognition that "the madman had the mastery" (525). The driver seems proud of his accomplishment, boasting that they are flying "faster than ever mortal man travelled since the world was a world," faster than "spirits" (525). Just as the narrator sees that they are about to crash into a station, he awakes with a start, to find that he has fallen asleep while waiting for his train. The insane pleasure of the "maniac" engine-driver in the idea of travelling faster than any man before him seems intended to suggest that this kind of hubris borders on lunacy. And yet the madman's actual statements use perfectly conventional images to express commonly held ideas, and so are hardly indicative of a certifiable disorder.

Not surprisingly, perhaps, the story ends when the expected crash is interrupted by a voice calling, "Tickets, please!" and the narrator realizes with relief that it was only a "railway nightmare" (528). The imagined experience seems to express a fear of surrendering control to a "monster" whose uncanny speed presents an image of impending death. The jaded professionalism of the narrator's tone at the opening of the story is transformed into a frantic horror that also embodies a frisson of pleasure. The complicated response of the narrator to this imagined situation mirrors the mixed feelings of the travelling public as a whole, which alternated between pride in the amazing speed of rail travel and terror at the physical risks it presented.

In addition to a fear of speed and, by extension, accidents, the fear of personal contact with unsavory fellow travellers forms the basis for "A Night in a First-Class Railway Carriage," an anonymous story that appeared in *Dublin*

University Magazine in 1867. It is written from the point of view of a young
bride on a wedding tour with her husband. She is trapped in an express train
to Marseilles with a woman who immediately makes her nervous. The narrator
establishes herself as a somewhat anxious sort in her description of the claus-
trophobic effect of the closed carriage, and the way in which her companion's
"cat-like watch" had "an irritating effect upon [her] nerves."

> I was in that excited state of mind when trifles assume an unnatural importance,
> and, although to some it may seem almost laughable, yet I am sure a nervous
> reader will understand me when I say that the unbroken stillness of the carriage,
> the regular breathing of my husband, the unceasing swing, swing of the lamp
> above my head, and above all, the presence of our fellow passenger in the corner,
> became to me perfectly intolerable. (420)

She falls fitfully to sleep and dreams that she sees the woman slithering along
the floor of the carriage toward her. Her shriek when she awakes arouses the
sympathy of her fellow traveller, who suggests, "after consulting with great
attention the Railway Guide," that as the train is scheduled to stop for a full
twenty minutes the husband should go fetch some coffee for his wife (420). The
bride's worst fears are confirmed when the train immediately leaves, with the
two women alone in the carriage.

The narrator's description of the various threats and actions of her companion seem to confirm her assessment of her as a "dreadful mad woman" (421).
The narrator once again falls asleep and dreams that she is "in prison, and under the sentence for death," but when she awakens, feigns sleep and catches her
companion in the act of assuming a disguise: "I see it all. Our companion has
been a man disguised as a woman. Overcome with horror, I gasp in very agony
of mind" (422). The narrator's characteristic borderline state, between sleep and
wakefulness, has in fact been revelatory. Her fear of this woman is justified by
her exposure as a man; a man, moreover, who steals her husband's clothes and
papers and expresses a desire to assume his identity and continue to travel with
her.

The constant inversions of dream and reality in this story culminate in
an ambiguous ending. When they alight at the station, the lady utters a "wild,
piercing shriek" that attracts attention, and her supposed abductor explains that
he is a doctor who noted the strange state of a lady whose "nerves are terribly
shaken" and has been "fancying all kinds of delusions." He disappears, and she
lapses into a "brain fever" that leaves her unconscious for many weeks. Her tact-

ful relatives never allude to these events, but her husband, she says, "sometimes teases me by saying he thinks the man was right and the whole thing a *delusion*" (423). The story is thus recast as the possible fantasy of a hysteric, with the kidnapped bride becoming an Adela Quested whose accidental confinement with a man in close quarters triggers a kind of sexual hysteria. Or is she the heroine of "The Yellow Wallpaper," with a husband who is blandly indifferent to her own subjective reality? In any case, the railway carriage provides the setting for a cautionary tale in which women travellers are taught that the corollary of this more mixed, interactive form of travel is the possibility that one's worst nightmares will be realized. The generalized fear of encountering strangers, and in particular, strangers of the opposite sex, is embodied in a tale that positions itself somewhere along the spectrum between fantasy, nightmare, and reality. The socially ambiguous space of the railway train seems to generate equally ambiguous psychological states and experiences. The railway traveller, poised uncertainly somewhere between here and there, turned his or her attention inward to fill the undefined space of the railway car with his or her own imagination.

6. THE MATRIX: RAILWAY JUNCTIONS AS NON-SPACES

Railway stations, particularly at major junctions, were a favorite subject of both verbal and pictorial representation, for they seemed to emblematize the connective power of the railway network. While it was understood that a major benefit of railway expansion was the opportunity it provided for wider circulation of goods, it was the circulation of people that caught the public imagination. Michael Freeman has pointed out that prints and paintings such as L. J. Cranstone's *Waiting at the Station* (1850), F. B. Barwell's *Parting Words* (1859), George Earl's *Going North, King's Cross Station* (1893), and, most famously, W. P. Frith's depiction of Paddington, *The Railway Station* (1863) conveyed "the measure of railway stations as hives of human activity" (237). Such scenes combined a wide range of social types with an emphasis on the personal dramas inherent in the partings and greetings that took place. In written accounts, too, the image of the junction emphasizes the capacity of the railway to bring together an assortment of people from a wide variety of places. The station forms a kind of nexus that seems to draw energy from the constant activity of drawing people in and spinning them out again.

Railway stations quickly developed their own identities as meeting places, often attracting people "for other purposes than travelling," according to one account. In addition to serving as "a lovers' trysting-place," they also performed an important function in providing a convenient, centrally located meeting place for people to "conduct business on the cheap" ("Railway Stations," 306). This author's claim that "every class of people make appointments at railway-stations" (306) is borne out by the suggestion of Marion Yule, in *New Grub Street,* that an editor who has missed her father at home might arrange to meet him before his departure: "He might just call, or even see you at the railway station?" (Gissing, 75). The Oliphant story mentioned above, "The Railway Junction," describes the junction as kind of "limbo," and many other writers echo this sense of it as a transitional space that merely holds people in suspension.

Jerome K. Jerome famously satirized the confusion and bustle of a major railway terminus in his description of Waterloo, where he and his friends try unsuccessfully to find their train. Asking is no help: "Of course nobody knew; nobody at Waterloo ever does know where a train is going to start from, or where a train when it does start is going to, or anything about it" (40). When they find an engine-driver who seems unsure of his assigned destination, they offer him half a crown to become the 11.05 for Kingston: "'Nobody will ever know, on this line,' we said, 'what you are, or where you're going. You know the way, you slip off quietly and go to Kingston'" (41). Jerome's facetious description reinforces the image of a system beyond individual control by imagining the impossible: a human response to a human appeal. Destination is almost irrelevant; all one can say is that trains come and go, forming a pattern Jerome finds indecipherable.

By contrast, Trollope's description of the mythical Tenway Junction in *The Prime Minister* also emphasizes the confusion of the scene but implies that there is an inner logic to the mechanism that is not visible to the individual traveller. The junction has "direct communication with every other line in and out of London," like a kind of central switchboard, and while it seems impossible to the traveller to imagine that "the best trained engine should know its own line," trains "flash" in and out like lightning, each landing in its appointed place. The whole scene is "quite unintelligible to the uninitiated," but experienced travellers finally come to recognize that "over all this apparent chaos there is presiding a great genius of order" (II: 191–92).

The railway junction is, like the cyberspace matrix imagined by William Gibson, a nexus of technological order and human desire. The network of predetermined routes that pass through it represent the opportunities and constraints of modernity. *Mugby Junction*, a collection of short stories by several authors that first appeared in the Extra Christmas Number of *All the Year Round* in 1866, contains several pieces by Dickens that focus on the junction as an image of the many kinds of crossroads one encounters in life. The idea of the station as a transitional passage, a non-space, is exemplified by the sobriquet bestowed upon the station's most regular customer by the workers who see him every day: "the gentleman for Nowhere." He comes to the station but never leaves it, because he is paralyzed by indecision about which of the many "iron roads" (487) to take. He asks himself, "Where shall I go next?" and thinks, "I can go anywhere from here." But he finds that "there were so many lines," he must spend some time getting to know the junction in order to decide if he "like[s] the look of one Line better than another" (483). The ability to go "anywhere" translates into a desire to go nowhere, because all roads are alike to him. N. Katharine Hayles has categorized virtual reality technologies as "phenomena that foreground pattern and randomness and make presence and absence seem irrelevant" (26). The railway experience, too, highlights the randomness of a body's physical presence in a world where one location can be so quickly exchanged for another.

The paralysis of the "gentleman for Nowhere" is paralleled by the immobility of Phoebe, the invalid daughter of a railway worker who enjoys looking out at the scenic junction from her bed, claiming that watching the "threads of railway, with their puffs of smoke . . . makes it so lively" for her. Surprisingly, she is not envious of the travellers: "I think of the number of people who *can* go where they wish, on their business, or their pleasure; I remember that the puffs make signs to me that they are actually going while I look" (490). Though unable to move herself, she is cheered by the sense of mobility, freedom, and choice associated with the junction, where people can go anywhere they wish. When the gentleman comes to know Phoebe well enough to give her a present, she asks him which line he travelled on to buy it, and then tells him to take that road again, because it has become so special to her. So, finally, "the gentleman for Nowhere took a ticket for Somewhere," having been taught how formerly interchangeable places can acquire a distinct value through personal associations. This outcome suggests that Dickens sees some possibility of humanizing even the vast, mechanized world of the railway, and turning its non-spaces and nowherelands into real places. And as we will see, the "nowhere" of the network can provide a unique and valuable vantage point. George Levine suggests that in Victorian narratives, detachment is an important precondition for discerning an authentic reality, and the "best way to acquire knowledge is to be nowhere," to be positioned, as reader, outside the story (149). In the next section, we will see that the railway network represents the possibility of being nowhere, and thus accessing information everywhere.

7. WORLD WIDE WEB:
INFORMATION NETWORKS IN
SHERLOCK HOLMES AND *DRACULA*

By the end of the century, novelists would use the railway as both example of, and metaphor for, the increasing interrelatedness and complexity of life, particularly urban life, and the endless pressure for improved communication. Although the development of the railway preceded that of the telegraph, the two modes of technology expanded in tandem within the country, with railway lines being primary telegraph routes. In literature, the two are often thematically linked, showing that the capacity to transmit information rapidly was in many ways as important as the capacity to transport oneself bodily from place to place. Indeed, rail travel in late nineteenth-century fiction is often figured not as a physical activity but as a mode of communication, a way of sending words or information over long distances.

There is a surprising sense of disembodiment to many fictional representations of the railway. Though there is, as Jill Matus demonstrates, an important strain of commentary on railway accidents that reveals a deep anxiety about the corporeal dangers of the railway, very little is said about the ordinary physical experience of railway travel, or the visual experience of landscape during a railway journey. Instead, the emphasis is on the subjective experience of the train traveller, who is likely to be reading, talking with a companion, or even, as we see in *Dracula*, writing the very text that records the journey. We saw earlier that railway guides constantly negotiated the space between providing essential information and creating an information overload. Complaints about the "exfoliation" of Bradshaw ("An Old Guide," 547) reflect a recognition that the untrammelled growth of railways was closely connected to increased speed in the circulation of news and other forms of information.

This improved or accelerated circulation of information had a crucial effect on business practices and also on social life. Tom Standage claims that "the information supplied by the telegraph was like a drug to businessmen, who swiftly became addicted. In combination with the railways, which could move goods quickly from one place to another, the rapid supply of information dramatically changed the way in which business was done" (156). The two technologies were seen as inextricably linked. By the mid-1840s, "electric telegraphy was well on the way to being established as a commonplace feature of the railways" (Morus, 367), being used primarily to signal the movements of railway apparatus up and down the line. The telegraph provided, according to Iwan Rhys Morus, "a 'birds eye view' that, by allowing the entire railway system to be seen as a whole, could allow the reliable regulation of its various components," improving safety and efficiency (364).

The concept of circulation has been recognized as a central metaphor in nineteenth-century England, and many critics have noted what Schivelbusch called the "biologization of social processes and institutions" that is reflected in the frequent use of circulatory metaphors to describe metropolitan life and the industrial economy in general (Schivelbusch, 187). Alexander Welsh has explored the prevalence of organic metaphors in descriptions of London's networks of railway lines, sewer lines, and communication systems, which seem to imply that a healthy civic body is one in which things flow in a free and fluid manner. Richard Menke suggests that in *Middlemarch* the idea of the web or network serves to link "the natural structures of bodies to technological structures for communication" (15). Others have linked this organicist vision of the nation with an emphasis on the disease and contagion that threaten to undermine the health of the body politic.[15] But it is important to note that references to the circulation of information in particular are often mechanical, rather than organic. There seemed to be some understanding that communication of information, ideas, and decisions between the far-flung places that now constituted the British Empire would require technological intervention.

The railroad presented a powerful image for this new circulation of information.[16] Its capacity to transport passengers, physical bodies, at a speed that matched or exceeded the speed of written communication made it possible to conceive of individuals as links in a chain of information. Richard Menke has suggested that the representation of telegraphy in nineteenth-century fiction shows that "fiction both embodied information and treated the body as an informatic text" (98). In fact, one of the commonest uses of the telegraph was initially to track the movements of people. While it is certainly the case that timely telegraphic conveyance of stock market information, for example, had an important effect on business, it is clear that a central role of the telegraph in the popular imagination was to locate people in space and time. Tom Standage repeats the story that Samuel Morse's invention of the telegraph supposedly derived in part from his personal experience of learning of his wife's illness too late to reach her deathbed, and many early commentators emphasized the power of the telegraph to convey personal or family news.

Queen Victoria and Prince Albert early formed the habit of telegraphing their arrival to each other when travelling separately. When Prince Albert travelled to York for an agricultural meeting, the newspaper reported, the queen was notified within ten minutes of his arrival (Salt, 103). When the queen was confronted by a man with a gun at Windsor in 1882, she immediately telegraphed all of her family members and close friends to let them know that she was fine (Melchiori, 11). The telegraph also allowed the queen's actions to be tracked publicly; when her son Alfred was born in 1844, the news was instantly telegraphed from Windsor to London.

Late nineteenth-century novels contain frequent references to telegrams sent to announce an impending arrival, and Conan Doyle's stories are full of references to Holmes telegraphing Watson, Lestrade, or others to let them know on which train they should expect him. In *Dracula*, flurries of telegrams fly back and forth between Jonathan Harker and his comrades. Sometimes these telegrams include urgent updates or respond to an emergency, but just as often they are sent for mere convenience. At the beginning of chapter XVII, for example, Mina telegraphs Van Helsing to say that she is coming by train with "important news," Van Helsing suggests that they "telegraph her *en route,* so that she may be prepared" to be met at the station, and Dr. Seward telegraphs his housekeeper to have rooms prepared for Mrs. Harker (261–62). Like modern travellers calling from their cell phones, Victorian travellers seem often to have telegraphed for the sheer pleasure of being able to say where they were and when they would be home.

The telegraph could also be used to overcome the railway's speed advantage by tracking passengers who did not want to be found. Standage and others have noted that easier apprehension of criminals was one of the first benefits noted by early proponents of the telegraph, and it received a great deal of free publicity when it played a pivotal role in several well-known criminal cases. The use of the Great Western telegraph in 1842 to capture John Tawell for the murder in Slough of his former mistress was highly touted in the press (Morus, 367), a pattern that would be repeated when the wireless was famously instrumental in capturing the murderer Crippen in 1910 (Early).[17] These examples of new information technologies being used in the service of law and order are mirrored in the connection between the telegraph and other forms of surveillance and detection in a number of late Victorian texts, most notably the Sherlock Holmes stories.[18]

Railways play a pivotal role in a number of nineteenth-century novels by serving as conduits of information. Casual or recreational travel by rail is seldom depicted; instead, the railway enables characters to move about quickly in search of crucial information and is thus integral to the development of genres that rely heavily on suspense. As Nicholas Daly has pointed out, the sensation novel is "the first subgenre in which a Bradshaw's railway schedule and a watch become necessary to the principal characters."[19] In *Lady Audley's Secret*, for example, Robert Audley takes a train ride that is one of many train rides, telegraphic messages, and letters that form part of his busy investigation into the supposed death of his friend. Braddon's description emphasizes the way in which his experience of the journey is conditioned by his efforts to make sense of a puzzling situation.

> Within an hour of receipt of this message Mr. Audley arrived at the King's Cross station, and took his ticket for Wildernsea by an express train that started at a quarter before two.
>
> The shrieking engine bore him on the dreary northward journey, whirling him over desert wastes of flat meadow-land and bare corn-fields, faintly tinted with fresh sprouting green. This northern road was strange and unfamiliar ... and the wide expanse of the wintry landscape chilled him by its aspect of bare loneliness. The knowledge of the purpose of his journey blighted every object upon which his absent glances fixed themselves for a moment; only to wander wearily away; only to turn inwards upon that far darker picture always presenting itself to his anxious mind. (242)

Landscapes that mirror a character's innermost thoughts are as old as fiction itself, of course, but this passage is noteworthy in its interplay between Audley's harried mental state and the rapid, fragmentary nature of the scene that surrounds him. The receipt of a telegram propels Audley into immediate action, but he finds himself acting before he has had time to assimilate the significance of the information he has received. He is passively borne over "unfamiliar" landscape but has no time to become familiar with it; his "absent" glance lights on objects for a moment before wandering away. The description seems to locate this failure of attention in Audley, whose anxiety has "blighted" every thing he sees, but it also seems as if the unfixable vastness of the landscape that whirls past him augments his sense of powerlessness. His journey continues with a transfer at a station where he is "led, bewildered and half asleep, to another train," from which he alights in a state of complete disorientation: "the train swept on to gayer scenes before the barrister had time to collect his scattered senses, or to pick up the portmanteau" (242). The railway journey both represents and contributes to a sense of instability that results from Audley's information overload.

The railway is also associated with problematic communication between individuals in *Middlemarch*. Among the reforms that are a source of conflict in this small provincial town, the coming of the railway stands as an image of the inevitability of change. As Caleb Garth pragmatically tells a group of angry countrymen, it "will be made whether you like it or not" (559). The unstoppability of a train that moves along a fixed track makes it an apt image for the inevitable collision between the inflexible perspectives of Rosamond and Lydgate. Their growing estrangement is described starkly as a "total missing of each other's mental track" (587). Rosamond, we are told, was very quick to see "causes and effects which lay within the track of her own tastes and interests" (588), but she is utterly incapable of deviating from that path. On the other hand, Rosamond's final conversation with Dorothea, which temporarily evokes in her some consciousness outside of her own needs, is described in terms that seem to subtly reflect the language applied to railways: under the influence of Dorothea's emotion, she is "hurried along in a new movement which gave all things some new, awful, undefined aspect" (797). The railway seems to represent a current of feeling or line of communication between individuals that is part of the network of relations or web of community that forms the backbone of human society in the novel. Like the "centres of self" which we all occupy, the tracks of our accustomed views and interests lie ahead of us, shaping our path, and to switch from one track to another requires great effort.

Conan Doyle's Sherlock Holmes stories have solidified a popular image of 1890s London that tends to evoke hansom cabs as the primary means of transportation. In fact, Holmes uses every possible means of transportation at his disposal: hansom cabs, trains, and even occasional boats on the Thames as interchangeable legs on endless journeys around London and the surrounding countryside. Most stories begin with his receiving a telegram, or a visitor, in Baker Street, thus relieving the ever-present threat of boredom that, as Watson notes with resignation, often leads Holmes to cocaine use. When not occupied by a case, Holmes needs a seven-per-cent solution to speed up his life. But when a new problem presents itself, he springs energetically into action, often jumping on the next train out to the suburb where a crime has taken place.

Trains form only one aspect of a vast communication network that has Holmes at its center. Holmes sends many telegrams to points far and near to gather necessary information, and he employs his own cadre of operatives, the boys known as the "Baker Street Irregulars," to act as his eyes and ears in the gathering of information on the streets. He makes a point of cultivating people who are themselves gatherers of information, such as Langdale Pike, a London clubman who "was the receiving-station, as well as the transmitter, for all the gossip of the Metropolis" ("Three Gables," *Case-Book*, 1065). His own brother Mycroft is occasionally useful to him in this capacity. Holmes describes his reclusive brother as a kind of organic computer in the service of the government.

> He has the tidiest and most orderly brain, with the greatest capacity for storing facts, of any man living. . . . The conclusions of every department are passed to him, and he is the central exchange, the clearing-house, which makes out the balance. All other men are specialists, but his specialism is omnipotence. . . . In that great brain of his everything is pigeon-holed, and can be handed out in an instant. ("Bruce-Partington Plans," *Case-Book*, 766)

Laura Otis has described Mycroft as the "nucleus" of an "imperial control center" that seeks to counter threats of contagion to "the national body" (100). The fantasy of centralized information embodied in the description of Mycroft is paradigmatic of the world of the Holmes stories, which present London as a vast network of seemingly unrelated phenomena that turn out to be linked. Holmes describes his nemesis Moriarty as a "foul spider" lurking in the center of a "web" made up of thefts, assaults, and "purposeless outrage" that "could be worked into one connected whole" only by the "man who held the clue"—himself ("The Norwood Builder," *Return*, 137). In fact, Watson's description of Holmes is not so different from Holmes's characterization of his enemy. Watson notes that to Holmes, all places, city and suburb, are alike.

> He loved to lie in the very centre of five millions of people, with his filaments stretching out and running through them, responsive to every little rumour or suspicion of unsolved crime. Appreciation of Nature found no place among his many gifts, and his only change was when he turned his mind from the evil-doer of the town to track down his brother of the country. ("The Cardboard Box," *Adventures*, 307)

Holmes stretches out his tentacles from his nerve center in Baker Street, grabbing people and data from wherever they may be, in an image that once again seems to blend the organic and the technological.

Holmes's sense of his own omniscience is often reflected in the elevated perspective he takes on the world around him, a perspective that evokes the panoramic views of London discussed in Part One. Several train journeys include views like the one Holmes and Watson see from a Portsmouth train. After they pass Clapham Junction, Holmes suddenly remarks, "'It's a very cheering thing to come into London by any of these lines which run high and allow you to look down upon the houses like this.'" Watson is surprised, finding the view "sordid enough," but Holmes calls his attention to "those big, isolated clumps of building rising up above the slates, like brick islands in a lead-coloured sea." When Watson identifies these as "the Board schools," Holmes corrects him: "'Lighthouses, my boy! Beacons of the future! Capsules, with hundreds of bright little seeds in each, out of which will spring the wiser, better England of the future'" ("Naval Treaty," *Adventures*, 420). These Board schools, created by the 1870 Education Act, were often added to already congested areas and thus had to be several stories high (Girouard, 198). From Holmes's bird's-eye perspective, schools can become lighthouses, and he feels confident in his own ability to see not only the present but the future with special insight. The association of trains with progress reinforces the sense of omniscience already generated by the panoramic perspective.

The elevated perspective of cities that was often provided by railway bridges is reflected in illustrations that provided a view of urban reality not previously available. Robert Bell describes this sort of comprehensive view in terms that are reminiscent of balloon descriptions like Henry Mayhew's.

> If we wanted to convey to a foreigner a succinct notion of the way in which the great hive of London is packed, chambered, and worked, we would take him to the railway terminus as Shoreditch or London Bridge. Here the miracle is accomplished of flying over the roofs and spires, the fantastical tiles, chimney pots, and drunken gables of a dense maze of streets, lanes, squares, crescents, blind alleys, shops, warehouses, and manufactories, enabling the curious explorer of vital statistics to take a bird's-eye view from his aerial car of a mass of human struggle, such as is not to be found elsewhere on the surface of the globe. (Bell, "Run on the Eastern Counties Railway," 448)

The streets become "a living tableau" in which one sees "the real drama of suffering and blight, labour, penury, and vice, which are here exhibited in incessant action" (448). This aerial view is not quite as distant as that provided by a balloon ride or a panorama: it is a view of the middle distance, broad but with a level of human detail missing from the panoramic perspective.

Sherlock Holmes is not blind to the realities of urban life. But standing above the scene allows him, like the balloon travellers of a few decades earlier, to see the city as a kind of map whose structure is only truly visible from afar—in this case, a map of human destinies, with all its emotional currents and inter-connections forming a kind of grid.

> If we could fly out of that window hand in hand, hover over this great city, gently remove the roofs, and peep in at the queer things which are going on, the strange coincidences, the plannings, the cross-purposes, the wonderful chains of events, working through generations, and leading to the most *outré* results, it would make all fiction with its conventionalities and foreseen conclusions most stale and unprofitable. ("Case of Identity," *Adventures*, 147)

The godlike perspective Holmes describes transcends space and time, allowing him to see connections that are invisible to those enmeshed in them, and conse-quences stretching from the past into the present and the future. The railway is one of many mechanisms that tie him into this network.

In Bram Stoker's *Dracula*, too, railways are an integral part of the patterns of communication that form the substance of the novel. Critics have recognized that different forms of media and communication play an important role. As Jennifer Wicke has shown, *Dracula* is a book obsessed with its own means of production, its manuscript composed of a "patchwork made up out of the com-bined journal entries, letters, professional records, and newspaper clippings" of the vampire hunters (469). These texts are transmitted not only by letter but by shorthand, gramophone, typewriting, and telegraph, and together suggest that "the social force most analogous to Count Dracula's . . . is none other than mass culture, the developing technologies of media in its many forms, as mass trans-port, tourism, photography and lithography in image-production, and mass-produced narrative" (Wicke, 469).[20]

A second major strand of recent commentary recognizes the thematic im-portance of the novel's emphasis on travel. Stephen Arata has suggested that *Dracula*, which appeared at a time of perceived "cultural decay" in Britain, "en-acts the period's most important and pervasive narrative of decline, a narra-tive of reverse colonization" (623). Arata sees the novel as a blending of two genres, the gothic and the travel narrative, in which Jonathan Harker's journal description of his trip to Transylvania displays many of the standard tropes of Victorian travel (635–66). Harker and Dracula, he argues, ultimately present mirror images of each other in their movement through the geography of the novel: Harker is an "Orientalist travelling East," while Dracula is presented as an "Occidentalist travelling West" (638). Wicke, too, describes Jonathan Harker as a "tourist manqué" in Transylvania, naively anxious to absorb local color (472).

Every form of travel imaginable is required to complete the book's many journeys: Harker's journey to Transylvania, the Count's journey back, and the many trips taken by the friends of Lucy Westenra in the course of investigating the Count's movements and, finally, destroying him. The many choices available to the modern traveller are acknowledged in Mina's detailed memorandum on the subject of how Count Dracula might be expected to return: "*Ground of inquiry.*—Count Dracula's problem is to get back to his own place. . . . (b) *How is he to be taken?*—Here a process of exclusion may help us. By road, by rail, or by water?" (417). Mina works methodically through a list of the pros and cons of each mode of travel from the unique perspective of a passenger who must spend part of each day confined in a wooden coffin.

While many of the book's most dramatic journeys are sea voyages, rail travel occupies a central thematic position. As Arata has noted, one of Jonathan Harker's first meetings with the Count finds him reading, "of all things in the world, an English Bradshaw's Guide" (34), which Arata sees as part of his successful impersonation of an English gentleman, a role that, as Harker himself demonstrates, includes a "fetish for punctual trains" (Arata, 638).

The Count, as it turns out, makes full use of the rail networks, sending coffins of earth by the Great Northern Railway after they have arrived from overseas; their receipt at King's Cross Station is dutifully noted by an exchange of letters between his solicitors and his shipping agents (119–20). Later, Harker is able to track Dracula through the King's Cross stationmaster (272). The novel is fanatical in its insistence on recording characters' movements, both through descriptions of voyages by sea or rail, and through casual references ("I know you will be anxious to hear all that has passed since we parted at the railway station at Whitby" [127]). There are frequent references to the timing of trains, as when Dr. Seward says, "I took my way to Paddington, where I arrived about fifteen minutes before the train came in" (262), or when Jonathan Harker gives some papers to Van Helsing but notes, "As you go by the 10.30 train, you will not have time to read them" (227). These references not only impart a sense of urgency to the hunt, they help to establish a context of modern "railway time" occupied by the vampire hunters that contrasts with the timeless world of the centuries-old vampire. Like the specific brand-names that contemporary fiction writers sprinkle throughout their stories, these references serve as markers of contemporary culture that help readers to orient themselves. While it would be difficult to label a novel about the supernatural a work of realism, the book blends its fantastic story with an aggressively up-to-date quality that gives it a surprisingly realistic texture. In both Doyle and Stoker we see the immersive strategies that earlier novelists used to locate the reader within their fictional worlds give way to a quasi-documentary emphasis on timetables, facts, and statements.

The almost supernatural power of the railway is embodied in the figure of Mina Harker, who describes herself as a "train fiend," an image that seems to align her with Dracula himself. She mentions her interest almost apologetically, like an addiction, to Dr. Seward: "You forget—or perhaps you do not know, though Jonathan does and so does Dr. Van Helsing—that I am a train fiend. At home in Exeter I always used to make up the timetables, so as to be helpful to my husband" (402). She is able to inform Seward, having made a study of local timetables, that any train to Castle Dracula would "go by Galatz, or any rate through Bucharest," and that the next train to Galatz leaves at 6:30 the following morning (402). Mina had noted earlier, after a conversation with Van Helsing: "he was surprised at my knowledge of the trains offhand, but he does not know that I have made up all the trains to and from Exeter, that I may help Jonathan in case he is in a hurry" (224). This image of Mina is reminiscent of Doyle's description of Mycroft Holmes: she is like a computer who stores up a wide array of information in order to be able to spit out one piece of data when it is needed. Yet she is also able to infiltrate invisible networks to retrieve key information.

Mina is presented throughout as possessed of an uncanny gift for communication, both in her mastery of modern technological media like shorthand and typing, and in her capacity to express her own thoughts and intuit the thoughts of others. Her first meeting with Van Helsing results in a kind of mystic communion in which his reading of her papers allows him to instantly "know" her: she admits to him, "You do not know me," but suggests that reading her diary and Jonathan's letters will allow him to "know [her] better," and the mere offer allows him to respond, "I know you now" (265). Later, her communication skills will be supernaturally enhanced by her experience with Dracula, as under Van Helsing's hypnosis she becomes a medium who can channel Dracula's movements (not his thoughts, significantly, but his physical location) and relay them to her friends. While in the end her role as a conduit forces her friends to hide information from her, Mina's combination of technogeek skills and intuitive grasp of the networks that will need to be negotiated in order to defeat Dracula give her a unique power.

The association of rail travel with the free circulation of information and people is highlighted by Dracula's exclusion from the mobility of the modern world. Once Harker has escaped from his initial confinement by the Count and returned to his own country, the freedom of movement enjoyed by himself and his friends is contrasted with the limited mobility of the Count, burdened by his coffins of soil, and the Count's henchman, Renfield, imprisoned in an insane asylum. The initial powerful image of the Count as a bat who can fly anywhere and see anything is qualified by increasing awareness of the many physical constraints that mark him as a creature not of this place or time. Van Helsing describes him as "more prisoner than the slave of the galley, than the madman in his cell" (287). Harker and his friends, by contrast, are very much products of a particular place and time, and they take full advantage of the freedom afforded by new technologies of travel as well as new technologies of communication. In the end, they manage to destroy the Count by denying him the resting place that he would need if he were to be transplanted to foreign soil, what Van Helsing calls "his earth-home, his coffin-home, his hell-home" (287), and pursuing him to his real home in Transylvania. Thus, the novel associates mobility, particularly the modern form of mobility represented by rail travel, with the forces of good, and immobility with evil. Count Dracula's rootedness in his own land is a symptom of the aristocratic decay that can only be expunged through the use of modern technology.

Thomas Richards has described the development of what he calls "the imperial archive" in the nineteenth century, a "fantasy of knowledge connected and united in the service of state and Empire" (1993, 6). Not only did the Victorians seek "a comprehensive knowledge of the world" in all aspects of scholarship and inquiry (4), they hoped to use that knowledge, Richards suggests, to hold together an empire that seemed in danger of disintegration. It is perhaps not surprising to find that the railway occupies a central place in this "collectively imagined junction of all that was known or knowable" (11). For the Victorians, the railway symbolized the networks of communication that would become the foundation of modern culture. In the Victorian imagination, the experience of railway travel was not about going somewhere in particular, it was about unmooring one's body from physical constraints and throwing it into the matrix. The process of sending oneself "like a parcel" was an exhilarating, even frightening, experience of the virtual that future media would attempt to emulate.

8. MOVING THROUGH MEDIA

The "mobility of vision" that, according to Schivelbusch, characterizes the visual experience of train travel has been linked to capitalism and the development of commodity culture in the nineteenth century. Schivelbusch suggests that the "commodity character of objects" (186)—even of passengers, as seen in the epigraph by Ruskin—is enforced by the railway's speed and efficiency, and he posits an analogy between "panoramic perception" and "the accelerated circulation of commodities," and the visual plenitude and "fragmentation" of department store displays (186). As we noted in Part One, Anne Friedberg, following Schivelbusch, also describes the "mobilized virtual gaze" as a key component of commodity culture (5).

This sense of the centrality of "panoramic" perception to emerging modernity has led critics to seek connections to other forms of consumer culture and mass entertainment. Many critics have posited a connection between the "panoramic" visual perception of train travel and the development of moving pictures at the turn of the century. Film historians have explored the continuities between nineteenth-century entertainment media, such as the panorama, kaleidoscope, and magic lantern, and the development of motion pictures, and generally seem to agree that film is less indebted to still photography than to these more dynamic forms of visual display. Thus the panorama can be seen as a conceptual hinge linking rail travel and cinema in the visual experience of movement that they both offer.

As Mary Anne Doane suggests, the essential modernity of film derives from the fact that cinema is "a privileged machine for the representation of temporality" (138), and its emphasis on the "present tense of the filmic flow" (140) evokes other modern forms of movement. More recently, film historians have noted direct connections between railway travel and early film, evident in the dominance of railway images and plots in early films like Lumière's famous *Train Entering a Station* (1895), the American Edwin S. Porter's *Romance of the Rail* (1903) and *The Great Train Robbery* (1903), and the Biograph Company's *Hold-up of the Rocky Mountain Express* (1906). Tom Gunning has suggested that the radical "transformation of experience" (1995, 15) created by the railway is similar to the magical transformations of cinema, and that this affinity was recognized and exploited by early filmmakers.

> The early genres of cinema, especially such seemingly diverse forms as travel actualities and trick films, visualized a modern experience of rapid alteration, whether by presenting foreign views from far-flung international locations or by creating through trick photography a succession of transformations which unmoored the stable identity of both objects and performers. (16)

Gunning notes that early actuality films frequently presented "a simulacrum of travel" not simply through foreign views but also through "'phantom rides' films, which were shot from the front of trains or prows of boats and which gave seated, stationary spectators a palpable sensation of motion" (16). The highly popular American phenomenon of "Hale's Tours" in 1905–6 represented the acme of this genre: viewers were seated in a simulated railway carriage, watching a film view from the front or rear window of a train, with "train clatter and the appropriate swaying" of the carriage (Musser, 129).[21] Such descriptions clearly evoke earlier responses to panoramas, which aimed at precisely similar effects. Lynne Kirby, following in Gunning's tracks, expounds this connection at length in a study of railways and the cinema that, while centered on American film and the very different development of the American railroad system, also notes many points of connection that seem equally true of British culture.

> As a machine of vision and an instrument for conquering space and time, the train is a mechanical double for the cinema and for the transport of the specta-tor into fiction, fantasy, and dream. . . . Like film's illusion of movement, the experience of the railroad is based on a fundamental paradox: simultaneous mo-tion and stillness. In both cases, passengers sit still as they rush through space and time, whether physically and visually, as on the train, or merely visually, as in the cinema. (2)

Kirby describes the railroad as "a significant cultural force influencing the emer-gence and development of the cinema during the silent period in both the Unit-ed States and Europe" (2).[22]

Cinema seems to emerge as the culmination of the panoramic tradition, both as represented by actual panoramas and as represented in the panoramic perspective associated, by Schivelbusch and others, with railway travel. Certain-ly the history of film demonstrates that the medium has much in common with characteristics that made panoramas so appealing in the nineteenth century. But without attempting to survey the complex theorizing of the spectator's gaze that has been undertaken by film critics over the last few decades, one could perhaps assert that the position of the viewer of most films, even early films, is far less stable and unitary than that of panorama audiences as described in Part One. Once editing technology had advanced to the point that filmmakers could offer multiple perspectives and rapid scene changes, they did.

There continues to be a popular subgenre of film that provides an expe-riential view of specific locations, usually in IMAX format. Such films, often educational or documentary in nature, seek to immerse the viewer in a wide-screen portrayal of a particular environment and are often produced for ongo-ing exhibition at educational venues. Current films combine IMAX with 3-D technology, as in *Galapagos in 3D*, and *Under the Sea 3D*. The IMAX website uses familiar rhetoric in describing one feature: "Through the power of IMAX 3D, *Hubble 3D* will enable moviegoers to journey through distant galaxies to ex-plore the grandeur and mysteries of our celestial surroundings, and accompany space-walking astronauts as they attempt the most difficult and important tasks in NASA's history." The film industry as a whole, however, did not cling to the panoramic paradigm by attempting to represent a continuous sequence as it appears from a fixed perspective. Instead, filmmakers quickly perceived that a far more complex and satisfying aesthetic experience could be created by abandoning that fixed perspective and using film, as nineteenth-century novelists used narrative, to play with different points of view and contrasting subjectivities.

As I have already suggested, video games may be the contemporary medium that most closely emulates the continuous, unitary perspective associated with panoramas, as they lead players through a sequence of scenes and situations. Though games as a genre present a variety of perspectives, most individual games maintain a single perspective that the player follows fluidly throughout. But while many theorists and players might argue that the most realistic games are those that present a "fully subjective perspective where character and player are unified into a first-person movement through virtual space" (161), to quote Martii Lahti again, some games create instead a separate perspective that is reminiscent of the "hypothetical traveller" we have seen in many of the Victorian texts, a hybrid perspective that helps create a sense of being between two worlds.

The many video games that follow a quest format, or simulate entire worlds, might seem to offer the most obvious analogues to the virtual travel described in this study. In fact, however, a good example is provided by the music game *The Beatles: Rock Band*. It promises "game play that takes players on a journey through the legacy and evolution of the band's legendary career" (Harmonix/MTV), a claim that may remind us of the panorama advertisements discussed in Part One. The game's setting is as elaborately realistic in many of its details as Banvard's Panorama of the Mississippi. Working closely with Apple Corps, the company controlled by the surviving Beatles and the widows of Lennon and Harrison, the creators used documentary films, archival materials, and personal photo collections to meticulously recreate the authentic concert venues and studio settings—the Cavern Club in Liverpool, Studio Two at Abbey Road, even the set of the *Ed Sullivan Show*—in which many Beatles songs were performed or recorded. The goal was to create "the most deeply immersive way of experiencing the music and the mythology of the Beatles" (Radosh, 2), and, as with Victorian panoramas, attention to detail becomes a marker for authenticity.

Situating the player in a realistic space is an important aspect of the game's immersiveness, and the fluid stream of notes that spill off the screen also helps to pull the player in. But a crucial difference between this game and predecessors like *Guitar Hero* is its triangulation of perspective. In *The Beatles: Rock*

Band, the home player is not the star. Nor are the pictured Beatles avatars for the player. The player watches, and plays with, the Beatles as they perform. This position offers the player a hybrid perspective that is quite different from the first-person role-playing of *Guitar Hero*. The player is inside and outside at the same time, much like the "participant observer" that James Buzard describes as satisfying the "ethnographic impulse" in Victorian fiction (*Disorienting Fiction*, 8). This game is not like watching a concert, nor is it like starring in a performance. It is something in between: what its creators call an "experiential journey" (Harmonix/MTV). Such games present a contemporary version of the same kind of virtuality the Victorians sought through their vicarious travel experiences: a sense of being in two places at once, constantly negotiating the space between them.[23]

CONCLUSION

I began this study with a question about why the mode of fictive experience I have called "virtual travel" was so appealing to the Victorians. In attempting to address that question, I have argued that the development of a culture of virtual travel in nineteenth-century England played a fundamental role in the evolution of the Victorian realist novel. But the question is not fully answered unless we ask ourselves what cultural work is being performed by the continuous project of inventing realism.

I suggested in the Introduction that literary realism involves, among other things, an interrogation of the relationship between subjective and objective experience. The forms of virtual travel that we have examined here embody a similar tension. In fact, I would argue, they exist precisely in order to identify and triangulate that relationship. The panoramic perspective, as we saw in Part One, presents the world from a fixed point of view, and the sensation of virtual travel it created was predicated on the viewer's assumption of that predetermined perspective.[24] Though a fixed perspective, it was not an entirely stable one; it sketched in a transitional space, creating a mediated, "hypothetical" point of view that spectators were expected to temporarily adopt and then discard. This hypothetical or contingent point of view, I have argued, is a paradigm for fictional representation that was exploited by nineteenth-century novelists. River travel on the Thames, with its self-conscious repetition of familiar itineraries, also generated a nonlocalized perspective that isolated the viewer from direct experience of the scene surveyed. Similarly, rail travel required spectators to place themselves in a kind of limbo, a transitional space in which their usual understanding of their own physical location was rendered irrelevant.

Yet as we have seen, the emphasis in many railway narratives on the importance of stations and junctions as points of connection between different parts of the network suggests a growing understanding that the significance of location was increasingly relational, rather than absolute. Individuals now had to position themselves, not in relation to established categories like "home" and "abroad," "close" and "far," but in relation to a vast interconnected system that would define its own coordinates in time and space. This recognition of the interconnectedness of places and individuals seems to gesture in the direction of a cosmopolitanism that, Vinay Dharwadker points out, "frequently differentiates itself from more than nationalism, arising out of clusters of cultural formations that are denser in their interactions than binary oppositions."[25] This mode of networked thinking is consistent with the general challenge to dualism, what I have called triangulation, represented by virtual travel.

By the end of the century, the Victorians had come to understand that the railway was not in fact a unique symbol of modernity but one strand in an evolving network of communication technology: technology that facilitated, not just the transfer of goods, but the transfer of information from one place to another. The abstraction of imaginative experience from physical context that fascinated the Victorians in train travel was simply one example of an increasing abstraction of information. Understanding the inherent value of information as a commodity separate from its instantiation in a specific form or medium was the first step in a process that has led to continuing development of new media, and of technology to facilitate its circulation.

Although most accounts of media history have, as noted earlier, been dominated by analysis of visual media, Friedrich Kittler has analyzed the role of technologies of transcription in creating the "discourse networks" that he sees as evolving over the course of the nineteenth century. His analysis depends on what David Wellbury calls a "presupposition of mediality" that includes literature among the contributors to the system of information circulation he describes.[26] This study also presupposes that literature circulates among other media. But where Kittler sees a "terror of novelty" registered in literature that responded to "gramophones, films, and typewriters—the first technological media,"[27] I am suggesting that if we expand our understanding of media to include not just technology but any artificial intervention between communicator and audience, then the Victorians first experienced media through the mediation of virtual travel, and found the experience exhilarating.

Ultimately, the project of this book has been to recover and explain the sense of exhilaration that the Victorians associated with virtual travel, and the almost physical sense of immersion it engendered. This analysis has demonstrated that in many ways, Victorian literature functioned like media: it virtually *was* media. The approach taken here may seem to simply apply a different vocabulary to the rhetoric of engagement that critics have long recognized as central to nineteenth-century realism. But looking at realism through the conceptual framework of media studies helps us to understand the cultural context of the communication strategies employed by Victorian novelists, and to map the continuities between distinctively nineteenth-century forms of representation and broader aesthetic questions that continue to intrigue us in the twenty-first century.

This effort to uncover resemblances and continuities between the Victorian period and the present takes its place among numerous studies that have, over the past decade, sought to connect the Victorian age with modernity, with post-modernity, or with the immediate present. Jay Clayton's *Charles Dickens in Cyberspace: The Afterlife of the Nineteenth Century in Postmodern Culture* (2003) set the stage for this trend with its analysis of the persistence of Victorian themes and affinities in postmodern literature. Clayton's effort at "combining history with current modes of cultural studies" leads him to conclude, "Postmodernism has a hidden or repressed connection with nineteenth-century culture" (5). By looking at intersections among literature, science, and technology, both in the Victorian period and in their "contemporary transformations" (13), Clayton seeks to redress what he sees as a gap in historical consciousness and to counter the "resolutely synchronic" trend in cultural studies (16). He allows himself to explore disjunctions as well as continuities, jumping back and forth between the nineteenth century and the present in his examples, an approach that illustrates his claim that affinities do not always manifest themselves in unbroken historical sequence but can become submerged and then unexpectedly resurface.

Other critical works have attempted to capture this sometimes elusive sense of resemblance, relying on terms like *afterlives*, which was institutionalized in John Kucich and Dianne Sadoff's edited collection, *Victorian Afterlife: Postmodern Culture Rewrites the Nineteenth Century* (2000), as well as in Robert Douglas-Fairhurst's *Victorian Afterlives: The Shaping of Influence in Nineteenth-Century Literature* (2002). Simon Joyce used a different image for this reflexivity with his 2007 book, *The Victorians in the Rearview Mirror*. Rohan McWilliam recently described this emerging critical trend as a "specter haunting the world of Victorian studies" and asked, "Why have we become so preoccupied with these Victorian afterlives?" He answers his own question by acknowledging that this interest reflects a desire to rewrite our understanding of the present as well

Fig. 8. Panoramic View from the London Eye. Photograph by Stephen Jensen, © 2011.

as the past." What is at stake in this agenda is a set of question marks about the so-called 'modernity' of the 20th century."[28]

Most recently, this trend has come to be known as "Neo-Victorian Studies," a term that was once used in quotation marks but is now the name of a new, peer-reviewed e-journal. Originally used in studies of contemporary novels that are pastiches or rewritings of Victorian fiction, the term has now grown to cover a field that includes studies of modern Victorianism, creative writing that references the Victorian, and explorations of the popular cultural dimension of neo-Victorianism known as "steampunk." In the 2008 inaugural issue of this journal, Mark Llewellyn notes current frustrations with the term *Victorian Studies*, "an interdisciplinary perspective that refuses to be tied to the chronological range of 1837–1901," and which faces "problematic implications about the 'global' nature of Victorian Studies and the various meanings attached to the first word, either through an associated colonial past, or its continued colonising presence as a form of academic discourse." Llewellyn offered this description of the journal's aim: "In regularly bringing together a critically-inflected creative writing strand with a creatively-aware criticism, it opens up different interpretations which, while they cannot and do not claim to be all-encompassing reconfigurations of the Victorian, can nevertheless illustrate conflict and difference through their very act of undermining the stability of a presumed hegemonic historical narrative."[29] The political implications of this definition set themselves against another thread of commentary about neo-Victorianism, which responds to the use of the same term to describe a nostalgic attachment to Victorian ideology.[30]

Though the present study is rooted in detailed examination of Victorian literature and cultural phenomena, its occasional flash-forwards to the present may reflect the same impatience with the constrictions of periodization that has generated the emerging field of Neo-Victorian Studies. My approach here has assumed that it is possible to examine a historically specific body of material with both an awareness of its immediate cultural context and an openness to the illumination offered by comparing it with contemporary aesthetic and cultural manifestations. My effort to trace the strand of the virtual that is woven into, and out of, the "particular web" of nineteenth-century realism arises out of my original question, why was realism so important to the Victorians? This book offers not an answer, but a partial response, which is to acknowledge that the project of locating one's place in the world—the essential project of realism—continues to be important to us, even as the technologies through which we travel, and the media through which we represent that world, continue to evolve.

NOTES

Introduction

1. Jack Simmons ([1951] 1969, 23) describes this process as beginning even before the railway, with the advent of the chaise and the stagecoach, which "made possible that 'opening-up' of England that is such a striking achievement of the eighteenth and nineteenth centuries." See Ian Ousby, *The Englishman's England: Taste, Travel, and the Rise of Tourism*, and James Buzard, *The Beaten Track: European Tourism, Literature, and the Ways to "Culture," 1800–1918*.

2. Buzard (1993, 18) describes the "origins of tourism as a modern cultural practice," focusing in particular on tourism abroad. I will have occasion throughout this study to rely on his insights about the distinction between tourist and traveller as deliberately constructed personae. I deliberately use the more generic term *travel* here, rather than *tourism*, as I am not attempting to retread the path Buzard has already laid out in his influential exploration of tourism as a cultural industry.

3. On advertising and imperialism, see Anne McClintock's *Imperial Leather: Race, Gender, and Sexuality in the Colonial Contest*; works that discuss visual culture in relation to gender include Deborah Cherry, *Beyond the Frame: Feminism and Visual Culture, 1850–2000*, and Lynda Nead, *Victorian Babylon: People, Streets, and Images in Nineteenth-Century London*. Numerous works on exhibitions and commodity culture include Jeffrey Auerbach, *The Great Exhibition of 1851: A Nation on Display*, and Timothy Mitchell, *Colonising Egypt*. A more direct link between the rise of consumer culture and fiction is made in Andrew Miller's *Novels Behind Glass: Commodity Culture and Victorian Narrative*.

In noting the relative scarcity of works that apply contemporary media theory to the Victorian period, I am distinguishing between application of contemporary media theory to narrative, and research on Victorian media. In addition to the seminal works of Friedrich Kittler, *Discourse Networks 1800/1900* and *Gramophone, Film, Typewriter*, one might cite David Thorburn and Henry Jenkins, *Rethinking Media Change: The Aesthetics of Transition*, Lisa Gitelman and Geoffrey B. Pingree, *New Media, 1740–1915*, and other works in MIT Press's now-defunct Media in Transition series, as well as Richard Menke's excellent *Telegraphic Realism*, a work that shares many preoccupations with the present study.

4. A number of contemporary narratologists who are trained as literary critics in fact write about multiple media. See Pat Harrigan and Noah Wardrip-Fruin, *Third Person*; Marie-Laure Ryan, *Narrative Across Media: The Languages of Storytelling*; David Herman, *Narratologies: New Perspectives on Narrative Analysis* and *The Cambridge Companion to Narrative*; and Sandra Heinen and Roy Sommer, *Narratology in the Age of Cross-Disciplinary Narrative Research*.

5. The role of nineteenth-century photography in relation to realism in literature is explored by Nancy Armstrong in *Fiction and the Age of Photography: The Legacy of British Realism*, which argues that literary realism and photography jointly authorized a perception of reality as the visually presentable, or that which can be photographed. Jennifer Green-Lewis, in *Framing the Victorians: Photography and the Culture of Realism*, notes that "photography frequently provided a locus for debates having to do with realism, especially literary realism," because of the photograph's "narrative potential," and also because of the "unusual relationship to truthfulness" implied in its means of production (19–20). See also Daniel A. Novak, *Realism, Photography, and Nineteenth-Century Fiction*.

6. For a history of the development of cinema that emphasizes its relationship to earlier media, see Leo Charney and Vanessa R. Schwartz, *Cinema and the Invention of Modern Life*; Tom Gunning's seminal essay, "The Cinema of Attractions: Early Film, Its Spectator and the Avant-Garde," as well as Gunning's subsequent work; and Anne Friedberg, *Window Shopping: Cinema and the Postmodern*. Friedberg's *The Virtual Window: From Alberti to Microsoft* explores windows and framing in both moving and non-moving visual art over several centuries.

The history of technologies of seeing and optical apparatuses from the nineteenth through the twentieth century has been thoroughly documented in Jonathan Crary's fascinating *Techniques of the Observer: On Vision and Modernity in the Nineteenth Century* and *Suspensions of Perception: Attention, Spectacle, and Modern Culture*.

7. As Lilian R. Furst (176) notes, in the realist novel, place "amounts to far more than an insistently acknowledged background, or an omnipresent context for the action. The interaction between the perceiving, feeling, reflecting self of the protagonists on the one hand and the consensus of their particular material and social world on the other is the ever reiterated and ever changing matter of realist narrative." J. Hillis Miller (19) describes the novel as a "figurative mapping" in which "the story traces out diachronically the movement of the characters from house to house and from time to time, as the crisscross of their relationships gradually creates an imaginary space."

8. See Edward Said, *Culture and Imperialism*; Patrick Brantlinger, *Rule of Darkness: British Literature and Imperialism, 1830–1914*; and Suvendrini Perera, *The Reaches of Empire: The English Novel from Edgeworth to Dickens*.

9. Studies of the body in extreme states—as in Athena Vrettos's *Somatic Fictions: Imagining Illness in Victorian Culture*, Janet Oppenheim's *Shattered Nerves: Doctors, Patients, and Depression in Victorian England*, and Jill Matus's *Shock, Memory, and the Unconscious in Victorian Fiction*—have been accompanied by a range of works about

sensation and perception, such as John Picker's *Victorian Soundscapes*, Janice Carlisle's *Common Scents*, and many works on visual perception that will be noted separately. A comprehensive look at sensory imagery and experience can be found in William Cohen's *Embodied: Victorian Literature and the Senses*. For an examination of materiality in general, see Daniel Hack, *The Material Interests of the Victorian Novel*.

10. See Ousby, *The Englishman's England*, and Buzard, *The Beaten Track*, particularly Buzard's account of the rise of "anti-tourism" as a reaction against travel by the "masses."

11. Nancy Armstrong notes that this is true not only of visual media but of the larger information culture. "The technologies of representation we consider most Victorian— for example, scientific and social-scientific description, reportage, statistics, graphs, new cartographic methods, as well as photography, exhibitions, and displays—were all ways of bringing to the literate public chunks of the world that could formerly be seen only by travelling to various sites throughout that world" (314).

12. See Benedict Anderson, *Imagined Communities: Reflections on the Origin and Spread of Nationalism*. In *Ornamentalism: How the British Saw Their Empire*, David Cannadine describes the way in which "a shared sense of Britishness" (122) was created by the movement of objects and rituals from the metropolis to the periphery and back again. John Plotz writes that "recreating home had become a nearly sacred injunction for English émigrés by the middle of the nineteenth century," suggesting that familiar objects served as a "mechanism of imperial expansion" (18).

13. Travel writing in general has always been seen as a genre that, insofar as it replicates the "strong historical connection of exploration with exploitation and occupation," seems to promote "the exercise of imperial power" (Clark, 3). It feeds, as Graham Huggan notes, into exoticism, "a mode of vision in which travel writing, fuelling European fantasy, has acted as the primary vehicle for the production and consumption of cultural 'otherness'" (56). See also David Spurr, *The Rhetoric of Empire: Colonial Discourse in Journalism, Travel Writing, and Imperial Administration*, and Ali Behdad, *Belated Travelers: Orientalism in the Age of Colonial Dissolution*.

14. Steve Clark (8) critiques Pratt's oft-quoted question "How has travel writing produced the rest of the world for European readerships at particular points in Europe's expansionist trajectory?" (Pratt 1992, 5) as "hyperbolic," noting that other representational practices are surely involved in "producing the rest of the world" and suggesting that a more nuanced reception argument is needed in order to justify large claims about readership.

15. See also Jonathan Arac and Harriet Ritvo's discussion of the spectacle of exoticism in *Macropolitics of Nineteenth-Century Literature: Nationalism, Exoticism, Imperialism*.

16. Alison Byerly, *Realism, Representation, and the Arts in Nineteenth Century Literature*.

17. Following the publication of Jay David Bolter and Richard Grusin's *Remediation: Understanding New Media* (1999), Grusin wrote a 2004 article and a 2010 book, *Premediation: Affect and Mediality after 9/11*, that focus on fictional works that represent imagined future technologies, and ways in which contemporary news media anticipate the

representation and significance of future events. Ultimately, he suggests, *premediation* represents "a desire to colonize the future by extending our networks of media technologies not only spatially across the globe and beyond, but also temporally into the future; in this sense, premediation seeks to make sure that the future is so fully mediated by new media forms that it is unable to emerge into the present without having already been remediated in the past" (2004, 36). Grusin uses the term to describe a process of control over the content of future representations, a kind of pre-spin, whereas I would like to use the word to describe the inverse of *remediation*. Where remediation involves refashioning old media, premediation would describe the anticipation of future media forms.

18. *Presence* is the name of a key journal in the field, based at MIT; and at Stanford, the interdisciplinary Presence Project brings together researchers in drama and performance theory, anthropological archaeology, and computer science to look at the "means by which 'presence' is achieved in live and mediated performance and simulated environments." In fact, communication theorist Frank Biocca has suggested that "quantity and quality of presence" is the one feature that distinguishes virtual reality from other media, past and present (1997, 5.2.1.1). Researchers evaluate success in creating presence in virtual environments not only by surveying participants about their experience but by measuring physiological signs of involvement and excitement (Schroeder, 3).

19. Of course, as many users would testify, the mobility of the cell phone is an illusion. A Sussex Technology Group study of cell phone use cites Baudrillard's "revenge of the object" in noting that a cell phone increases one's accountability, so that the user of these light, mobile devices is in fact "pinned down" by the "weight of self-responsibility" (220).

20. Three-dimensional (3-D) representation, too, has become more common owing to rapid improvement in graphic interfaces that can render 3-D images from two-dimensional drawings, photographs, or diagrams. Video and computer games, of course, have been among the most consistent users of 3-D perspective, and fully stereoscopic video-game display is now possible with a combination of 3-D-ready LCD display, glasses, and powerful GPU processors. Within the film industry, the jury is still out on whether 3-D cinema is poised to become a transformative phenomenon on the scale of "talkies," as the success of *Avatar* and a few 3-D films has been followed by some disappointing results for other 3-D productions. Three-dimensionality is still the twenty-first-century equivalent of the moving panorama: a realistic technology that in and of itself is a novelty rather than an art form.

21. A number of games, such as Electronic Arts' *Mirror's Edge*, consist primarily of searches and escapes that challenge the player's ability to move in a fluid, *parkour*-like manner across a complex landscape of obstacles. Even when the focus is on combat, movement is a crucial aspect of the perceived realism of an environment. Epic Games' *Gears of War*, for example, has been praised for the subtlety of motion the game requires as a player attempts to seek cover, and the way in which the distorted camera perspective offered when the player is running creates an overall effect of "intense panic" (Bisell, 82) that strengthens the illusion of running.

22. The development of "force feedback technologies" for game consoles that make them rumble and shake in response to game action contributes to the player's sense of physical engagement, making the transaction between reality and game a two-way street. "Instead of just drawing gamers *into* the virtual worlds represented onscreen," one critic notes, "contemporary video games also extend the space of the game out into the space traditionally reserved for televisual spectatorship and consumption" (Murphy, 224).

23. In virtual reality settings, this interaction might involve a physical interface such as a stereoscopic head-mounted display that rotates images in response to turns of the head, datagloves that translate hand gestures into information, or other ways of registering and responding to bodily movement. Conversely, a user might enter a CAVE, an immersive projection-room system involving multiple displays that are responsive to the movement of a viewer or viewers through the space.

Video games, multi-user dungeons (MUDs), and other computer-generated displays are often called "interactive" when they offer the player or viewer a range of options and react to the specific choices made. In addition, games or collaborative environments that allow users to interact not just with a system but with each other have been shown to create an enhanced sense of presence (Regenbrecht and Schubert, 429; Sallnas, 177). Many of the most sophisticated games, such as *World of Warcraft*, create opportunities for voice communication among players and encourage them to form guilds or collaborate and interact in other ways.

24. Multiplayer games typically involve the creation of an avatar, a graphical representation of the player that allows him or her to participate. (Computer-created characters are generally referred to as "embodied agents," whereas "avatars" are "digital models driven by real-time humans" [Bailenson, Yee, et al., 359]). Games that utilize computer-generated characters attempt to create programs that allow those characters to interact with users' avatars in a manner that closely replicates human social behavior, and some game designers suggest that this is their greatest challenge (Vick 2007, 55).

25. Views on this differ. N. Katherine Hayles disputes Jerome McGann's assessment that hypertext, though a valuable tool for scholarship, has not produced high-quality literature. Hayles argues that such assessments reflect "a tendency to apply to electronic literature the same reading strategies one uses for print, while underappreciating or perhaps simply not recognizing the new strategies available to electronic literature: animation, rollovers, screen design, navigation strategies, and so on" (1999, 38).

26. For example, a company that specializes in creating three-dimensional simulated environments partnered with the University of Southern California to create a "virtual Iraq" used for treating soldiers with post-traumatic stress syndrome; the full portal includes "a head-mounted display (a helmet with a pair of video goggles), earphones, a scent-producing machine, and a modified version of Full Spectrum Warrior, a popular video game" (Halpern). Therapists can also utilize simulations of New York City and the collapse of the Twin Towers for treatment of 9/11 survivors. Cornell University's Weill Medical Center offers a range of Virtual Reality Exposure Therapy treatments,

with a web page featuring such scenarios as Virtual Airplane, Virtual Storm, Virtual Vietnam, and Virtual Audience. Virtual reality environments have been used by medical students practicing delicate procedures, by scientists who find it helpful to visualize certain kinds of complex processes or information, and by architects, archaeologists, engineers, and urban planners, who are able to recreate or test physical environments by using technology to create three-dimensional models that can be "entered."

27. Nick Yee et al. have suggested that massively multiplayer online role-playing games (MMOs) "could potentially be unique research platforms for the social sciences and clinical therapy," with the important caveat, however, that "it is crucial to first establish that social behavior and norms in virtual environments are comparable to those in the physical world" (115).

28. For example, Yellowstone National Park, one of the most popular destinations in America, can be visited through the Active Worlds web browser. Visitors to the site see real-time webcam images of Old Faithful, and can chat with a park ranger or other visitors if they wish. Given that overcrowding is a significant problem that contributes to diminished air quality and degradation of the park environment in a variety of ways, park authorities might well hope that providing simulated visits can help preserve the original.

29. Edward Castronova's work on the economics of online games emphasizes the way in which successful games create a self-enclosed, coherent world, one that includes the same characteristics and dynamics as the real world. The online economy of many games has spilled out into a real market, as virtual goods are bought and sold on the Internet. This external validation of the game world earns it a reality status derived from its success at not just replicating but generating real-world behavior. See Castronova's *Synthetic Worlds: The Business and Culture of Online Games,* as well as Julian Dibbell, *Play Money: Or, How I Quit My Day Job and Made Millions Trading Virtual Loot.*

30. George Landow presents an excellent summary of this debate in *Hypertext 3.0* (250–54). This battle may represent a false dichotomy, however. Henry Jenkins (2004) has tried to sketch out "a middle ground position" that "respects the particularity of this emerging medium—examining games less as stories than as spaces ripe with narrative possibility" (118). He notes that "discussion of the narrative potentials of games need not imply a privileging of storytelling over all the other possible things games can do" (120) and suggests that ludologists who reject claims of narrative influence often operate with a limited view of linear narrative that does not include modernist and postmodern narrative structures. Jesper Juul (121) points out that videogames do "present fictional worlds" but also "have game rules" that control the player's actions. "Rules and fiction are attractive for opposite reasons," he suggests, and it is the unique blend offered by video games that makes them appealing.

31. Baudrillard (2000) described the increasing "virtualization" of our society as a "murder of the Real," lamenting this "blind point of reversal, where nothing is true or false any longer and everything is drifting indifferently between cause and effect, between origin and finality" (62). An "excess of Reality" leads to the end of reality, just as

"the excess of information puts an end to information, or the excess of communication puts an end to communication" (66). Baudrillard suggests that in the absence of a contrast between reality and nonreality, reality itself loses its meaning. He sees the "compulsion" toward an "unconditional realization of the real" (65) as a state of continual paradox in which all dreams and ideas are "operationalized" and cease to exist as concepts (66). Reality becomes "a sort of sphinx, enigmatic in its hyperconformity, simulating itself as virtuality or reality show." Reality becomes "hyperreality—paroxysm and parody all at once" (77). A clear understanding of reality and valuing of illusion as its radical counterpart is replaced by the "simulacrum, which consecrates the unhappy non-distinction between true and false, between the real and its signs, and the unhappy, necessarily unhappy, destiny of meaning in our culture" (1996, 17). As critics have noted, Baudrillard's critique assumes the complete victory of the hyperreal over the true or the real, describing "budding trends" as "a full-blown or completely fixed social order" and generally underrating "the tenacity of the real" (Luke, 31).

Slavoj Žižek, too, emphasizes the idea that virtual reality threatens reality, not by standing in opposition to it but by absorbing it. Cyberspace complicates identity and subjectivity by allowing us to construct our own personae; it complicates reality by identifying reality with illusion, and hence eliminating any role for "appearance," or, in Lacanian terms, the Symbolic (111). Both Baudrillard and Žižek see virtual reality as assuming the functions of everyday reality, and thereby obscuring the layer that underlies that appearance, what Baudrillard calls "dreams and ideas," and what Žižek calls "the Real," the symbolic or psychological reality that is normally accessed through dreams or fantasy (122).

Baudrillard and Žižek are concerned about the implications of creating a layer of simulation that triangulates the already complex relationship between the real and the not-real. Their critiques rest on the assumption that in surrendering ourselves to the illusion of virtual reality, we lose the ability to use reality as a reference point against which to calibrate other kinds of experience. This study suggests that, on the contrary, a major benefit of virtual reality is that it extends the conceptual space available to accommodate different levels of representation and allows the viewer or reader to move freely between them.

32. Victor Nell, *Lost in a Book* (213), paraphrasing Josephine Hilgard, *Personality and Hypnosis: A Study of Imaginative Involvement* (Chicago: University of Chicago Press, 1979). A similar argument is made by psycholinguist Richard J. Gerrig, who writes in *Experiencing Narrative Worlds* about the metaphor of being "transported" by a literary work, and outlines a six-part sequence of steps involved, emphasizing the traveller's temporary alienation from his world of origin, and his return as someone changed by the journey (11).

Part One

1. Matt Leone, "From Unreal Warfare to Gears of War," 1UP.com, 5-19-2005, 1.

2. The terms *panorama* and *diorama* were often used more or less interchangeably, but technically a panorama is an expansive, completely circular painting, usually of a city or natural landscape; or conversely, a large, moving scroll containing a linear representation of a scene or series of scenes. The term *panorama* was also used for linear depictions on a much smaller scale, for example the foldout panoramas often included in guidebooks. *Diorama* refers to a scenic representation that uses light effects, sounds, and/or sculpted figures to enhance the realism of the picture by adding a sense of depth and temporality. The general, nontechnical sense of a "panorama" as a broad (real) vista seems to have developed soon after painted panoramas came into being. Not long after that, *panorama* also attained its current usage as a name for a broad survey of any subject.

3. See, for example, Wolfgang Schivelbusch, *The Railway Journey: The Industrialization of Time and Space*, and Stephen Kern, *The Culture of Time and Space, 1880–1910*.

4. This characterization of the picturesque derives in part from the work of Ann Bermingham, *Landscape and Ideology: The English Rustic Tradition, 1740–1860*, and Kim Ian Michasiw, "Nine Revisionist Theses on the Picturesque," and is explored in detail in Byerly, *Realism, Representation, and the Arts in Nineteenth-Century Literature* (18–25).

5. Altick's discussion remains the best exposition of the place of the panorama within the entertainment culture of nineteenth-century England. Ralph Hyde's *Panoramania!*, the catalog of the 1998 Barbican Art Gallery exhibition of panorama materials, provides a well-illustrated overview of panoramas and related artifacts (such as toys and games) of the period. In addition, two recent books have presented surveys of the panorama genre from the eighteenth century through the present, as seen in England, America, and Europe. Stephan Oettermann's *The Panorama: History of a Mass Medium* cogently describes its origins, technical features, and development in each of the countries (England, France, Germany, Austria, and the United States) where it played a significant role in the history of mass entertainment. Bernard Comment's *The Panorama* covers much of the same territory but is organized thematically, with somewhat more emphasis on the panorama's relation to eighteenth- and nineteenth-century aesthetic theories and practices. Comment's book is more lavishly illustrated and includes several full-color foldouts of panoramic paintings and preparatory sketches. My focus here is less on the history of the panorama than on written accounts of panoramas, and the ways in which the language and perspective of those accounts is reflected in other British writing of the period. In particular, I make no attempt to discuss the rich history and influence of the panorama in countries other than England. The fact that Oettermann's book originally appeared in German, and Comment's book in French, suggests the importance of the panorama in European culture.

6. This part will make frequent reference to advertisements, handbills, and guidebooks from the British Library (BL), the Museum of London (ML), and the John Johnson Collection of Printed Ephemera at the Bodleian Library, Oxford (JJ Coll). Guidebooks or multipage pamphlets with publication information are listed in the Works Cited and will be referred to by title. For advertisements and other pieces of printed

matter, I will give a parenthetical reference to the location of the material (e.g., JJ Coll, Dioramas 1).

7. The touristic popularity of St. Paul's is reflected in the fact that Peggotty owns a work-box with St. Paul's painted on the lid. Clare Pettit suggests the work-box was probably "an early Victorian souvenir," one of many "memorial-commodities recently placed within the reach of a new class of tourist" (paragraph 2).

8. These three Victorian coronation panoramas from the Royal Archives / Royal Library were displayed in 2003 in the Drawings Gallery of Windsor Castle as part of a "Coronations" exhibition to mark Queen Elizabeth's Golden Jubilee. Pocket-sized cardboard copies of "Robins' panoramic presentation of the Queen's Coronation Procession from the Palace to the Abbey on the 28th June 1838, Delineating every portion of that splendid scene" can be purchased at the Victoria and Albert Museum shop.

9. For discussions of panoramas in America and in particular their influence on American writers, see Oettermann, 313–44; Robert L. Carothers and John L. Marsh, "The Whale and the Panorama," *Nineteenth-Century Fiction* 26 (1971): 319–28; Charles Zarobila, "Walt Whitman and the Panorama," *Walt Whitman Review* 25 (1979): 51–59; and Joseph Moldenhauer, "Thoreau, Hawthorne, and the Seven-Mile Panorama," *ESQ: A Journal of the American Renaissance* 44 (1998): 227–73.

10. This pattern continued well into the twentieth century in the popular format of film travelogues accompanied by a live lecturer. Charles Musser has noted the transition in America from travel lecturers using stereopticon slides in the 1890s to early twentieth-century film exhibitors screening travel films with their own commentary. Musser suggests that "audience identification" with showmen-travellers allowed "those who lacked the time, money, or fortitude" to enjoy the "vicarious experience" of travel (126–27).

11. Kate Flint, among others, notes the importance of distinguishing between the hypothetically constructed reader referred to in the text and Thackeray's actual, intended readers. She suggests that in *Vanity Fair*, Thackeray associates an emotional or affective response to literature with women's novel-reading, while characterizing male readers as more capable of detached irony and self-reflexivity ("Women, Men and the Reading of *Vanity Fair*," in *The Practice and Representation of Reading in England*, ed. James Raven, Helen Small, and Naomi Tadmor, 246–62. [Cambridge: Cambridge University Press, 1996]). The above essay shows Thackeray registering both of these dimensions: emotion and irony, immersion and detachment.

12. See John M. L. Drew's two substantial essays on Dickens and travel: "Voyages Extraordinaires: Dickens's 'Travelling Essays' and *The Uncommercial Traveller*," Part I, *Dickens Quarterly* 13, no. 2 (1996): 76–99; and Part II, *Dickens Quarterly* 13, no. 3 (1996): 127–51. Drew notes that Dickens was very familiar with the literary tradition of the creation of a narrator or persona who was an "insubstantial, peripatetic entity" known as "The Rambler . . . The Spectator . . . the Idler," etc. (I, 78), and suggests that this influenced his frequent use of a framework resembling a "récit de voyage" in essays that "consist in the account of a journey, tour, walk, ramble, strut, stroll, or 'lounge' through

some familiar . . . landscape (often urban) which derives humor and often a satirical component from invoking the narrative of 'real' voyages and travels" (I, 79). See also Clotilde de Stasio, "The Traveller as Liar: Dickens and the 'Invisible Towns' in Northern Italy," *Dickensian* 96 (2000): 5–13. For further discussion of Dickens as a "flâneur," see also Michael Hollington's "Dickens the Flâneur," *Dickensian* 77 (1981): 71–87, and Alison Byerly, "Effortless Art: The Sketch in Nineteenth-Century Painting and Literature," *Criticism* 41 (1999): 349–64.

13. Helen Small disputes the notion that the audiences for Dickens's readings were genuinely working-class to any significant degree, but notes that the perception of Dickens's readership as being "universal" was part of a "crucial stage in the development about the relationship between the culture and class in Britain: one in which the middle-classes exerted and consolidated unprecedented control over the cultural sphere" ("A Pulse of 124: Charles Dickens and a Pathology of the Mid-Victorian Reading Public," in *The Practice and Representation of Reading in England*, ed. James Raven, Helen Small, and Naomi Tadmor, 268 [Cambridge: Cambridge University Press, 1996]). See also Philip Collins, introduction to *Charles Dickens: The Public Readings* (Oxford: Oxford University Press, 1975).

14. Elaine Freedgood's excellent account of Victorian ballooning in *Victorian Writing about Risk* suggests that it was an activity that, by creating a kind of "perspectival enlargement of the self," served as both "a rehearsal for and re-enactment of empire building" (91). "The needs and interests of egos, England, and empire meshed in the upper air where the highly pleasurable experience of regression, in which the self is momentarily sublime and therefore experienced as maximally powerful and even indestructible, becomes the emotional basis for the heroic action associated with imperial and colonial adventures" (93).

15. Both Oettermann and Comment make this irresistible comparison. Oettermann notes that when Robert Barker coined the term *panorama* in 1792, Bentham's idea of the panopticon had been appearing in print for several years. Both terms describe "round structures built around a central observation platform that is isolated from the periphery" (51). Oetterman also cites Foucault's own footnote, in *Discipline and Punish*, querying, "'Was Bentham aware of the Panoramas that Barker was constructing at exactly the same period (?)'" (Oettermann 41n.108). Comment connects the "all-knowing and all-seeing" (142) perspective of both the panorama and the panopticon with other architectural manifestations of the "*Überblick*, the gaze from above" (141).

16. Timothy Mitchell notes that the Egyptian exhibit at the 1889 Paris Exposition Universelle, a display of "great historical confidence" on the part of an imperial power, impressed even Egyptian visitors. "Exhibitions, museums, and other spectacles were not just reflections of this certainty, however, but the means of its production, by their technique of rendering history, progress, culture and empire in 'objective' form" (7).

17. Many critics have discussed spectatorship in Hardy's novels, as well as the complex visual perspective of the narrator himself, but these have generally been treated as separate issues. Thus, Sheila Berger ascribes the "hypothetical observer" point of view

to the narrator, who "pretends to nothing more than the ability to see surfaces" (*Thomas Hardy and Visual Structures* [New York: New York University Press, 1990], 98), while David Lodge characterizes this purely visual perspective as "cinematic." ("Thomas Hardy as a Cinematic Novelist," in *Thomas Hardy after Fifty Years*, ed. Lance St. John Butler [London: Macmillan, 1977], 78–89).

The point of view I am describing here seems to me to combine the point of view of a typical spectator (that is, a character) with an omniscient narrative perspective. Thus, it does not fall into the category of description analyzed by, for example, Julie Grossman in her essay "Thomas Hardy and the Role of the Observer" (*ELH* 58 [1989]: 619–39).

18. *Bleak House* is of course noted for its shifts in perspective, and many critics have commented upon its thematic tension between what Daniel Hack calls "the preference for the proximate" and more remote objects of reform (2008, 748). See also Bruce Robbins, "Telescopic Philanthropy: Professionalism and Philanthropy in Bleak House," in *Nation and Narration*, ed. Homi K. Bhabha (London: Routledge, 1990), 213–30.

19. Eliot may have chosen to honor Albert Smith with a presentation copy because Blackwood had reported some months earlier that Smith had been so moved by the serial publication of "Amos Barton," the first story in the collection, that he "blubber[ed] like a boy" (Haight, 220).

Part Two

1. I pursue this idea in an earlier essay that prefigures and incorporates portions of my argument here: "Rivers, Journeys, and the Construction of Place in Nineteenth Century English Literature," in *The Greening of Literary Scholarship: Literature, Theory, and the Environment*, ed. Steven Rosendale (Iowa University Press, 2002), 77–94.

2. Ruskin writes, "The traveller on his happy journey, as his foot springs from the deep turf and strikes the pebbles gaily . . . sees with a glance of delight the clusters of nut-brown cottages. . . . Here, it may well seem to him, if there be sometimes hardship, there must be at least innocence and peace, and fellowship of the human soul with nature. It is not so. . . . Enter the street of one of those villages, and you will find it foul with that gloomy foulness that is suffered only by torpor, or by anguish of soul" (312). For these cottagers, Ruskin claims, there is "neither hope nor passion of spirit" (314). He goes on to note the irony of theatrical representations that convert such squalor into rustic charm. He might be describing one of Albert Smith's Alpine cottages for "The Ascent of Mont Blanc" when he writes:

> Is it not strange to reflect, that hardly an evening passes in London or Paris but one of those cottages is painted for the better amusement of the fair and idle, and shaded with pasteboard pines by the scene-shifter; and that good and kind people,—poetically minded—delight themselves by imagining the happy life led by peasants who dwell by Alpine fountains. . . . If all the gold that has gone forth to paint the simulacra of the cottages, and to put new songs in the mouths of the

simulacra of the peasants, had gone to brighten the existent cottages . . . it might, in the end, have turned out better so, not only for the peasants, but even for the audience. (315)

Ruskin's explicit linkage of the tourist's perspective with the theatergoer's perspective suggests that the detached, aestheticized view of the tourist renders the real sights he views as unreal as a stage set.

3. David S. J. Hodgson, *Halo 3 ODST: Prima Official Game Guide* (New York: Random House/Prima Games, 2009), 1.

4. Anne Friedberg, *Window Shopping: Cinema and the Postmodern* (Berkeley: University of California Press, 1993). See also Friedberg, *The Virtual Window: From Alberti to Microsoft* (Cambridge: MIT Press, 2006).

5. It is perhaps worth noting that the "official" biography of Whistler, *The Life of James McNeill Whistler* (London, 1908), was written, with the cooperation of the artist, by fellow Thames enthusiasts Joseph and Elizabeth Robins Pennell, authors of *Stream of Pleasure.* Joseph Pennell was an artist, and the Pennells were avid collectors of Whistler's work. Joseph Pennell also illustrated Henry James's *English Hours* (1877), with its description of the Thames cited below.

6. The relationship between the geographic status and the ontological status of a utopia is a larger topic than my argument here can accommodate, but Louis Marin offers a contrasting perspective to Rancière's, suggesting in relation to More's *Utopia* that it is place defined entirely by its name: "*Utopia is not a topography but a topic.* It is often said that it is an imaginary place. Rather, it is an indetermined place. Better yet, it is the very indetermination of place" (115). Both of these views encapsulate the essential point about utopias, which is that they seek to give a local habitation and a name to an abstract vision of the world.

7. In an essay on the meaning of "the waves" in *Dombey and Son,* Malvern Van Wyck Smith links the novel's use of the image of the sea with mercantile imperialism and sees the complementary image of the river as providing a vision of "indifferent private and public misery" that is a counterpoint to "imperial triumph" (132). Smith briefly connects *Dombey and Son's* "uncertainty and ambivalence" about imperialism with Dickens's 1848 review of Willam Allen and Thomas Thompson's account of Thomas Fowell Buxton's "disastrous" Niger River expedition of 1841–42 (128), a connection that reminds us of the pervasive influence of exotic river-exploration accounts on the Victorian sense of the symbolic dimensions of river journeys.

8. Harry Stone sees Gaffer's comment as one of many examples of a "cannibalistic theme" in Dickens. Stone connects Gaffer's comment, as well as Eugene's later remarks about the taste of "river-wash," with a passage in Dickens's essay "Travelling Abroad" in which Dickens is revolted by having accidentally swallowed some water while swimming in the Seine, shortly after viewing the body of a drowned man at the morgue. Stone also notes that in *A Tale of Two Cities,* Jerry Cruncher "calls his nocturnal body snatching 'fishing,' and claims that this sinister 'fishing' is meat and drink to his family" (Stone, 151–53).

9. See *London's Riverscape Lost and Found: A Photographic Panorama of the River Thames from 1937 and Today* (London: The Found Riverscape Partnership, Checkmate at Art Books International, 2000), 44. The photographs comprising the 1937 panorama can also be viewed on the Museum of London website.

10. G. H. Lewes's diary for Feb. 2, 1875, notes that Eliot and Lewes drove one afternoon "to Kew Bridge and walked along the river to Richmond, choosing a spot for the meeting of De Ronda [*sic*] & Mirah'" (Haight 1968, 476).

11. Though rowing is characterized as a typical young gentleman's activity, it could be enjoyed by young women as well: a letter from Eliot to Mr. and Mrs. Charles Bray in August 1849 apologizes for her delay in writing, noting that she has "almost lost the use of my arms with rowing, and my pen straggles anywhere but in the right place" (Haight 1954, I, 300).

12. See Amanda Anderson's chapter on *Daniel Deronda* in *The Powers of Distance*. This passage has striking similarities to several scenes in Hardy, including the moment in *Tess of the D'Urbervilles* in which Tess describes looking up at the stars and feeling her self stand outside her body. Among many who have discussed the relationship between visual perception and subjectivity in Hardy, the most relevant recent commentaries include John Plotz's discussion of Hardy's emphasis on "individuated perception" (128). Plotz sees this as integral to Hardy's "obsession with how different individuals orient themselves in the world" (123).

13. The *Princess Alice* disaster, like many railway accidents and similarly dramatic examples of sudden death, instantly became fodder for religious tracts like *Are You Prepared?, or the Thames Catastrophe* (1878); its hold on the public imagination was perhaps intensified by the death of Princess Alice herself, at the age of thirty-five, three months later.

Part Three

1. The telegraph might seem a more obvious analogy, and Tom Standage's *The Victorian Internet: The Remarkable Story of the Telegraph and the Nineteenth Century's Online Pioneers* (London: Phoenix, 1998) has popularized the comparison. I would argue, however, that the railway had a more dramatic effect on the daily lives of individuals than the telegraph and hence was more influential and visible as an emblem of change. But the two technologies developed in a symbiotic relationship that allows similar points to be made about both.

2. Schivelbusch followed Dolf Sternberger in describing the view from a railway window as "panoramic," a point to which we will return. Sternberger emphasizes that railway travel "turned the eye of travelers outward, offering them a rich diet of changing tableaux" (122), whereas my discussion will emphasize the interiority of the experience. See Sternberger, *Panorama of the Nineteenth Century*, trans. Joachim Neugroschel (Oxford: Basil Blackwell, 1977; orig. pub. as *Panorama oder Ansichten vom 19. Jahrhundert*, 1938).

3. This large colored print, reproduced in several places, including Simmons's *The Railway Journey*, is found in the John Johnson Collection, Railways Folder 2.

4. John Carey and David Quirk, "The Mythos of the Electronic Revolution," *Communication as Culture: Essays on Media and Society* (Routledge, 2008), 87–108; David Nye, *American Technological Sublime* (MIT, 1996).

5. Michael Freeman has noted the pervasiveness of images of flight, particularly supernatural flight, in descriptions of rail travel (38).

6. For a detailed discussion of Ruskin's attitude toward railways, which he described as "the loathsomest form of devilry now extant," see Jeffrey Richards, "The Role of the Railways." Richards notes that Ruskin objected to the railway for several reasons: "It interfered with the process of detailed observation, it encouraged mental torpor and it destroyed the very scenery that the traveller should be observing" (Richards, 135).

7. See Kern, 11–15, and Freeman. For an overview of the development of standardized time, and discussion of the meaning of time at the turn of the century, see Peter Galison, "Einstein's Clocks: The Place of Time," *Critical Inquiry* 26, no. 2 (2000): 355–89.

8. See, for example, "Ministerial Crisis," *Illustrated London News*, May 1, 1880, 1.

9. Richard D. Altick, *The English Common Reader* (1957), 89, 305; Simmons, *The Victorian Railway*, 245–49; Schivelbusch, 66–71.

10. When the Tay Bridge collapsed on December 28, 1879, during a violent storm, killing some seventy-five passengers whose train plunged into the Firth of Tay, the *Illustrated London News* noted the chilling fact that the queen had herself crossed the bridge recently, reminding readers that "we gave an illustration of the Royal Train . . . with the Queen looking out of the window, surveying the expanse of water far below and the opposite shore two miles apart." *Illustrated London News*, Jan. 3, 1880, 18.

11. For an overview of the development of excursion trains, see Simmons, 270–308; for a discussion of the effect of railways on the mobility of workers, see Simmons, 318–32.

12. *Illustrated London News*, Sept. 4, 1880, 244–45.

13. *Punch* 51 (1866): 70.

14. Matus, "Trauma, Memory, and Railway Disaster: The Dickensian Connection," *Victorian Studies* 43 (2001): 11. See also Matus, *Shock, Memory and the Unconscious*. The trauma of railway accidents as represented in the *Illustrated London News* is also discussed by Peter Sinnema, *Dynamics of the Pictured Page* (Ashgate, 1998), 120ff, as well as by Nicholas Daly, as noted in text.

15. This image is explored in detail by Laura Otis, in *Metaphors of Invasion in Nineteenth-Century Science, Literature, and Politics* (Johns Hopkins University Press, 1999). See also Tina Young Choi, "Writing the Victorian City: Discourses of Risk, Connection, and Inevitability," *Victorian Studies* 43, no. 4 (2001): 561–90.

16. An older system of information circulation that contains many parallels is the postal system. See Derek Gregory, "The Friction of Distance? Information Circulation and the Mails in Early Nineteenth-Century England," *Journal of Historical Geography* 13, no. 2 (1987): 130–54.

17. Standage, 54. Erik Larsen's 2006 book *Thunderstruck* pairs the story of Marconi's experiments in telegraphy with Dr. Crippen's famous murder of his wife, exploring the way in which telegraphic communication allowed Crippen's flight to become a worldwide media sensation even as Crippen's isolation on a transatlantic crossing prevented him from knowing that he was being pursued.

18. Among the first and best discussions of the role of telegraphs in nineteenth-century literature is Jay Clayton's "The Voice in the Machine: Hazlitt, Hardy, and James," which appeared as a chapter in *Language Machines: Technologies of Literary and Cultural Production*, ed. Jeffrey Masten, Peter Stallybrass, and Nancy Vickers (Routledge, 1997), and subsequently became a chapter in his *Charles Dickens in Cyberspace: The Afterlife of the Nineteenth Century in Postmodern Culture* (Oxford, 2003). Clayton makes a case for the fundamental importance of the telegraph in the history of modern media and faults Friedrich Kittler for failing to account for the role of the telegraph, which he sees as symptomatic of Kittler's tendency to focus on media as recording and storage mechanisms, while "neglect[ing] their communicative functions" (51).

More recently, Richard Menke's *Telegraphic Realism: Victorian Fiction and Other Information Systems* (Stanford, 2008) discusses both the Penny Post and the development of telegraphy as alternative models for the circulation of information. Menke's "examination of how fiction could begin imagining itself as a medium and information system in an age of new media" (3) has many affinities with my own study. Henry James's short story "In the Cage" is a focal point for these discussions, and for N. Katharine Hayles, in *My Mother Was a Computer*, 65–83.

19. Daly, *Literature, Technology, and Modernity*, 47. Daly emphasizes the role of the sensation novel in reinforcing the "transformation of human experience of time and space being effected by the railways" (47), stressing the treatment of time in particular. He outlines the importance of dramatic time limits and deadlines in creating sensation fiction's characteristic effects on the nerves (49). More generally, Daly sees "speed, suspense, and mystery" as "the first hallmarks" of an "early literature of modernization" (4).

20. Ronald R. Thomas has pointed out that Francis Ford Coppola's 1992 film *Bram Stoker's Dracula* foregrounds "Stoker's preoccupation with turn-of-the-century media and textuality" by using "a series of complex dissolves and superimpositions" to weave "montages of handwriting, typewriting, and phonograph recording with the shifting settings and dramatic action of the narrative throughout the film" (299).

21. Gunning discusses the "exhibitionism" of such "non-narrative" subgenres of film, which he sees as relating more to "the attractions of the fairground than to the traditions of legitimate theatre" (58), in "The Cinema of Attractions: Early Film, the Spectator, and the Avant-Garde."

22. Further discussion of travel and film may be found in Charles Musser, "The Travel Genre in 1903–4: Moving toward Fictional Narrative," *Iris* 2 (1984): 47–60.

23. Daniel Radosh notes that music video games are often criticized as a poor substitute for reality precisely because they seem tantalizingly close to the experience of playing music: "People who play *Halo* or Gran Turismo are rarely asked why they don't pick

up a real gun or race real cars. You rarely hear that Monopoly is a waste of time because it doesn't actually teach anything about buying hotels. The disparagement of Rock Band and Guitar Hero, then, suggests that music games *do* resemble actual performance, at least enough so that people feel the need to point out that they are not" (26).

24. This fixed perspective is replicated in a modern re-creation of the "Rhinebeck" Panorama recently installed in the Docklands Museum in London, which helpfully provides not only a guardrail but an X on the floor to direct viewers to the ideal vantage point.

25. Vinay Dharwadker, Introduction, *Cosmopolitan Geographies: New Locations in Literature and Culture* (Routledge, 2001), 7. For further commentary on Victorian cosmopolitanism, see Bruce Robbins, *Cosmopolitics: Thinking and Feeling Beyond the Nation* (Minnesota, 1998); Amanda Anderson, *The Powers of Distance: Cosmopolitanism and the Cultivation of Detachment* (Princeton, 2001); and the special section on "Victorian Cosmopolitanisms" in *Victorian Literature and Culture* 38, no. 2 (September 2010), which contains articles by James Buzard, Judith Walkowitz, and Bruce Robbins, among others.

26. David Wellbury, Introduction, *Friedrich Kittler, Discourse Networks 1800/1900*, trans. Michael Meteer (Stanford University Press, 1990), xiii.

27. Friedrich Kittler, *Gramophone, Film, Typewriter*, trans. Geoffrey Winthrop-Young and Michael Wutz (Stanford University Press, 1996), xl.

28. Rowan McWilliam, "Victorian Sensations, Neo-Victorian Romances: Response," *Victorian Studies* 52, no. 1 (2009): 106–13.

29. Mark Llewellyn, "What Is Neo-Victorian Studies?" *Neo-Victorian Studies* 1, no. 1 (Autumn 2008): 164–85.

30. See Elaine Hadley, "The Past is a Foreign Country: The Neo-Conservative Romance with Victorian Liberalism," *Yale Journal of Criticism* 10, no. 1 (1997): 7–38.

WORKS CITED

Adams, Paul. "Network Topologies and Virtual Place." *Annals of the Association of American Geographers* 88, no. 1 (1998): 88–101.

"All Round St. Paul's." *Punch* 18 (1850): 179.

Allen, John Naule. "Railway Reading." *Ainsworth's Magazine* 24 (December 1853): 483–87.

Altick, Richard. *The Shows of London*. Cambridge: Harvard University Press, 1978.

Anderson, Alexander. *Songs of the Rail*. London: Simpkin, Marshall, 1878.

Anderson, Amanda. *The Powers of Distance: Cosmopolitanism and the Cultivation of Detachment*. Princeton: Princeton University Press, 2001.

Anderson, Benedict. *Imagined Communities*. London: Verso, 1983.

Arac, Jonathan, and Harriet Ritvo, eds. *Macropolitics of Nineteenth-Century Literature: Nationalism, Exoticism, Imperialism*. Philadelphia: University of Pennsylvania Press, 1991.

Arata, Stephen D. "The Occidental Tourist: Dracula and the Anxiety of Reverse Colonization." *Victorian Studies* 33 (1990): 621–45.

Are You Prepared? Or, the Thames Catastrophe. A Tract. London: Hall, 1878.

Armour, M[argaret]. *Thames Sonnets and Semblances*. With Illustrations by W. B. McDougall. London: Elkin Mathews, 1897.

Armstrong, Nancy. *Fiction and the Age of Photography: The Legacy of British Realism*. Cambridge: Harvard University Press, 2000.

Auerbach, Jeffrey. *The Great Exhibition of 1851: A Nation on Display*. New Haven: Yale University Press, 1999.

Augé, Marc. *Non-Places: An Introduction to Supermodernity*. Translated by John Howe. New York: Verso, 1995.

Bailenson, Jeremy, Jim Blascovich, Andrew Beall, and Beth Noveck. "Courtroom Applications of Virtual Environments, Immersive Virtual Environments, and Collaborative Virtual Environments." *Law and Policy* 28, no. 2 (April 2006): 249–70.

Bailenson, Jeremy, Nick Yee, Dan Merget, and Ralph Schroeder. "The Effect of Behavioral Realism and Form Realism of Real-Time Avatar Faces on Verbal Disclosure, Nonverbal Disclosure, Emotion Recognition, and Copresence in Dyadic Interaction." *Presence* 15, no. 4 (2006): 359–72.

Baines, Dudley, Nicholas Craft, and Tim Leunig. "Railways and the Electronic Age." London School of Economics and Political Science. 2003. N.p. Accessed at www.fathom.com/feature/122057.

Baucom, Ian. *Out of Place: Englishness, Empire, and the Location of Identity.* Princeton: Princeton University Press, 1999.

Baudrillard, Jean. *The Perfect Crime.* 1995. Translated by Chris Turner. London: Verso, 1996.

Baudrillard, Jean. *Simulacra and Simulation.* 1981. Translated by Sheila Faria Glaser. Ann Arbor: University of Michigan Press, 1994.

Baudrillard, Jean. *Simulations.* Translated by Paul Foss, Paul Patton, and Philip Beitchman. New York: Semiotext(e), 1983.

Baudrillard, Jean. *The Vital Illusion.* Edited by Julia Witwer. New York: Columbia University Press, 2000.

Baumgarten, Murray. "Railway/Reading/Time: *Dombey & Son* and the Industrialized World." *Dickens Studies Annual* 19 (1990): 65–89.

Beaumont, Matthew, ed. *Adventures in Realism.* Malden: Blackwell, 2007.

Behdad, Ali. *Belated Travelers: Orientalism in the Age of Colonial Dissolution.* Durham: Duke University Press, 1994.

Bell, Robert. *The Ladder of Gold: An English Story.* London: Richard Bentley, 1850.

Bell, Robert. "A Run on the Eastern Counties Railway." *Bentley's Miscellany* 28 (October 1850): 448–59.

Benjamin, Walter. *The Arcades Project.* Translated by Howard Eiland and Kevin McLaughlin. Cambridge: Belknap Press of Harvard University Press, 1999.

Benjamin, Walter. *Illuminations.* Edited by Hannah Arendt. Translated by Harry Zohn. London: Cape, 1970.

Benko, Georges, and Ulf Strohmeyer. *Space and Social Theory: Interpreting Modernity and Postmodernity.* Oxford: Blackwell, 1997.

Bermingham, Ann. *Landscape and Ideology: The English Rustic Tradition, 1740–1860.* Berkeley: University of California Press, 1986.

Bhabha, Homi K. "Dissemination: Time, Narrative, and the Margins of the Modern Nation." In *Nation and Narration,* edited by Homi K. Bhabha, 291–322. London: Routledge, 1990.

Bhabha, Homi K. "Introduction: Narrating the Nation." In Bhabha, ed., *Nation and Narration,* 1–7. London: Routledge, 1990.

Bhabha, Homi K. *The Location of Culture.* London: Routledge, 1984.

Biocca, Frank. "The Cyborg's Dilemma: Progressive Embodiment in Virtual Environments." *Journal of Computer-Mediated Communication* 3, no. 2 (September 1997). Accessed October 15, 2008, http://jcmc.indiana.edu/vol3/issue2/biocca2.html.

Birkerts, Sven. *The Gutenberg Elegies: The Fate of Reading in an Electronic Age.* Boston: Faber and Faber, 1994.

Bissell, Tom. "The Grammar of Fun." *The New Yorker,* November 3, 2008, 78–84.

Bittanti, Matteo. "All Too Urban: To Live and Die in *SimCity.*" In *Videogame, Player, Text,* edited by Barry Atkins and Tanya Krzywinska, 29–51. Manchester: Manchester University Press, 2007.

Blascovich, Jim, and Jeremy N. Bailenson. *Infinite Reality: Avatars, Eternal Life, New Worlds, and the Dawn of the Virtual Revolution.* New York: HarperCollins, 2011.

Blascovich, Jim, Jack Loomis, Andrew C. Beall, Kimberly R. Swinth, Crystal L. Hoyt, and Jeremy N. Bailenson. "Immersive Virtual Environment Technology as a Methodological Tool for Social Psychology." *Psychological Inquiry* 13, no. 2 (2002): 103–24.

"Boaters on the Way to Henley Regatta." *Illustrated London News.* July 3, 1886: 10.

Boellstorf, Tom. *Coming of Age in Second Life: An Anthropologist Explores the Virtually Human.* Princeton: Princeton University Press, 2008.

Bogost, Ian. *Unit Operations: An Approach to Videogame Criticism.* Cambridge: MIT Press, 2006.

Bolland, R. R. *Victorians on the Thames.* Tunbridge Wells: Midas Books, 1974.

Bolter, Jay David, and Richard Grusin. *Remediation: Understanding New Media.* Cambridge: MIT Press, 1999.

Booth, Michael. *Victorian Spectacular Theater, 1850–1910.* Boston: Routledge, 1981.

Bosson, Olaf E. *Slang and Cant in Jerome K. Jerome's Works.* Cambridge: Heffner, 1911.

Boyd, A. K. H. "How I Mused in the Railway Train." *Fraser's Magazine* 59 (1859): 146–48.

Boyle's Thames Guide. London: G. Boyle, 1840.

Braddon, Mary Elizabeth. *Lady Audley's Secret.* 1862. Edited by David Skilton. Oxford: Oxford University Press, 1987.

"Bradshaws." *British Quarterly Review* 43 (1866): 367–414.

Bradshaw's London Railway Guide, Commercial Companion and Advertiser. London: W. J. Adams, 1862.

Bradshaw's Monthly Descriptive Railway Guide and Illustrated Hand-Book of England, Wales, Scotland, and Ireland. London: W. J. Adams, 1857.

Bradshaw's Pocket Handbook to the London, Brighton, and South Coast Railway, its Various Branches and Connections, Describing Every Place and Object of Interest. London: W. J. Adams, [1873].

Brantlinger, Patrick. "'News from Nowhere': Morris's Socialist Anti-Novel." *Victorian Studies* 19 (1975): 35–79.

Brantlinger, Patrick. *Rule of Darkness: British Literature and Imperialism, 1830–1914.* Ithaca: Cornell University Press, 1988.

Brontë, Charlotte. *Villette.* 1853. Edited by Herbert Rosengarten and Margaret Smith. Oxford: Clarendon Press, 1984.

Brown, William Wells. *The Travels of William Wells Brown. Including Narrative of William Wells Brown, a Fugitive Slave, and The American Fugitive in Europe: Sketches of Places and People Abroad.* Edited by Paul Jefferson. Edinburgh: Edinburgh University Press, 1991. Originally published in 1852 as *Three Years in Europe: Places I Have Seen and People I Have Met.*

Buck-Morss, Susan. *The Dialectics of Seeing: Walter Benjamin and the Arcades Project.* Cambridge: MIT Press, 1989.

"Burford's Panorama of Paris." *Illustrated London News* 12 (June 1848): 373.

[Burgoyne, Margaret]. "The Balloon. An 'Excursion Trip,' but not by Railway, by a Lady." *Bentley's Miscellany* 30 (November 1851): 528–34.

Burton, Sir Richard F. *Personal Narrative of a Pilgrimage to Al-Madinah and Meccah.* London: Longmans, 1855.

Buzard, James. *The Beaten Track: European Tourism, Literature, and the Ways to "Culture,"* *1800–1918.* Oxford: Clarendon Press, 1993.

Buzard, James. *Disorienting Fiction: The Autoethnographic Work of Nineteenth-Century British Novels.* Princeton: Princeton University Press, 2005.

Buzard, James. "Ethnography as Interruption: *News from Nowhere*, Narrative, and the Modern Romance of Authority." *Victorian Studies* 40, no. 3 (1997): 445–74.

"By the Underground Railway." *Temple Bar* 77 (1886): 496–508.

Byerly, Alison. "'A Prodigious Map Beneath His Feet': Virtual Travel and the Panoramic Perspective." *Nineteenth-Century Contexts* 29, nos. 2–3 (June–September 2007): 151–69.

Byerly, Alison. *Realism, Representation, and the Arts in Nineteenth Century Literature.* Cambridge: Cambridge University Press, 1998.

Byerly, Alison. "Rivers, Journeys, and the Construction of Place in Nineteenth-Century English Literature." In Steven Rosendale, ed., *The Greening of Literary Scholarship: Literature, Theory, and the Environment*, 77–94. Iowa City: Iowa University Press, 2002.

Cannadine, David. *Ornamentalism: How the British Saw Their Empire.* Harmondsworth, UK: Penguin, 2001.

Carey, James W., and John J. Quirk. "The Mythos of the Electronic Revolution." *Communication as Culture: Essays on Media and Society*, 87–108. New York: Routledge, 2009. Reprint.

Carlisle, Janice. *Common Scents: Comparative Encounters in High-Victorian Fiction.* New York: Oxford University Press, 2004.

Carroll, David. *George Eliot and the Conflict of Interpretations.* Cambridge: Cambridge University Press, 1992.

Castronova, Edward. *Exodus to the Virtual World: How Online Fun Is Changing Reality.* New York: Palgrave Macmillan, 2007.

Castronova, Edward. *Synthetic Worlds: The Business and Culture of Online Games.* Chicago: University of Chicago Press, 2005.

Chaouli, Michael. "How Interactive Can Fiction Be?" *Critical Inquiry* 31 (Spring 2005): 599–617.

Charney, Leo, and Vanessa R. Schwartz, eds. *Cinema and the Invention of Modern Life.* Berkeley: University of California Press, 1995.

Cherry, Deborah. *Beyond the Frame: Feminism and Visual Culture, 1850–2000.* London: Routledge, 2000.

Choi, Tina Young. "Writing the Victorian City: Discourses of Risk, Connection, and Inevitability." *Victorian Studies* 43, no. 4 (2001): 561–90.

Clark, Steve, ed. *Travel Writing and Empire: Postcolonial Theory in Transit.* London: Zed Books, 1999.

Clayton, Jay. *Charles Dickens in Cyberspace: The Afterlife of the Nineteenth Century in Postmodern Culture.* New York: Oxford University Press, 2003.

Clayton, Jay. "Hacking the Nineteenth Century." In *Victorian Afterlife: Postmodern Culture Rewrites the Nineteenth Century,* edited by John Kucich and Dianne Sadoff, 186–210. Minneapolis: University of Minnesota Press, 2000.

Cohen, William A. *Embodied: Victorian Literature and the Senses.* Minneapolis: University of Minnesota Press, 2009.

"The Colosseum." *Illustrated London News* 12 (1848): 312.

"Comical Christmas Chronicle." A supplement to the *Illustrated London News. ILN* 13, December 23, 1848.

Comment, Bernard. *The Panorama.* London: Reaktion, 2001.

Conrad, Joseph. *Heart of Darkness.* 1899. Oxford: Oxford University Press, 2008.

"Constantinople Removed to Regent Street." *Punch* 19 (1850): 97.

Cornish, Thomas Hartree. *The Thames: A Descriptive Poem.* London: William Pickering, 1842.

Crary, Jonathan. *Suspensions of Perception: Attention, Spectacle, and Modern Culture.* Cambridge: MIT Press, 1999.

Crary, Jonathan. *Techniques of the Observer: On Vision and Modernity in the Nineteenth Century.* Cambridge: MIT Press, 1990.

Curtis, Barry, and Claire Pajaczkowska. "'Getting There': Travel, Time, and Narrative." In *Travellers' Tales: Narratives of Home and Displacement,* edited by George Robertson, Melinda Mash, Lisa Tickner, Jon Bird, Barry Curtis, and Tim Putnamet, 199–215. London: Routledge, 1998.

Daly, Nicholas. "Blood on the Tracks: Sensation Drama, the Railway, and the Dark Face of Modernity." *Victorian Studies* 42 (1999): 47–76.

Daly, Nicholas. *Literature, Technology, and Modernity, 1860–2000.* Cambridge: Cambridge University Press, 2004.

Daly, Nicholas. "Railway Novels: Sensation Fiction and the Modernization of the Senses." *ELH* 66 (1999): 461–87.

De Cauter, Lieven. "The Capsule and the Network: Notes toward a General Theory." In *The Cybercities Reader,* edited by Stephen Graham, 94–97. New York: Routledge, 2004.

Description of Banvard's Panorama of the Mississippi and Missouri Rivers. Extensively known as the "Three-Mile Painting . . ." London: W. J. Golbourn, Leicester Square, 1848.

"A Description of the Colosseum, as Reopened in MCCCXLV." With Numerous Illustrations, and Eight Colored Sections of the Panorama of London, Embossed by Mssrs. Dobbs, Bailey, and Co. London: J. Wertheimer and Co., n.d.

"Description of a Painting of Jerusalem and the Surrounding Country, As it Appears at this Time from the Mount of Olives." Painted by E. Donovan. View Taken in the year 1811, 1812. London Museum, Fleet-Street. [JJ Coll, Dioramas 1.]

"Description of a View of the City of Coblentz." London, 1843. [ML Dioramas, Panoramas A2.]

"Descriptive Book of the Tour of Europe." Frankfurt, 1853. [John Johnson Collection of Printed Ephemera, Dioramas Box 3, The Bodleian Library, Oxford.]

De Vries, Leonard. *Victorian Inventions*. London: John Murray, 1971.

Dias, Nelia. "Looking at Objects: Memory, Knowledge, in Nineteenth-Century Ethnographic Displays." In *Travellers' Tales: Narratives of Home and Displacement*, edited by George Robertson, Melinda Mash, Lisa Tickner, Jon Bird, Barry Curtis, and Tim Putnam. 164–76. London: Routledge, 1998.

Dibbell, Julian. *Play Money: Or, How I Quit My Day Job and Made Millions Trading Virtual Loot*. New York: Basic Books, 2006.

Dickens, Charles. *American Notes*. 1842. Oxford: Oxford University Press, 1966.

Dickens, Charles. *Bleak House*. 1853. Oxford: Oxford University Press, 1966.

Dickens, Charles. *David Copperfield*. 1838. Oxford: Oxford University Press, 1966.

Dickens, Charles. *Great Expectations*. 1861. Oxford: Oxford University Press, 1966.

Dickens, Charles. *Mugby Junction*. 1866. Foreword by Robert McFarlane-Harpers Classics, 2005.

Dickens, Charles. *Oliver Twist*. 1839. Oxford: Oxford University Press, 1966.

Dickens, Charles. *Sketches by Boz*. 1839. New York: Oxford University Press, 1957.

Dickens, Charles. *The Uncommercial Traveller and Reprinted Pieces*. Oxford: Oxford University Press, 1958.

Dickens, Charles, Jr. (the Younger). *Dickens's Dictionary of the Thames*. London: Macmillan, 1887. Facsimile reprint. Moretonhampstead: Old House Books, 1994.

Doane, Mary Anne. "Screening Time." In *Language Machines: Technologies of Literary and Cultural Production*, edited by Jeffrey Masten, Peter Stallybrass, and Nancy Vickers. Routledge, 1997.

Doel, Marcus A., and David B. Clarke. "Virtual Worlds: Simulation, Suppletion, S(ed)uction and Simulacra." In *Jean Baudrillard*, vol. 1, edited by Mike Gane, 191–215. Sage Masters of Modern Social Thought. London: Sage, 2000.

Domenichetti, Richard Hippesley. *The Thames*. Newdigate Prize Poem, 1885. Oxford: A. Thomas Shrimpton and Son, 1885.

Douglas-Fairhurst, Robert. *Victorian Afterlives: The Shaping of Influence in Nineteenth-Century Literature*. Oxford: Oxford University Press, 2002.

Dovey, Kimberly. "The Quest for Authenticity and the Replication of Environmental Meaning." *Dwelling, Place, and Environment: Towards a Phenomenology of Person and World*, 42–48. New York: Columbia University Press, 1985.

Doyle, Sir Arthur Conan. *The Adventures of Sherlock Holmes*. 1887–93. Ware: Wordsworth Classics, 1996.

Doyle, Sir Arthur Conan. *The Case-Book of Sherlock Holmes*. 1908–27. Ware: Wordsworth Classics, 1993.

Doyle, Sir Arthur Conan. *The Return of Sherlock Holmes*. 1901–4. Ware: Wordsworth Classics, 1996.

Doyle, Audrey. "Steamboy [review]." *Area.autodesk.com*. October 22, 2007.

Duncan, James, and Derek Gregory. *Writes of Passage: Reading Travel Writing*. London: Routledge, 1999.

Eade, Brian. *Forgotten Thames*. Phoenix Mill: Thrupp, 2002.

Early, Julie English. "Technology, Modernity, and the 'Little Man': Crippen's Capture by Wireless." *Victorian Studies* 39 (1996): 309–38.

Eliot, George. *Adam Bede*. 1859. London: Virtue, n.d.

Eliot, George. *Daniel Deronda*. 1876. Harmondsworth: Penguin Books, 1996.

Eliot, George. *Felix Holt: The Radical*. 1866. Harmondsworth: Penguin Books, 1995.

Eliot, George. *Letters of George Eliot*. Edited by Gordon Haight. 7 vols. New Haven: Yale University Press, 1954–55.

Eliot, George. *Middlemarch*. 1872. Harmondsworth: Penguin Books, 2003.

Eliot, George. *The Mill on the Floss*. 1860. Harmondsworth: Penguin Books, 2003.

Eliot, George. *Scenes of Clerical Life*. 1859. Harmondsworth: Penguin Books, 1999.

Foucault, Michel. "Of Other Spaces." *Diacritics* 16, no. 1 (1986): 22–27.

Foucault, Michel. *This is not a pipe. With illustrations and Letters by René Magritte*. Translated and edited by James Harkness. Berkeley and Los Angeles: University of California Press, 1983.

Foxwell, E. *Two Papers on Express Trains*. London: Edward Stanford, 1884.

Freedgood, Elaine. *Victorian Writing about Risk: Imagining a Safe England in a Dangerous World*. Cambridge: Cambridge University Press, 2000.

Freeling, Arthur. *The Railway Companion, from London to Birmingham, Liverpool, and Manchester; With Guides to the Objects Worthy of Notice in Liverpool, Manchester, and Birmingham*. London: Whittaker, 1838.

Freeman, Michael. *Railways and the Victorian Imagination*. New Haven: Yale University Press, 1999.

Friedberg, Anne. *The Virtual Window: From Alberti to Microsoft*. Cambridge: MIT Press, 2006.

Friedberg, Anne. *Window Shopping: Cinema and the Postmodern*. Berkeley: University of California Press, 1993.

Froude, J. A. "A Siding at a Railway Station." *Fraser's Magazine*, o.s., 100 (1879): 622–33.

Furst, Lilian R. *All Is True: The Claims and Strategies of Realist Fiction*. Durham: Duke University Press, 1995.

Gagnier, Regenia. *Subjectivities: A History of Self-Representation in Britain, 1832–1920*. New York: Oxford University Press, 1991.

Gaskell, Elizabeth. *Cranford; and other Tales*. 1853. London: Smith, Elder, 1906.

Gerrig, Richard J. *Experiencing Narrative Worlds: On the Psychological Activities of Reading*. New Haven: Yale University Press, 1993.

The Ghost of John Bull; or, the Devil's Railroad: A Marvellously Strange Narrative. London: James Pattie, 1838.

Gibson, William. *Neuromancer.* New York: Berkley, 1984.

Gilbert, Helen. "Belated Journeys: Ecotourism as a Style of Travel Performance." In *In Transit: Travel, Text Empire*, 255–74. New York: Peter Lang, 2002.

Gilbert, Helen, and Anna Johnston, eds. *In Transit: Travel, Text, Empire.* New York: Peter Lang, 2002.

Girouard, Mark. *The English Town.* New Haven: Yale University Press, 1990.

Gissing, George. *New Grub Street.* 1891. Harmondsworth: Penguin Books, 1968.

Gissing, George. *The Odd Women.* 1893. Ed. Elaine Showalter. New York: New American Library, 1983.

Gitelman, Lisa, and Geoffrey B. Pingree, eds. *New Media, 1740–1915.* Cambridge: MIT Press, 2003.

Glaisher, James. *Travels in the Air.* London: Richard Bentley, 1871.

Goldsack, Paul. *River Thames: In the Footsteps of the Famous.* Chalfont St. Peter, UK: Bradt Travel Guides, 2003.

"Grand Panorama of the Great Exhibition." Foldout engraving in two parts. *Illustrated London News* 19, November 22, 1851: 632–33; December 6, 1851: 691–92.

"A Grand View of a Lake and Waterfall in Switzerland . . ." Advertising handbill. Whitechapel: W. Buck, 1831. [John Johnson Collection of Printed Ephemera, Dioramas Box 3, The Bodleian Library, Oxford.]

Green-Lewis, Jennifer. *Framing the Victorians: Photography and the Culture of Realism.* Ithaca: Cornell University Press, 1997.

Gregory, Derek, and John Urry, eds. *Social Relations and Spatial Structures.* Palgrave Macmillan, 1985.

Grusin, Richard. "Premediation." *Criticism* 46, no. 1 (2004): 17–39.

Grusin, Richard. *Premediation: Affect and Mediality after 9/11.* New York: Palgrave Macmillan, 2010.

Guidebook to Mr. Washington Friend's Grand Tour of Five Thousand Miles in Canada and the United States of America. Nottingham: Stafford and Co., n.d. [Museum of London, Dioramas, Panoramas A3.]

Gunning, Tom. "The Birth of Film Out of the Spirit of Modernity." *Masterpieces of Modernist Cinema*, edited by Ted Perry, 13–40. Bloomington: Indiana University Press, 2006.

Gunning, Tom. "The Cinema of Attractions: Early Film, Its Spectator, and the Avant-Garde." In *Early Cinema: Space/Frame/Narrative*, edited by Thomas Elsaesser and Adam Barker, 56–62. London: British Film Institute, 1990.

Gunning, Tom. "Tracing the Individual Body: Photography, Detectives, and the Early Cinema." In *Cinema and the Invention of Modern Life,*. edited by Leo Charney and Vanessa R. Schwartz, 15–42. Berkeley: University of California Press, 1995.

Hack, Daniel. "Close Reading at a Distance: The African Americanization of Bleak House." *Critical Inquiry* 34 (2008): 729–53.

Hack, Daniel. *The Material Interests of the Victorian Novel.* Charlottesville: University of Virginia Press, 2005.

Haight, Gordon. *George Eliot: A Biography.* 1968. London: Penguin, 1997.

Haight, Gordon, ed. *George Eliot Letters.* Vol. I. New Haven: Yale University Press, 1954.

Haliburton, T. C. "'The Season Ticket': A Train of Thought, and Thoughts in a Train." *Dublin University Magazine* 54 (1859): 105–16.

Hall, N. John. *Anthony Trollope: A Biography.* Oxford: Oxford University Press, 1993.

Hapgood, Lynne. "The Literature of the Suburbs: Versions of Repression in the Novels of George Gissing, Arthur Conan Doyle and William Pett Ridge, 1890–99." *Journal of Victorian Culture* 5, no. 2 (2000): 287–310.

Halpern, Sue. "Virtual Iraq: Using Simulation to Treat a New Generation of Traumatized Veterans." *New Yorker,* May 19, 2008, 32–37.

Hansen, Mark B. N. *Bodies in Code: Interfaces with Digital Media.* New York: Routledge, 2006.

Hardy, Thomas. *Far from the Madding Crowd.* 1874. London: Macmillan, 1912.

Hardy, Thomas. *Jude the Obscure.* 1896. London: Penguin, 1978.

Hardy, Thomas. *The Mayor of Casterbridge.* 1886. London: Macmillan, 1912.

Hardy, Thomas. *Tess of the D'Urbervilles.* 1891. London: Macmillan, 1912.

Hardy, Thomas. *The Woodlanders.* 1887. London: Macmillan, 1912.

Harrigan, Pat, and Noah Wardrip-Fruin, eds. *Third Person: Authoring and Exploring Vast Narratives.* Cambridge: MIT Press, 2009.

Harvey, David. "The Cartographic Imagination: Balzac in Paris." *Cosmopolitan Geographies.* New York: Routledge, 2001.

Harvey, Geoffrey. "Introduction." Jerome K. Jerome, *Three Men in a Boat.* Oxford: Oxford University Press, 1998.

"Have You Seen Niagara Falls?" Undated handbill, Bodleian Libraries, University of Oxford, John Johnson Collection of Printed Ephemera: Shelfmark Dioramas 1 (21).

Hayles, N. Katharine. *How We Became Posthuman: Virtual Bodies in Cybernetics, Literature, and Informatics.* Chicago: University of Chicago Press, 1999.

Heim, Michael. *Virtual Realism.* New York: Oxford University Press, 1998.

Heinen, Sandra, and Roy Sommer, eds. *Narratology in the Age of Cross-Disciplinary Narrative Research.* Berlin: Walter de Gruyter, 2009.

Hemingway, Andrew. *Landscape Imagery and Urban Culture in Nineteenth-Century Britain.* Cambridge: Cambridge University Press, 1992.

Hemyng, Bracebridge, "ed." *Secrets of the River. By a Thames Policeman.* London: J. A. Berger, 1870.

Henry, Charles B. "The Night Train." *Ainsworth's Magazine* 21 (1852): 197–203.

Herbert, Christopher. *Culture and Anomie: Ethnographic Imagination in the Nineteenth Century.* Chicago: University of Chicago Press, 1991.

Herendeen, W. H. "The Rhetoric of Rivers: The River and the Pursuit of Knowledge." *Studies in Philology* 78 (1981): 107–27.

Herman, David, ed. *The Cambridge Companion to Narrative.* Cambridge: Cambridge University Press, 2007.

Herman, David, ed. *Narratologies: New Perspectives on Narrative Analysis.* Columbus: Ohio State University Press, 1999.

Herman, David. *Story Logic: Problems and Possibilities of Narrative.* Lincoln: University of Nebraska Press, 2002.

Hewitt, Martin. "Why the Notion of Victorian Britain Does Make Sense." *Victorian Studies* 48, no. 3 (2006): 395–438.

Hill, David. *Turner on the Thames: River Journeys in the Year 1805.* New Haven: Yale University Press, 1999.

Hodgson, David S. J. *Halo 3 ODST: Prima Official Game Guide.* New York: Random House/Prima Games, 2009.

Holden, Donald. *Whistler: Landscapes and Seascapes.* New York: Watson-Guptill, 1969.

Hollingshead, John. "The Excursion Train." *Cornhill Magazine* 4 (1861): 727–34.

Home and Country Scenes on Each Side of the Line of the London and Birmingham and Grand Junction Railways. N.d. [1839, per National Railway Museum catalog]. London: Charles Tilt, Fleet Street.

Hooper, H. G. *A Poetical Sketch of the Thames from the Seven Springs to the Nore.* Cheltenham: T. Hailing, 1885.

Horner, David Sanford. "Cyborgs and Cyberspace: Personal Identity and Moral Agency." *Technospaces: Inside the New Media,* edited by Sally R. Munt, 71–84. London: Continuum, 2001.

"How Father Thames Appeared to the Cabinet, on the Road to the Whitebait Dinner, and What He Said to Them." *Punch* 35 (July 31, 1858): 47.

Huggan, Graham. "Counter-Travel Writing and Post-Coloniality." In *Being/s in Transit: Travelling, Migration, Dislocation,* edited by Liselotte Glage, 37–59. Amsterdam: Editions Rodopi B. V., 2000.

Hyde, Ralph. *Panoramania! The Art and Entertainment of the "All-Embracing" View. An Exhibit at Barbican Art Gallery from 3rd November 1988 to 15th January 1989.* London: Trefoil in association with Barbican Art Gallery, 1988.

"An Illustrated Description of the Diorama of the Ganges. With Foldout Panorama of Calcutta." T. C. Dibden Pianist, Lecturer. London: Portland Gallery, 1850. [John Johnson Collection of Printed Ephemera, Dioramas Box 1, The Bodleian Library, Oxford.]

Imken, Otto. "The Convergence of Virtual and Actual in the Global Matrix: Artificial Life, Geo-Economics, and Psychogeography." *Virtual Geographies: Bodies, Spaces, and Relations,* edited by Mike Crang, Phil Crang, and Jon May, 92–106. New York: Routledge, 1999. Jacobsen, Wendy, ed. *Dickens and the Children of Empire.* Basingstoke: Palgrave, 2000.

Jaffe, Audrey. *Vanishing Points: Dickens, Narrative, and the Subject of Omniscience.* Berkeley: University of California Press, 1991.

James, Henry. *English Hours.* 1877. Edited by Alma Louise Lowe. New York: Orion Press, 1960.

Jameson, Fredric. *Postmodernism, or, the Cultural Logic of Late Capitalism*. London: Verso, 1991.

Jenkins, Henry. *Convergence Culture: Where Old and New Media Collide*. New York: New York University Press, 2006.

Jenkins, Henry. "Game Design as Narrative Architecture." In *First Person: New Media as Story, Performance, and Game*, edited by Noah Wardrip-Fruin and Pat Harrigan, 118–130. Cambridge: MIT Press, 2004. http://web.mit.edu/cms/People/henry3/games&narrative.html.

Jenkins, Henry, and David Thorburn. *Rethinking Media Change: The Aesthetics of Transition*. Cambridge: MIT Press, 2003.

Jennings, Humphrey, and Mary-Lou Jennings. *Pandaemonium, 1660–1886: The Coming of the Machine Age as Seen by Contemporary Observers*. 1985. London: Papermac, 1995.

Jerome, Jerome K. *My Life and Times*. London: John Murray, 1926. Reprint, 1983.

Jerome, Jerome K. *Three Men in a Boat; Three Men on the Bummel*. 1889; 1900. Edited by Geoffrey Harvey. Oxford: Oxford University Press, 1998.

Jerrold, Douglas. "Christmas Thoughts of the Crystal Palace." *Illustrated London News* 19 (December 20, 1851): 738–39.

John Johnson Collection of Printed Ephemera [JJ Coll], Bodleian Library, Oxford. Diorama Box 1, Diorama Box 2, Diorama Box 3. Railway Box 6, Railway Box 7, Railway Box 8, Railway Box 10, Railway Box 11, Railway Box 12, Railway Box 16, Railway Box 19, Railway Box 24. Railway Folder 1, Railway Folder 2.

Joyce, Simon. *The Victorians in the Rearview Mirror*. Athens: Ohio University Press, 2007.

Juul, Jesper. *Half-Real: Video Games between Real Rules and Fictional Worlds*. Cambridge: MIT Press, 2005.

Kern, Stephen. *The Culture of Time and Space, 1880–1910*. London: Weidenfeld and Nicolson, 1983.

Kerridge, Richard. "Ecologies of Desire: Travel Writing and Nature Writing as Travelogue." In *Travel Writing and Empire: Postcolonial Theory in Transit*, edited by Steve Clark, 164–82. London: Zed Books, 1999.

King, Geoff. "Play, Modality, and Claims of Realism in *Full Spectrum Warrior*." *Videogame, Player, Text*. Edited by Barry Atkins and Tanya Krzywinska, 52–65. Manchester: Manchester University Press, 2007.

King, Geoff, and Tanya Krzywinska. *Tomb Raiders and Space Invaders: Videogame Forms and Contexts*. London: I. B. Tauris, 2006.

Kirby, Lynne. *Parallel Tracks: The Railroad and Silent Cinema*. Exeter: University of Exeter Press, 1997.

Kittler, Friedrich A. *Discourse Networks 1800/1900*. 1985. Translated by Michael Mettler. Stanford: Stanford University Press, 1990.

Kittler, Friedrich A. *Gramophone, Film, Typewriter*. 1986. Translated by Geoffrey Winthrop-Young and Michael Wutz. Stanford: Stanford University Press, 1999.

Koerner, Joseph Leo. *Casper David Friedrich and the Subject of Landscape*. New Haven: Yale University Press, 1990.

Kucich, John, and Dianne Sadoff, eds. *Victorian Afterlife: Postmodern Culture Rewrites the Nineteenth Century*. Minneapolis: University of Minnesota Press, 2000.

"Ladies in Railway Carriages." *Sala's Journal* 1, no. 5 (1892): 97–98.

Lahti, Martti. "As We Become Machines: Corporealized Pleasures in Video Games." In *The Video Game Theory Reader*, edited by Mark J. P. Wolf and Bernard Perron, 157–70. New York: Routledge, 2003.

Landow, George. *Hypertext 3.0: Critical Theory and New Media in an Age of Globalization*. Baltimore: Johns Hopkins University Press, 2006.

Landow, George, ed. *Hyper/Text/Theory*. Baltimore: Johns Hopkins University Press, 1994.

Lee, Debbie, and Tim Fulford. "Virtual Empires." *Cultural Critique* 44 (Winter 2000): 3–28.

Le Quesne, Nicholas. "Let the Arguments Begin." *Time*, November 11, 2002, 75.

Leslie, George D. *Our River*. Illustrations by the Author. London: Bradbury, Agnew, 1881.

Lever, Charles James. *Tales of the Trains, Being Some Chapters of Railroad Romance, by Tilbury Tramp*. London: W. S. Orr, 1845.

Levine, George. *Dying to Know: Scientific Epistemology and Narrative in Victorian England*. Chicago: University of Chicago Press, 2002.

Lévy, Pierre. *Becoming Virtual: Reality in the Digital Age*. Translated by Robert Bonomo. New York: Plenum, 1998.

Lévy, Pierre. *Cyberculture*. Translated by Robert Bonomo. Minneapolis: University of Minnesota Press, 2001.

Livingstone, David. *Missionary Travels and Researches in South Africa*. London: John Murray, 1857.

Lock, Charles. "Hardy and the Railway." *Essays in Criticism* 50 (2000): 44–66.

"London: River Thames Guide and Audio for iPhone, iPod." By Way2Go Guides. http://itunes.apple.com/us/app/london-river-thames-guide/id330004600?mt=8.

London's Riverscape: Lost and Found. A Photographic Panorama of the River Thames from 1937 and Today. London: Found Riverscape Partnership, Checkmate at Art Books International, 2000.

Luke, Timothy W. "Power and Politics in Hyperreality: The Critical Project of Jean Baudrillard." In *Jean Baudrillard*, vol. 2, edited by Mike Gane, 26–48. Sage Masters of Modern Social Thought. London: Sage Publications, 2000.

Lunenfeld, Peter. *The Digital Dialectic: New Essays on New Media*. Cambridge: MIT Press, 1999.

Mackay, Charles. "Rambles Among the Rivers: The Thames and its Tributaries." *Bentley's Miscellany* V, no. I: 372–80; no. II: 508–16; no. III: 602–9. "The Manchester and Liverpool Rail-Road." *Monthly Supplement of the Penny Magazine of the Society for the Diffusion of Useful Knowledge.* March 31 to April 30, 1833. London: Charles Knight, 1833.

Marin, Louis. *Utopics: Spatial Play.* Translated by Robert A. Vollrath. Atlantic Highlands, NJ: Humanities Press, 1984.

Matus, Jill. *Shock, Memory, and the Unconscious in Victorian Fiction.* Cambridge: Cambridge University Press, 2009.

Matus, Jill. "Trauma, Memory, and Railway Disaster: The Dickensian Connection." *Victorian Studies* 43 (2001): 413–36.

Mayhew, Henry. "A Balloon View of London." 1852. Reprinted in Humphrey Jennings, *Pandaemonium 1660–1886: The Coming of the Machine as Seen by Contemporary Observers,* edited by Mary-Lou Jennings and Charles Madge. London: Andre Deutsch, 1985.

Mayhew, Henry. *London Labour and the London Poor.* 1849–50. Edited and selected by Victor Neuberg. Harmondsworth, UK: Penguin, 1985.

McClintock, Anne. *Imperial Leather: Race, Gender, and Sexuality in the Colonial Contest.* New York: Routledge, 1995.

McGann, Jerome. *Radiant Textuality: Literature after the World Wide Web.* New York: Palgrave, 2001.

Measom, George. *The Official Illustrated Guide to the South Eastern Railway.* London: W. H. Smith, Booksellers to the Company, [1853].

Meisel, Martin. *Realizations: Narrative, Pictorial, and Theatrical Arts in Nineteenth-Century England.* Princeton: Princeton University Press, 1983.

Melchiori, Barbara Arnett. *Terrorism in the Late Victorian Novel.* London: Croom Helm, 1985.

Menke, Richard. *Telegraphic Realism: Victorian Fiction and Other Information Systems.* Stanford: Stanford University Press, 2008.

Michasiw, Kim Ian. "Nine Revisionist Theses on the Picturesque." *Representations* 38 (1992): 76–100.

Michie, Elsie B. "Buying Brains: Trollope, Oliphant, and Vulgar Victorian Commerce." *Victorian Studies* 44 (2001): 77–98.

Miller, Andrew. *Novels behind Glass: Commodity Culture and Victorian Narrative.* Cambridge: Cambridge University Press, 1995.

Miller, J. Hillis. *Topographies.* Stanford: Stanford University Press, 1995.

"Mission Statement." *Illustrated London News.* May 1842, 1.

Mitchell, Timothy. *Colonising Egypt.* Cambridge: Cambridge University Press, 1988.

Moretti, Franco. *Atlas of the European Novel, 1800–1900.* London: Verso, 1998.

Morus, Iwan Rhys. *Frankenstein's Children: Electricity, Exhibition, and Experiment in Early Nineteenth-Century London.* Princeton: Princeton University Press, 1998.

"Moving and Most Popular Panorama of the Voyage to Australia." Handbill, 1853. The Bodleian Libraries, University of Oxford, John Johnson Collection of Printed Ephemera: Shelfmark Dioramas 4 (60).

"Mr. William Johnson's Grand Balloon Ascent." *Ainsworth's Magazine* 23 (April 1853): 347–53.

Murphy, Sheila C. "'Live in Your World, Play in Ours': The Spaces of Video Game Identity." *Journal of Visual Culture* 3, no. 2 (2004): 223–38. http://vcu.sagepub.com/cgi/content/abstract/3/2/223.

Murray, Janet. *Hamlet on the Holodeck: The Future of Narrative in Cyberspace*. New York: Free Press, 1997.

Murray, John. *A Picturesque Tour of the River Thames in its Western Course; Including Particular Descriptions of Richmond, Windsor, and Hampton Court*. London: Henry Bohn, 1849.

Museum of London Collection [ML]. Dioramas, Panoramas Box A1; Dioramas, Panoramas Box A2; Dioramas, Panoramas Box A3; Oversized Panoramas/Dioramas Box C1.

Musser, Charles. "The Travel Genre in 1903–4: Moving Towards Fictional Narrative." In *Early Cinema: Space/Frame/Narrative*, edited by Thomas Elsaesser and Adam Barker, 123–32. London: British Film Institute, 1990.

Naylor, Maria, ed. *Etchings of James McNeill Whistler*. Mineloa, NY: Dover, 1975.

Nead, Lynda. *Victorian Babylon: People, Streets, and Images in Nineteenth-Century London*. New Haven: Yale University Press, 2000.

Negroponte, Nicholas. *Being Digital*. New York: Vintage, 1995.

Nell, Victor. *Lost in a Book: The Psychology of Reading for Pleasure*. New Haven: Yale University Press, 1988.

Nelson, Harland S. "Staggs's Gardens: The Railway through Dickens's World." *Dickens Studies Annual* 3 (1974): 41–54.

"Nightmare on the Rails." *Fraser's Magazine* 34 (1846): 522–28.

Novak, Daniel A. *Realism, Photography, and Nineteenth-Century Fiction*. Cambridge: Cambridge University Press, 2008.

Nunes, Mark. "Virtual Topographies: Smooth and Striated Cyberspace." In *Cyberspace Textuality: Computer Technology and Literary Theory*, edited by Marie-Laure Ryan, 61–77. Bloomington: Indiana University Press, 1999.

Oettermann, Stephan. *The Panorama: History of a Mass Medium*. Translated by D. L. Schneider. New York: Zone Books, 1997.

The Official Guide to the Midland Railway. London: Cassell, 1884.

The Old Arm-Chair: A Retrospective Panorama of Travels by Land and Sea. Anonymous. London: Society for Promoting Christian Knowledge, 1854.

"An Old Guide." *Temple Bar* 5 (1862): 542–48.

"An Old Question Settled at Last." *Punch* 18 (1850): 69.

Oliphant, Margaret. "Boating on the Thames." *Blackwood's Edinburgh Magazine* 108 (1870): 460–77.

Oliphant, Margaret. "A Railway Junction; or, the Romance of Ladybank." *Blackwood's Edinburgh Magazine* 114 (1873): 419–41.

Ollier, Edmund. In *The Royal River: The Thames, from Source to Sea*. London: Cassell, 1885.

Oppenheim, Janet. *Shattered Nerves: Doctors, Patients, and Depression in Victorian England*. New York: Oxford University Press, 1991.

Otis, Laura. *Metaphors of Invasion in Nineteenth-Century Science, Literature, and Politics*. Baltimore: Johns Hopkins University Press, 1999.

Ottley, George. *A Bibliography of British Railway History*. London: George Allen and Unwin, 1965. 2nd ed. 1983.

Ousby, Ian. *The Englishman's England: Taste, Travel, and the Rise of Tourism*. Cambridge: Cambridge University Press, 1990.

"Panorama of London by Night. Projected and carried out by Mr. William Bradwell, painted by Mr. Danson and Mr. Telbin." N.p., n.d. [British Library].

"Panorama of the British Constitution." *Punch* 19 (1850): 70.

"A Panorama of the Maine . . . designed by nature by F. W. Delkeskamp, engraved by John Clarke." 1830. [John Johnson Collection of Printed Ephemera, Dioramas Box 1, The Bodleian Library, Oxford.]

Panorama of the Thames, from London to Richmond. London: Samuel Leigh, n.d. (ca. 1840).

Parrinder, Patrick. "From Mary Shelley to *The War of the Worlds*: The Thames Valley Catastrophe." *Anticipations: Essays on Early Science Fiction and Its Precursors*, edited by David Seed. Liverpool: Liverpool University Press, 1995.

Parsons, Deborah L. *Streetwalking the Metropolis: Women, the City, and Modernity*. Oxford: Oxford University Press, 2000.

Peacock, Thomas Love. *The Genius of the Thames*. Thomas and Edward Hookham, 1810.

Pennell, Joseph, and Elizabeth Robins Pennell. *The Stream of Pleasure: A Narrative of a Journey on the Thames from Oxford to London*. London: T. Fisher Unwin, 1891.

Perera, Suvendrini. *The Reaches of Empire: The English Novel from Edgeworth to Dickens*. New York: Columbia University Press, 1991.

Pettit, Clare. "Peggotty's Work-Box: Victorian Souvenirs and Material Memory." *Romanticism and Victorianism on the Net*, 53 (February 2009). www.erudit.org/revue/ravon/2009/v/n53/029896ar.html. Accessed March 10, 2011.

Philips, John. "Lagging Behind: Bhabha, Post-colonial Theory and the Future." *Travel Writing and Empire*, edited by Steve Clark. New York: Zed Books, 1999.

Picker, John. *Victorian Soundscapes*. New York: Oxford University Press, 2003.

Pike, Richard, ed. *Railway Adventures and Anecdotes: Extending Over More than Fifty Years*. London: Hamilton, Adams, 1884.

Plotz, John. *Portable Property: Victorian Culture on the Move*. Princeton: Princeton University Press, 2008.

Poole, Steven. "William Gibson: Tomorrow's Man." *The Guardian*, March 5, 2003, 20–23.

Porter, Dale H. *The Thames Embankment: Environment, Technology, and Society in Victorian London*. Akron: University of Akron Press, 1998.

Poster, Mark. "Theorizing Virtual Reality: Baudrillard and Derrida." *Cyberspace Textuality: Computer Technology and Literary Theory*, edited by Marie-Laure Ryan, 42–60. Indianapolis: Indiana University Press, 1999.

Poulet, Georges. "The Phenomenology of Reading." *New Literary History* 1, no. 1 (Oct. 1969): 53–68.

Pratt, Mary Louise. *Imperial Eyes: Travel Writing and Transculturation*. Boston: Routledge, 1992.

The Presence Project. "Performing Presence: From the Live to the Simulated." Accessed October 1, 2008. www.humantieslab.stanford.edu/presence/home.

Quin, Michael J. *Steam Voyages on the Seine, the Moselle, and the Rhine; with Railroad Visits to the Principal Cities of Belgium*. 2 vols. London: Henry Colburn, 1843.

Radosh, Daniel. "While My Guitar Gently Beeps." *New York Times Magazine*, Aug. 11, 2009: 26–37, 44–47. http://www.nytimes.com/2009/08/16/magazine/16beatles-t.html.

Railroad Eclogues. London: William Pickering, 1846.

"A Railway Glance at the Corn Laws." *Fraser's Magazine* 19 (1839): 254–60.

"Railway Literature." *Dublin University Magazine* 34 (1849): 280–91.

"Railway Stations." *Chambers's Journal* 7 (1890): 305–6.

"A Railway Trip, by Miles Ryder, Esq." *Fraser's Magazine* 22 (1840): 238–42.

"Rambles Round Travel." *Blackwood's Magazine* 121 (May 1877): 605–26.

Rancière, Jacques. "Discovering New Worlds: Politics of Travel and Metaphors of Space." In *Traveller's Tales: Narratives of Home and Displacement*, edited by George Robertson et al. London: Routledge, 1994; reprint,. 1998.

Regenbrecht, Holger, and Thomas Schubert. "Real and Illusory Interactions Enhance Presence in Virtual Environments." *Presence* 11, no. 4 (2002): 425–34.

Rheingold, Howard. *Virtual Reality*. New York: Touchstone, 1991.

Richards, Jeffrey. "The Role of the Railways." *Ruskin and Environment: The Storm-Cloud of the Nineteenth Century*, edited by Michael Wheeler, 123–43. Manchester: Manchester University Press, 1995.

Richards, Thomas. *The Commodity Culture of Victorian England: Advertising and Spectacle, 1851–1914*. Stanford: Stanford University Press, 1990.

Richards, Thomas. *The Imperial Archive: Knowledge and the Fantasy of Empire*. London: Verso, 1993.

Robbins, Bruce. "Telescopic Philanthropy: Professionalism and Philanthropy in Bleak House." In *Nation and Narration*, edited by Homi K. Bhabha, 213–30. London: Routledge, 1990.

Robertson, George, et al. *Traveller's Tales: Narratives of Home and Displacement*. London: Routledge, 1994; reprint, 1998.

Robins, Kevin. "Cyberspace and the World We Live In." *Cyberspace, Cyberbodies, Cyberpunk: Cultures of Technological Embodiment*, edited by Michael Featherstone and Roger Burrows. Thousand Oaks, CA: Sage, 1996.

Robison, Roselee. "Time, Death, and the River in Dickens' Novels." *English Studies* 53 (1972): 436–54.

Rogers, Pat. "*Windsor-Forest, Britannia,* and River Poetry." *Studies in Philology* 77 (1980): 283–99.

Rojek, Chris, and John Urry. "Transformations of Travel and Theory." In *Touring Cultures: Transformations of Travel and Theory,* edited by Chris Rojek and John Urry, 1–22. London: Routledge, 1997.

The Royal River: The Thames from Source to Sea. London: Cassell and Co., 1885. Including chapters by W. Senior, T. G. Bonney, H. Schutz Wilson, Godfrey Turner, Edmund Ollier, Aaron Watson, J. Runciman.

Ruskin, John. *Modern Painters.* 1843–60. 5 vols. London: Cook and Wedderburn, 1904.

Ryan, Marie-Laure. *Avatars of Story.* Minneapolis: University of Minnesota Press, 2006.

Ryan, Marie-Laure, ed. *Cyberspace Textuality: Computer Technology and Literary Theory.* Bloomington: Indiana University Press, 1999.

Ryan, Marie-Laure, ed. *Narrative Across Media: The Languages of Storytelling.* Lincoln: University of Nebraska Press, 2004.

Ryan, Marie-Laure. *Narrative as Virtual Reality: Immersion and Interactivity in Literature and Electronic Media.* Baltimore: Johns Hopkins University Press, 2001.

Said, Edward. *Culture and Imperialism.* New York: Vintage, 1994.

Sallnas, Eva-Lotta. "Collaboration in Multi-Modal Virtual Worlds: Comparing Touch, Text, Voice, and Video." In *The Social Life of Avatars: Presence and Interaction in Shared Virtual Environments,* edited by Ralph Schroeder, 172–88. London: Springer-Verlag, 2002.

Salt, Samuel. *Railway and Commercial Information.* London: W. H. Smith, 1850.

Saltz, David Z. "The Art of Interaction: Interactivity, Performativity, and Computers." *Journal of Aesthetics and Art Criticism* 55, no. 2 (Spring 1997): 117–27.

Sanders, Andrew. *Charles Dickens: Resurrectionist.* London: Macmillan Press, 1982.

Schama, Simon. *Landscape and Memory.* London: Fontana Press, 1995.

Schivelbusch, Wolfgang. *The Railway Journey: The Industrialization of Time and Space in the Nineteenth Century.* 1977. Berkeley: University of California Press, 1986.

Schroeder, Ralph. "Social Interaction in Virtual Environments: Key Issues, Common Themes, and a Framework for Research." In *The Social Life of Avatars: Presence and Interaction in Shared Virtual Environments,* edited by Ralph Schroeder, 1–18. London: Springer-Verlag, 2002.

Schroeder, Ralph, and Ann-Sofie Axelsson, eds. *Avatars at Work and Play: Collaboration and Interaction in Shared Virtual Environments.* London: Springer-Verlag, 2006.

Schwarzbach, F. S. *Dickens and the City.* London: Athlone Press, 1979.

Sen, Sambudha. "Bleak House, Vanity Fair, and the Making of an Urban Aesthetic." *Nineteenth-Century Literature* 54, no. 4 (2000): 480–502.

Shanes, Eric. *Turner's Rivers, Harbours, and Coasts.* London: Chatto and Windus, 1981.

"The Sights of London" [William Thackeray, unsigned]. *Punch* 18 (1850): 132.

Simmons, Jack, ed. *Journeys in England: An Anthology.* 1951. Trowbridge: David and Charles, 1969.

Simmons, Jack. *The Victorian Railway.* London: Thames and Hudson, 1991.

Singer, Ben. "Modernity, Hyperstimulus, and the Rise of Popular Sensationalism." *Cinema and the Invention of Modern Life*, edited by Leo Charney and Vanessa R. Schwartz, 72–102. Berkeley: University of California Press, 1995.

Sinnema, Peter. *Dynamics of the Pictured Page: Representing the Nation in* The Illustrated London News. Aldershot, UK: Ashgate, 1998.

Slater, Michael, ed. *Dickens' Journalism Volume II: The Amusements of the People and Other Papers: Reports, Essays and Reviews 1834–51.* London: J. M. Dent, 1996.

Smith, Malvern Van Wyck. "'What the Waves Were Always Saying': *Dombey and Son* and Textual Ripples on an African Shore." In Wendy S. Jacobson, *Dickens and the Children of Empire*, 128–52. Palgrave Macmillan, 2000.

Spurr, David. *The Rhetoric of Empire: Colonial Discourse in Journalism, Travel Writing, and Imperial Administration.* Durham: Duke University Press, 1993.

Standage, Tom. *The Victorian Internet: The Remarkable Story of the Telegraph and the Nineteenth Century's Online Pioneers.* London: Phoenix, 1998.

Stapleton, John. *The Thames: A Poem.* London: C. Kegan Paul, 1878.

Steiner, Wendy. *The Scandal of Pleasure: Art in an Age of Fundamentalism.* Chicago: University of Chicago Press, 1995.

Sternberger, Dolf. *Panorama of the Nineteenth Century.* Translated by Joachim Neugroschel. Oxford: Basil Blackwell, 1977. Originally published as *Panorama oder Ansichten vom 19. Jahrhundert*, 1938.

Stevenson, Robert Louis. *The Letters of Robert Louis Stevenson*, edited by Bradford A. Booth and Ernest Mehew. 8 vols. New Haven: Yale University Press, 1995.

Stewart, Garrett. *Dear Reader: The Conscripted Audience in Nineteenth-Century British Fiction.* Baltimore: Johns Hopkins University Press, 1996.

Stoker, Bram. *Dracula.* 1897. Harmondsworth: Penguin Books, 2003.

Stone, Alluquére Rosanne. "Will the Real Body Stand Up? Boundary Stories about Virtual Cultures." In *Cyberspace: First Steps*, edited by Michael Bendikt, 81–118. Cambridge: MIT University Press, 1992.

Stone, Harry. *The Night Side of Dickens: Cannibalism, Passion, Necessity.* Columbus: Ohio State University Press, 1994.

Strobel, Susanne. "Floating into Heaven or Hell: The River Journey in Mary Kingsley's *Travels in West Africa* and Joseph Conrad's *Heart of Darkness*." In *Being/s in Transit: Travelling, Migration, Dislocation*, edited by Lisolette Gage, 69–82. Amsterdam: Rodopi, 2000.

Sussex Technology Group. "In the Company of Strangers: Mobile Phones and the Conception of Space." In *Technospaces: Inside the New Media*, edited by Sally R. Munt, 205–23. London: Continuum, 2001.

Taylor, Jonathan. "The Emerging Geographies of Virtual Worlds." *Geographical Review* 87, no. 2 (1997): 172–92.

Taylor, Mark C. *The Moment of Complexity: Emerging Network Culture.* Chicago: University of Chicago Press, 2001.

Taylor, T. L. "Living Digitally: Embodiment in Virtual Worlds." In *The Social Life of Avatars: Presence and Interaction in Shared Virtual Environments,* edited by Ralph Schroeder, 40–62. London: Springer-Verlag, 2002.

Thackeray, William. "Dumas on the Rhine." *Foreign Quarterly* October 1842. In *The Irish Sketch Book and Contributions to the 'Foreign Quarterly Review,' 1842–4,* edited by George Saintsbury, 418–39. Oxford: Oxford University Press, n.d.

Thackeray, William. *The Irish Sketch Book and Contributions to the 'Foreign Quarterly Review,' 1842–4.* Edited by George Saintsbury. Oxford: Oxford University Press, n.d.

[Thackeray, William]. *The Kickleburys on the Rhine.* By M. A. Titmarsh. London: Smith, Elder, 1850.

[Thackeray, William]. *The Newcomes.* 1855. Edited by George Saintsbury. Oxford: Oxford University Press, n.d.

[Thackeray, William]. *The Paris Sketch-Book.* 1840. Edited by George Saintsbury. Oxford: Oxford University Press, n.d.

[Thackeray, William]. "'The Rhine' by Victor Hugo." *Foreign Quarterly* April 1842. In *The Irish Sketch Book and Contributions to the 'Foreign Quarterly Review,' 1842–4,* edited by George Saintsbury, 369–401. Oxford: Oxford University Press, n.d.

[Thackeray, William]. *Vanity Fair: A Novel Without a Hero.* 1848. Edited by Peter Shillingsburg. New York: Garland, 1989.

"The Thames." *Saint Paul's* 5 (Dec. 1869): 306–19.

"'There Be Land Pirates.'" *Punch* 18 (1850): 163.

Thomas, Ronald R. "Specters of the Novel: *Dracula* and the Cinematic Afterlife of the Victorian Novel." In *Victorian Afterlife,* edited by John Kucich and Dianne Sadoff, 288–319. Minneapolis: University of Minnesota Press, 2000.

Thorburn, David, and Henry Jenkins, eds. *Rethinking Media Change: The Aesthetics of Transition.* Cambridge: MIT Press, 2003.

Thorne, James. *Rambles by Rivers.* Vol. 1, *The Thames.* London: C. Cox, 1847.

Thurston, Gavin. *The Great Thames Disaster.* London: George Allen and Unwin, 1965.

"To the Thames!" *Punch* 35 (July 3, 1858), 7.

The Tour of the Thames; or, the Sights and Songs of the King of Rivers. London: John Kendrick, 1849.

Trollope, Anthony. *The Prime Minister.* 1873. 2 vols. London: Oxford University Press, 1952.

Trollope, Anthony. *The Way We Live Now.* 1875. London: Penguin, 1994.

Turkle, Sherry. *Alone Together: Why We Expect More from Technology and Less from Each Other.* New York: Basic Books, 2011.

Turkle, Sherry. *Life on the Screen.* London: Weidenfeld and Nicolson, 1996.

Turner, Fred. *From Counterculture to Cyberculture: Steward Brand, the Whole Earth Network, and the Rise of Digital Utopianism*. Chicago: University of Chicago Press, 2006.

Up the River from Westminster to Windsor. A Panorama in Pen and Ink. Illustrated with Eight-One Engravings and a Map. London: Hardwicke and Bogue, 1876.

Verne, Jules. *Around the World in Eighty Days; and Five Weeks in A Balloon*. 1873 and 1863. Ware, UK: Wordsworth Classics, 1984.

Vick, Erik Henry. "Designing Intentional, Emotional Characters: Personality and Personality Dynamics in Videogames." *Journal of Game Development* 2, no. 3 (2007): 53–61.

Vrettos, Athena. *Somatic Fictions: Imagining Illness in Victorian Culture*. Stanford: Stanford University Press, 1995.

Waithe, Marcus. "*News from Nowhere*, Utopia, and Bakhtin's Idyllic Chronotope." *Textual Practice* 16 (2002): 459–72.

Weber, Samuel. *Mass Mediauras: Form, Technics, Media*. Stanford: Stanford University Press, 1996.

Welsh, Alexander. *The City of Dickens*. Oxford: Clarendon Press, 1971.

"What are We Coming To?—A Conversation in a Railway Carriage." *Fraser's Magazine* 61 (1860): 583–92.

Wicke, Jennifer. "Vampiric Typewriting: *Dracula* and Its Media." *ELH* 59 (1992): 467–93.

Williamson, Elizabeth, and Nikolaus Pevsner. *London: Docklands*. New York: Viking Penguin, 1998.

Wilson, D. G. *The Victorian Thames*. Oxfordshire: Alan Sutton, 1993.

Wynter, Andrew. "Sensations of a Summer Night and Morning on the Thames." *Fraser's Magazine* 36 (1847): 62–67.

Yee, Nick, Jeremy Bailenson, Mark Urbanek, Francis Chang, and Dan Merget. "The Unbearable Likeness of Being Digital: The Persistence of Nonverbal Social Norms in Online Virtual Environments." *CyberPsychology and Behavior* 10, no. 1 (2007): 115–21.

Yuan, Xinpu, and Mary Madden. "Virtual Space Is the Place." Pew Internet and American Life Project, 11/27/2006 Report. http://www.pewresearch.org/pubs/97/virtual_space_is_the_place. Accessed 8/30/2008.

Žižek, Slavoj. "Is It Possible to Traverse the Fantasy in Cyberspace?" In *The Žižek Reader*, edited by Elizabeth Wright and Edmond Wright, 102–24. Oxford: Blackwell, 1999.

INDEX